SHINTO: THE UNCONQUERED ENEMY

OTHER BOOKS BY ROBERT O. BALLOU

The Viking Portable Library World Bible (EDITOR)

The Bible of the World (EDITOR)

This I Believe

Shinto

THE UNCONQUERED ENEMY

Japan's Doctrine
of Racial Superiority and
World Conquest

WITH SELECTIONS FROM JAPANESE TEXTS

By Robert O. Ballou

NEW YORK

The Viking Press

1945

TO

G. M. L. Brown, Elsy Becherer, and Helen Pinkerton, of Orientalia, who, in their appreciation of the social and cultural functions of bookselling, have made a fine art of a business, and whose helpfulness has been very great indeed. This is their book.

ACKNOWLEDGEMENT

The author wishes to express his gratitude and indebtedness to Horace L. Friess and D. C. Holtom for suggestions as to sources and directions, and to the publishers and authors who have granted permission to quote from their works. Detailed Credits will be found in Notes following the texts.

Contents

X CONTENTS

Part I

THE HISTORY AND MEANING OF SHINTO

1. Why Shinto Concerns Us

WHEN, on December 7, 1941, Japanese bombs fell on Pearl Harbor, the United States and Britain, nations committed to the ideals of democracy and universalism, set their feet upon the long hard road which would lead to eventual victory over the armed forces of the Land of the Rising Sun, thereby joining hands with China, land of the sages Confucius and Lao Tze, both of whom taught universalism twenty-five hundred years ago. In entering the war we, peoples who based our hopes for civilization upon the triumph of universalism and human freedom, were sending our armed forces against a mighty war machine. But of even greater importance, from a long range point of view, is the fact that we were opposing our ideals of the equality of man, of self-government, of freedom, and of peace, to powerful and contradictory ideas which must be charged with much of the responsibility for Japan's aggressive militarism— the Shinto conceptions that the islands of Japan, the people, and their ruler are divine, that their mission is to conquer the world, and that all peoples owe homage to the divine emperor whose authority is absolute.

In spite of terrifying initial setbacks, eventual military victory was, from the first, a foregone conclusion to every loyal American, Briton, and Chinese—a matter of resources, of the ability to manufacture military supplies well and quickly in previously unconceived quantities, of transportation, of advanced military strategy, and of epic courage in the freeborn sons of liberty-loving peoples.

Now, at the cost of hundreds of thousands of lives, and with the help of the atomic bomb, we have "won the war"—in so far as the surrender of an opponent's armed forces and government may be considered a victory. But surely the human race is by now old enough and war-wise enough to know that a military decision is not, in itself, ever a final decision between two opposing points of view. Pan-Germanism, the motivating power behind the German Army of 1914 was not destroyed by the Allies' military victory of 1918, but lived to spawn its pyromaniac child, Nazism, who set Europe ablaze in 1939. Nor were the Nazi armies, at the height of their power, able to destroy the love of liberty of the French, the Belgians, the Dutch, the Czechoslovakians, the Danes, the Norwegians, through overcoming their armies and occupying their countries. Two thousand years of persecution of the Jews has but strengthened their solidarity and increased the power of Judaism. Communism has never been suppressed by the imprisonment or execution of Communists. The submergence of individuals and the destruction of armies are simpler matters than the destruction of ideas.

In the war against Japan the United Nations were fighting not only against an army, a navy, and an air force, but also against an ideological force which was more than a thousand years old when Pan-Germanism was born, which, through many vicissitudes, has never been supplanted in Japan by vigorously opposing ideas, and which is more powerful in conditioning a people than Nazism could ever be, because it has behind it the strength of an ancient and undying religious reverence. Victory over the armed forces of Japan does not mean that we have conquered the aggressive, war-making, power of Shinto which gave them their life, their strength, and their purpose of world domination. Indeed, in view of the hatred which our bombing—and especially the use of the atomic bomb—has instilled in the Japanese, it may well be that we have only strengthened, through our military victory, some of the concepts which have grown out of Shinto. Unless we understand this, unless we proceed in the peace on the basis of this understanding, we have, when all is said and done, won no victory but merely a vain postponement of the true decision that must one day be made between the concept of international tolerance and co-operation, which marks the desires of the vast majority of peoples of the United Nations, and Japan's doctrine of race superiority and conquest, originating in and perpetuated by State Shinto, the religion of all of Japan.

It was not merely men and airplanes, machine guns and bombs, which attacked Pearl Harbor on December 7, 1941, nor merely wily diplomats who talked of peace in Washington while the planes were actually flying their lethal mission from Japan. Kurusu and Nomura, the bombs on Pearl Harbor, and the later Banzai-shouting infantry-men and *kami-kaze* * ("divine wind") suicide pilots—all were in-dividual expressions of the force of Shinto, a religion which has never emerged from primitivism, the ancient emperor-worshiping religion of self-styled "divine" Japan, with its heaven-established mission to conquer the world.

The task of inflicting military defeat upon Japan was perhaps the greatest, the most complex, and the most costly ever undertaken by the United States of America, who was called upon to bear the brunt of the Pacific War. That which lies ahead for the United Nations, the necessary task of winning an ideological victory over Shinto, is perhaps even greater and more complex, though properly approached its cost should be a small fraction of that of the war between the armed forces. It must be successfully accomplished if the world is to enjoy the fruits of a true victory and purge itself of the constant threat to world harmony which is innate in the existence of the Shinto-conditioned Japanese.

"The old communal form of religion that was normal in the West two thousand years ago exists in Japan today as a powerful social and religious force," writes D. C. Holtom, an outstanding contemporary Western scholar.

Into this religion the Japanese individual is born; loyalty to its belief and practice is his first qualification as a "good Japanese." It is not his by election; even when he chooses to attach himself to a universal re-ligion like Buddhism or Christianity, the old is ever there as a vital, all pervading influence, fundamentally conditioning his mentality and con-

---

* This appellation now applied to Japanese suicide pilots has been used by the Japanese under far different circumstances and with different meanings.

In 1281 Kublai Khan sent a great Mongol naval force against the Japanese coast of Hizen and Tikuzen. During the battle which raged between the invaders and the defenders a tremendous storm at sea overturned all of the Mongol ships. The Japanese called the storm a *kami-kaze*, or "god-sent wind." (*See* p. 127 for a Japanese account of the event.) When Perry and his flotilla entered a Japanese harbor in 1853, the reigning emperor prayed in vain to Amaterasu Omikami for a *kami-kaze* to destroy the "Western barbarians." The typhoon which destroyed a part of Admiral Halsey's fleet in 1945 was doubtless considered a *kami-kaze* by history-conscious Japanese. The province of Ise, where the great Shrine of Ise is located, is called in the *Nihongi* the "*kami-kaze* province [province of the divine wind], whither repair the waves from the eternal world."

duct and supplying a pattern to which all else must be accommodated. It permeates his home life, his agriculture, his business, his industry, his education, even his sports, and above all, his conception of the state and his duty to it. . . .

At the root of Japan's dedication to what she calls her "holy war" in East Asia lies the conviction that she is sent to be the savior of the world. Hand in hand with her deep economic need goes the belief that she is ordained by the divine forces that work through her history to share with less fortunate nations the blessings of her peerless institutions. Indeed, the doctrine that her state structure is the strongest and most excellent of all the world must have as its corollary the idea that non-Japanese people can only benefit by being brought under its sway. It would be misreading the facts if we should be content to account for the vigor and steadfastness with which this conviction of mission is asserted, merely as a search for compensation in the presence of frustration and insecurity, or as a pious verbiage that cloaks desperate economic need, on the one hand, and bitterly inconsistent severity toward conquered peoples, on the other.[1]

When Hideyoshi, the Japanese regent and powerful military dictator, failed to conquer Korea, China, and the Philippines in the sixteenth century, Japan received what, in her Shinto-dictated philosophy, was a temporary setback to her plans of conquest and domination. The plan and pattern of conquest remained the same. During the twentieth century, after widespread and terrifying successes *in her attempts to carry out the same plan according to the same pattern,* she has received another defeat, but it has cost those who have opposed her a staggering price. Will this defeat also be for her only a temporary setback? It will be if we do not fully understand the strong ideological base on which the plan of conquest rests, and find a way to induce the Japanese to build upon that base another form of structure which can fit into the general edifice of a civilized and peace-needing world. This is a task which cannot be accomplished by military might alone or merely by such tangible restraints as economic and geographic restrictions.

That military, political, geographic, and industrial control are essential goes without saying; yet, in view of the part which Japan has played in modern world history, and the part that the Japanese national religion has played in shaping and supporting Japan's conduct, no survey of forces destined to determine international affairs in the

Pacific can be adequate unless it includes thoughtful examination of this powerful cultus.

To begin such an examination, one must go back to the beginnings of Japanese history.

2. Beginnings of the Japanese, and of Shinto

THERE is no exact knowledge of when the peoples who were later to form the Japanese race came, as conquerors, to the islands which are now Japan, whence they came, or who they were. It is probable that most of them migrated from Northern Asia by way of Korea and that their migrations covered several centuries before the beginning of the Christian Era. There is evidence that the invaders may have included Chinese, Malay tribesmen, Koreans, and possibly dark-skinned natives of the Pacific South Sea Islands. Conquering the aboriginal tribes they found there, through a combination of destruction and amalgamation, the invaders, some time after their arrival, established the nation which we now know as Japan.

The name "Japan" is the result of a series of transitions. During the earliest, legendary days of the country's existence it was called by the poetical name "The Country in the Midst of Luxuriant Reed-Plains," probably because of the prevalence of marshes upon it. After the ascension of the first emperor, Jimmu Tenno, it was called Yamato (for which Inazo Nitobe hesitantly suggests the possible translation "Mountain Portal"). During the Middle Ages official Japanese correspondence with China called it "Hi-no-moto," or "The Source of the Sun" (from which comes the modern appellation, "The Land of the Rising Sun"). The Chinese characters for "Hi-no-moto" came to be pronounced "Nippon," which was perverted by Marco Polo, who spelled it "Jipangu," from which all Western designations of the name of the country, including the English "Japan," arise.[1]

In Japanese chronology Jimmu Tenno, the first Japanese emperor, ascended the throne in 660 B.C., now reckoned as the first year in the Japanese national era, but Western scholars set the date much later than that, the consensus of opinion being that the founding of the state and the beginnings of Japanese cultural history were at about the time of the opening of the Christian Era.

Confucianism, Taoism, Buddhism, and Zoroastrianism had already passed through more than half a millennium of establishment, growth, and modification. The *Rig-Veda,* earliest scripture of the Hindus, had been compiled more than a thousand years earlier than this. All of the Old Testament of Judaism had been written, and those events which the Gospels of the New Testament were to record were already taking place in the region of the Sea of Galilee. The great library at Alexandria was over three hundred years old. The Mayan civilization of Mexico and Central America had been established for five hundred years.

But as yet the Japanese had no books, and indeed, not until more than five centuries later—probably about the time of the coming of Buddhism to Japan—did they have a written language. Their first writing was done in Chinese, then in a combination of Chinese symbols and a calligraphy of their own development. Often Chinese characters were used, not in their original meanings, but as signs for Japanese words which had the same sounds but quite different meanings, a fact which has made translation of early Japanese records a challenging task, not only for Westerners, but for Japanese scholars as well. Conclusions have been based upon archaeological research and later records, often of questionable reliability.

Evidence thus disclosed suggests that the primary sources of the early Japanese religious beliefs are rather in Northern Asia than in China. Some of their earliest gods are Korean and others have Korean associations. There was nothing to correspond to the divine ruling force called *Shangti* and *Tien* in China (both translated as "Heaven," but meaning the divine and all-powerful force ruling the universe). In early Japan "Heaven" was not a force, but simply a plain very like the earth, though somewhat elevated above it, where the higher classes of gods dwelt.

An archaeologist makes an interesting case for his statement of the possibility that much of the early Japanese religion came by slow stages across the Pacific from the Royal God Cult of the Mayans, and cites, among other things, the similarity between the name of the Mayan ruler of the sky and son of the first god, *Itasamna,* with the name of the female of the Japanese creator pair of gods, *Izanami,* and draws many parallels between the rites and sacrifices of the two primitive religions.[2]

To be sure, such evidence must be examined with caution, for in many respects Japanese worship and Japanese cosmology were much like those of many other primitive religions. The universal creative force can be easily identified with the almost universal concept of a sky-father and earth-mother, the processes of creation resulting from a union between them. All of the primary deities were personifications of nature, with the sun at the center of all. (This adoration of the solar deity was later crystallized in homage to the very personal central goddess of the Shinto pantheon, but worship of the actual sun itself by the common people seems never to have been completely discontinued.)

At first the religion was nameless. The term *Shinto,* or *Shintau* (Way of the Gods), of Chinese origin, was apparently applied to it after infiltration of Confucianism and Buddhism made it necessary to distinguish between the indigenous religion and foreign faiths.

The influence of the ancient Chinese faith is also evident in Japanese beliefs. The primordial universe was believed to be pervaded by the two opposed, yet complementary, forces—the bright, the heavenly, the masculine (the *Yang* in China), and the dark, the earthly, the feminine (the *Yin* in China). But in an early personification of individual manifestations the Japanese created a voluminous pantheon.

The gods, or *kami,* were (and are) innumerable. Their number is spoken of in different records as eighty myriads, eight hundred myriads, and fifteen hundred myriads. Many of these were simple and direct personifications of the forces of nature (earthquake, thunder, rain, etc.). Many were individual natural bodies (the sun, the moon, trees, mountains). Some were the deified souls of individual human dead. Others were personified deifications of human qualities. Their natures and attributes as gods seem but vaguely conceived, and even Japanese scholars have, in the recent past, confessed the greatest difficulty in understanding the exact meaning of the word *kami,* which in some usages is translated as god or gods, but in others more simply as possessed of divinity or sacredness or even in earlier research as embodying merely superior and unusual powers. In some cases it means simply "above" or "superior" in space. It is used to designate the upper reaches of a river, the upper regions of a country, the hairs of the human head (but not the hairs on any other part of the body), the higher parts of mountains. It also means simply "paper." It is used to designate the emperor in other sense than that of his sacredness, as an indication of rank, and is applied to nobles and high government officials. The secular and religious meanings of the word have, in the past, been so frequently confused that often it has seemed impossible to tell which is intended, and the word has been the subject of scholarly discussion from the time of the earliest serious Japanese studies.

However, Japanese and Western scholars, working in Japan just before the outbreak of World War II, were making new and clarifying interpretations based on recent research, which indicate that *kami* meaning "deity" or "sacred" and *kami* meaning "superior" are two different words.[3] Dr. Saeki Ariyoshi, a contemporary Japanese scholar, in commenting on the sacred meaning, says:

Kami . . . means a personal and transcendant awe-inspiring spirit which is made the object of religious worship. . . . From ancient times onward, beginning with the Grand Shrine of Ise, shrines have been established throughout the country in each district, city, town and village, and the deities worshipped therein are many. If we group them in classes we find that individual ancestors who are worshipped as *kami* are most numerous. In addition to these there are numerous *kami* who are worshipped as the spiritual powers that guard the necessities of life. In foreign countries a single sovereign god is recognized, and apart therefrom no other gods are known. In our country, however, not only are deities of creation worshipped, but also it is believed that spirit exists in all things and this is worshipped as *kami*. Those who have given their lives in the service of the state are worshipped as *kami* by the state. There are also cases in which people who excel in virtue are worshipped as *kami* while still living.[4]

In recent years the Japanese government, in its insistence that Japanese have freedom of religion, and that the enforced doctrines of State Shinto do not constitute a religion, have inspired statements to the effect that *kami* is not at all, in the Western sense, a religious word. (*See* statement from the Transactions of the Meiji Japan Society among the selections from State Shinto doctrine following this discussion.) Holtom, however, in the light of his own findings and those of modern Japanese scholars, sums up the situation as follows:

We can state that *kami* in its characteristic content is a religious term through and through. It is not what some would have us believe it is, a "secular" expression, or one that connotes a non-religious or an extra-religious background and meaning. . . . If we accept the guidance of the Japanese experts . . . and everything points to the decision that we must—then *kami* is a word which in origin and development is saturated with the atmosphere of the divine, the sacred and the holy. It calls forth emotions of awe and mystery, of restraint and dedication, of dependence and obligation that are characteristically religious. . . . This is not to say that *kami* does not have a unique content. . . . We know that it does. It has preserved in a remarkable manner, through a long history, a characteristically Japanese pattern. But we know too that the primary emotions which the term *kami* registers are not exclusively Japanese, but rather they are attributes of universal human nature.[5]

He goes on to say that *kami* and *mana,* a term widely understood throughout the Pacific islands, mean the same thing—a power or influence, not physical, but which often shows itself in physical force. In Maori *mana* means authority, influence, prestige, effectiveness, supernatural power, divine authority.

In early Shinto celestial *kami* seemed to be simply more powerful than earthly men, and possessed of distinctly human attributes, both good and bad, along with extraordinary capabilities borrowed from nature. In the seventh century A.D., when a system of official ranks was introduced into Japan from China, and applied to gods as well as men, many of the gods were placed lower in the hierarchy than the highest grades of government officials. Later, when a god seemed to be instrumental in especially favorable occurrences, he was promoted. Inanimate things, such as stones, fields, houses, mud, sand, kitchen utensils—indeed almost anything useful to man—were thought of as living things and *kami*.

Deities were approached ritualistically at primitive sanctuaries in groves, on mountains, beneath great trees, beside rivers or springs or great rocks, any one of which symbolized the divine power of nature and might itself be the dwelling place of a god. Later, shrines were built at such spots to give the attendant god an alternate habitation. Rituals were designed to increase the harvest, to ward off pestilence, drought, flood, earthquake, illness, and other misfortunes. They sometimes included human sacrifices, which are re-enacted symbolically in some Shinto ceremonies today. Signs were read into unusual occurrences. A fox biting off a creeper and carrying the end away, and a dog carrying the arm and hand of a dead man, are recorded in the *Nihongi* as evidence that an Empress was about to die. A white pheasant, a white sparrow, a white crow, a crow with three legs, were all omens favorable to the emperor. A migration of rats betokened the imminent removal of the imperial palace.

Worship of the food goddess developed the widespread and complicated cult of *Inari,* in which the fox symbolizes the spirit of the rice and is revered as such. The cult includes much superstition and magic and is strongly mixed with phallicism.

Dreams were considered of the greatest importance as revelations of truth. (A strangely prophetic dream was reported by the twelfth-century Mikado Gotoba-no-Im. Waking from a dream under the inspiration of the Shrine of Ise, he said, "In the last days the world will be disturbed and all men troubled. The sovereign house will show respect for the military house.")

There was widespread phallic worship. Many male gods were represented by symbolic phalli of stone, wood, terra cotta, iron, or gold, and mushrooms and shells were used as phallic emblems. Phalloid boulders and carved wooden pillars were set up along highways, especially at crossroads, and phallic deities became gods of the highways. Offerings of phallic emblems were made in the shrines, especially to gods connected with agriculture, and large rocks, naturally phalloid, were worshiped.

W. G. Aston, in *Shinto, the Way of the Gods,* quotes the *To-yu-ki,* a work published in 1795, as authority for a description of wooden phalli seven or eight feet in length which were placed in large numbers along a highway in the province of Deha every year on the fifteenth day of the first month. The women of the district strung slips of paper above them as prayers for handsome lovers. Aston also cites from an earlier Japanese text evidence of the practice of laying phallic shapes in the runnels of a nonproductive rice field to improve the harvest.

This emphasis on phallicism was the natural outcome of the thought of a simple people to whom there was no clear distinction between procreation and creation. To them the creative power lay in sexual processes, and so the symbol of sexual power became the symbol of creation, and thus worshipful. There is nothing unusual in the fact that phallicism was part of a primitive religion; it has been connected with many and may still be found in India, Asia Minor, and other places. But rarely has it been as powerful and widespread a cult as in Japan (where it persisted openly until late in the nineteenth century when the government caused removal of the public phallic symbols) and there is plenty of residual evidence of it in the Land of the Rising Sun today.

In view of the close relationship which Japanese religious concepts have always held with every aspect of Japanese life, the persistence of phallicism in Shinto may at least partially explain the seemingly disproportionate consciousness of sex in adult Japanese. Geoffrey Gorer [6] says that "a major portion of the work of their most famed artists [is] so pornographic that much of it has never been seen in Europe or America." He also points out that no attempt is made to curb sex expression in children or their verbal obscenities.

Other evidences of a survival of ancient nature worship are found throughout Japan, especially in rural regions where the *yama-no-kami,* or mountain gods, are still appeased. The villagers report often hearing these gods voice their displeasure during the night, when sounds such as might be made by gigantic men felling tremendous trees are heard. But in the morning no sign is found to evidence the work of the celestial woodsmen. In some districts certain trees are believed to be inhabited by *yama-no-kami,* and no one would think of touching them with an ax. If there is any doubt in a woodsman's mind, he will lean his ax against the tree he wishes to cut and leave it there overnight. If it is still erect in the morning, he knows that he may safely fell the tree, for if a deity inhabits it, the god will throw the ax over.

These and many other customs still current in Japan and not mentioned in the basic books of Shinto testify to beliefs and practices which perhaps antedate even that shadowy time when the ancestors of the present Japanese came to the islands. Again, as with phallicism, there is nothing unusual about tree worship in a primitive religion. The glittering colored lights on spruce or hemlock trees which brighten Christian homes and churches at Christmas time illuminate a surviving evidence of widespread belief in the gods of the forest. The distinctive element in Shinto lies in the strength which has kept worship of trees alive to the present day.

Many a shrine of Shinto nestles closely under the branches of an ancient tree—not merely as evidence of aesthetic sensitiveness and the desire to plant trees about public buildings. The tree was there first. The shrine or "god house" was built later as a convenient alternate habitation for the deity of the tree.

The distinctive sacred tree of Shinto is the evergreen *sakaki*. It is commonly found, protected by sacred ropes, on the grounds of the shrines. Branches of it are used in many Shinto ceremonies.

Within every Shinto shrine, within the innermost recesses of the chief sanctuary, or *honden,* there is kept an object called the *shintai,* or "god body." It is carefully concealed from all eyes, even from those of the priests, for in it the god of the shrine is believed to dwell. When its wrapping becomes soiled or frayed, new coverings are sewed over it without removing the old, for fear that it may be seen. It may be a stone, a phallic emblem, an ancient sword or mirror, a sacred text, a lock of human hair, or a typical example of local craftsmanship. Often it is a branch of the *sakaki*. Branches of *sakaki* are also put, with water and food, on the "god shelves" of Japanese homes, where the spirits of ancestors are believed to dwell. Buddhist-Shinto priests of medieval times are reported as having been able to gain instant audience with the emperor by marching to the imperial palace in a body, each bearing a branch of *sakaki*.

A giant *icho* tree, many centuries old, in the eastern suburbs of Sendai and called the "Nurse Goddess Tree of Miyagi Field," is worshiped because of hanging formations somewhat resembling breasts, from which moisture drips in wet weather. These are believed to have the power of restoring milk to a woman who is unable to nurse her child, or to cure one who is suffering from a disease of the breast. The shrine, which now almost touches the bole of the great tree, is of minor importance, for in this case the tree itself is thought of as a god rather than merely the habitation of one. A stone tablet, erected near by in 1915, tells the history of the tree and the story of its miraculous powers. Believed to embody the spirit of a Buddhist nun of the eighth century A.D., who was wet nurse to an emperor, it was originally an object of reverence to Japanese Buddhists, but today Japanese women of all sects come to it to bring prayers, to drink the drops of moisture which drip from its pendulous "breasts," and to take away from the priest of the shrine tokens to place on their "god shelves."

Often tree worship and phallic worship overlapped. Phallic stones were laid (or large ones erected) at the base of a sacred tree as offerings. At Aoyama Harajuku in Tokyo an exceedingly old Chinese nettle tree with a peculiarly shaped crotch suggestive of the human female body is worshiped as a female deity and petitioned for recovery from sexual diseases. Again in a suburb of Tokyo, in a sacred compound surrounding a temple erected by the Taisei sect of modern Shinto, is the split stump of another ancient nettle tree rising fifteen feet. It is worshiped as the god of divorce, and every day petitions are brought to it written on tiny slips of paper, asking for severance of burdensome marriage relationships or, more frequently, for the removal of the amorous power which an interloper is exercising on the spouse of the petitioner.

But to go back to a day of which these survivals are evidence.

About A.D. 400, after the entrance of Confucianism, Japan became subject for the first time to the influence of a religion which had passed the primitive stage. In the Confucian tradition the state was regarded as one family whose father and mother are combined in the emperor and his spouse, appointed by heaven as benevolent patriarchs because of transcendent virtue. Further, it stated the primary axiom that man's nature is good—with the implication that in order to achieve righteousness one must be natural. Family loyalty and obedience to government were stressed. These doctrines, modified and distorted as they have been by the Japanese, made their impress upon the religious consciousness of a people still in the throes of establishing a state and pacifying it. Reflections of them are found in every form of Shinto from the earliest times to the present.

Some time during the early stages of pacification there grew up the legend that one of the gods had descended from heaven to rule over the people of the islands and to beget a line of emperors who would reign over them and their descendants "for ages eternal." Perhaps this was even then a political device concocted and used by the most powerful of the Japanese clans as a means of impressing the aboriginals with the futility of mortal resistance and the rival aspirants for leadership of the Japanese race with the superior claims of the imperial family.

For certainly Jimmu Tenno, the traditional first emperor—if indeed there ever was such an individual—was not the sole contestant for supreme authority, nor recognized as the ruler of all of the Japanese people. He was, more probably, merely a clan chief—one of several—who fulfilled the double function of priest and head man within his immediate clan and exercised authority only over a given locality, while fighting with other clans to extend that authority. It is likely that the claim of this clan to descent from the illustrious sun goddess, chief of celestial offspring of Izanagi and Izanami, was pressed as justification for supremacy over the other clans who perhaps claimed descent from gods less exalted than Amaterasu Omikami. As the head of the clan he was supposedly in intimate communication with the goddess, thus knowing her will, and was also titular holder of all of the lands which had been created by Izanagi and Izanami.

During the seventh century there was an attempt by the powerful Soga clan to overthrow the imperial clan and take over the latter's growing authority. But in the military trial of strength the imperial clan proved its greater power. In the Taikwa Reform which followed, the imperial clan consolidated its position by a concentration of political power, by laying a foundation in law for the ownership and control of all Japanese lands by the emperor, and by decreeing that the gods of the imperial clan were the national gods and were to be worshiped as such by the people who were themselves likewise descended from these gods. Thus the position of the emperor—himself by tradition a god incarnate—was strengthened, and reverence for the emperor, which has been so heightened during the years of modern State Shinto indoctrination, was firmly established.

It was also during the Taikwa Reform that the Fujiwara family, so influential a part of the Restoration in the nineteenth century, and strongly entrenched in Japanese government affairs today, consolidated its position as a mighty power behind the throne. Claiming descent from a god only a little lower in the pantheon than the sun goddess herself, the Fujiwaras supplied wives for the emperors. Thus the father-in-law and the maternal grandfather and grandmother of the emperor were Fujiwaras with all of the authority over the ruler given them by the doctrine of filial piety that had been imported from China.

The Taikwa Reform did not, however, settle the struggle for dominance of the rival clans. This was to continue throughout feudal times late into the nineteenth century and beyond. A reflection of the attempt to impress the clans with the indisputable position of the imperial family is in an edict of the Emperor Kotoku, issued in A.D. 807:

The empire was entrusted by the Sun Goddess to her descendants with the words "My children, in their capacity of deities, shall rule it." For this reason this country, since heaven and earth began, has been a monarchy. From the time that our Imperial Ancestor first ruled the land, there has been great concord in the empire and there has never been any factiousness. In recent times, however, the names, first of the gods, and then of the Emperors, have in some cases been separated from their proper applications. . . . In consequence of this, the mind of the people of the whole country take a strong partisan bias, and, conceiving a deep sense of the me and thee, hold firmly each to their names. . . . The duty has therefore devolved upon us in our capacity as Celestial Divinity, to regulate these things.[7]

Certainly the Chinese doctrine that the emperor was the "Son of Heaven" had something to do with the origin of the Japanese legend of the Mikado's divinity, but there was a marked difference between the Chinese and the Japanese conceptions. In the Confucian tradition the emperor, appointed by heaven because of his surpassing virtue, was a mortal, and need not be in direct line of descent from earlier "Sons of Heaven." Further, there was definitely placed upon him, by the assumption of his office, a responsibility to rule with wisdom, righteousness, and benevolence in order to retain his right to be called a "Son of Heaven" and continue as ruler. His "divinity" was not innately of his person, but something conferred upon him by heaven so long as he ruled well, in view of the solemn duty which devolved upon him to provide for the welfare of his people. It was the office rather than the man that was divine. If the emperor became an incompetent, a personally ambitious or otherwise bad ruler, it became

clearly evident that heaven had withdrawn its mandate and benison.
The remedy in the hands of the people, in the Confucian doctrine,
was the right of revolution, plainly stated by Mencius, the great
follower and expositor of the ancient sage. That the emperor's responsibility to his people was clearly recognized by both rulers and
people is evident in the humble tone in which Imperial Mandates of
the Confucian period are couched, and the critical candor exhibited
by advisers to the emperor.

But in this matter, as in others, the Japanese absorbed the superficial
aspects of a doctrine without accepting its underlying meaning. In
their application of the "Son of Heaven" conception, the first ruler of
the islands of Japan was a celestial god descended from heaven, and
every emperor who followed him has been a direct lineal descendant
of this divinity. Thus his virtue was peculiar, innate, and inevitable
through lineage, and not a matter which arose from his office or which
needed proof through righteous conduct.

Says D. C. Holtom:

It is biological and historical, a divinity and sacredness preserved in
the germ plasm, hence the indispensability of the doctrine of unbroken
lineage reaching back to the very beginning of the foundation of the
state. The Emperor is divine because he is the living extension in time
of the very bodies and souls of the great divine ancestors of the past and,
in particular, of the physical and spiritual attributes of the sun goddess,
Amaterasu Omikami, by whose will and wisdom the state was originally
founded. . . . It is obvious that, when we reach this kind of interpretation of imperial divinity we have transcended the limits of logic and history and find ourselves in the presence of assertions of religious faith
that represent sentimental attachments to traditional survivals out of
ancient folkways and mythology. The existence of these ancient sentiments and the national capacities for belief which support them open
to the Japanese state an extraordinary field for political cultivation and
equip it with an emotional integration that cannot be duplicated the
world over.[8]

Not a little of Japan's centuries-old ideological antagonism to
China arises from the direct conflict between these two interpretations
of a single concept that attributes a measure of divinity to an earthly
ruler. And in the directions taken by the two interpretations there
may be seen clearly one of the reasons why in the final alignment of

nations in World War II the Western democracies felt at home in an alliance with China, while Japan was most natually allied with authoritarian Germany and Italy, in both of which countries all pretense at government by the people had been abandoned.

For even though the government of China in the days of Confucius was in form an absolute monarchy, the Confucian doctrine—so annoying to the Japanese—which made the "Son of Heaven" responsible to his people, and conceded to the people the right of revolution against a monarch who had ceased to govern as a "Son of Heaven" should, was essentially a concept which established the final authority in the governed, whereas the Japanese "Son of Heaven" was responsible to no one save, perhaps, his divine ancestors, and the voice of the people spoke with no recognized authority whatever.

3. The Basic Myth of Racial Superiority

THE TWO oldest books of Japan, which are also the two basic books of Shinto, the *Kojiki* and the *Nihongi,* contain the first written record of this legend, which obviously existed long before it was set down. Compiled in A.D. 712 and A.D. 720, both tell the story of creation, tell of the birth of many gods and of the conquests of early Japanese emperors and armies. The chronology of both books begins with the creation. The *Kojiki* brings the record down to the close of the reign of the Empress Suiko in A.D. 628. The *Nihongi* repeats the story of the *Kojiki,* with variant versions of many of the episodes, and continues to the events of the year A.D. 697.

Since all the modifications of Shinto are based upon the same cosmogony—that of the *Kojiki* and *Nihongi*—and since that cosmogony has an incomparable importance in the national life, it is essential to begin the examination of Shinto with knowledge of this basic legend, which is briefly as follows:

After heaven and earth were formed from chaos, six generations of gods (who apparently didn't amount to much) were spontaneously produced. The seventh generation were Izanagi ("the male who invites") and Izanami ("the female who invites"). Some scholars believe that these were personifications of the Chinese *Yang* and *Yin*. In their creation there occurred the first differentiation of sex. Izanagi was given the "jewel spear of heaven" by the gods, apparently a phallic symbol, clearly so represented in early Japanese drawings and connected with early Japanese phallic worship.* Standing on the "bridge of heaven," Izanagi thrust the "jewel spear" into the ocean beneath him. As he raised it the brine which dripped from it congealed and formed the island of Onogoro-jima ("the island of the congealed drop"), supposedly a small island adjacent to the modern Awaji, lying at the entrance to the Inland Sea between Honshu and Shikoku.

Descending to Onogoro-jima, Izanagi and Izanami united as man and wife and gave birth to the eight islands of Japan and to numerous gods. It is interesting to note that (with the exception of Onogoro-jima) the islands of Japan, according to the myth, were actually "born" of the union of male and female deities, thus achieving divinity themselves, and a living reality impossible to the soil of other countries, for all other lands (according to Shinto commentaries) were later merely created of sea-foam and mud, and thus were dead and grossly inferior.

Of the gods born to Izanagi and Izanami, both jointly and individually (for while they produced gods through sexual union, each also produced many alone—through washing, through weeping, through vomiting, through killing other gods, through undressing, through urination and defecation, through breaking combs, through throwing peaches—Japanese symbol of the female sexual organs—

---

* "The *Ame-no-nuboko*, or 'heavenly jewel spear' which the ancestral deities in heaven bestowed upon Izanagi and Izanami had the shape of a phallus, so that the divine couple received a suggestion from it and were overjoyed in their nuptial union, begetting different gods successively. For the jewel spear is the root of heaven and earth."—Sato-Shinen, a Japanese scholar of the Tokugawa regime. Cited by Genchi Kato, *A Study of the Development of Religious Ideas Among the Japanese People as Illustrated by Japanese Phallicism,* in *Transactions of the Asiatic Society of Japan,* Supplement to Vol. I, 2nd Series (London: Kegan Paul, Trench, Trubner and Co., 1924). In later notations the *Transactions* will be referred to as *T.A.S.J.*

and Izanami through the putrefaction of her body after death), by far the most illustrious was Amaterasu Omikami (produced by Izanagi when he washed his left eye, according to the *Kojiki*), the sun goddess, to whom was assigned the rule of heaven.

In giving birth to the fire god, Izanami was so badly burnt that she died and went to the region of Yomi, or darkness. Following her, Izanagi found himself in a land of pollution. Leaving it hastily, pursued by Izanagi after he had shamed her by seeing her "rotting and swarming with maggots," he purified himself by washing, thereby creating a number of gods. Among them was Susa no Wo, the storm god who was produced when Izanagi washed his nose.

To heaven, whither Amaterasu, the sun goddess, had gone, went Susa no Wo, the turbulent one, accompanied by a groaning of the hills and mountains and a violent disturbance in the sea. Following a stormy argument with Amaterasu Omikami, Susa no Wo broke down the divisions between the rice fields belonging to his sister Amaterasu, let loose the "piebald colt of heaven," defecated in the hall where Amaterasu was celebrating the rites of first fruits, then flayed "the piebald colt of heaven with a backward flaying" and cast it into the hall where Amaterasu was weaving. So startled and angry was she at this indignity that she pricked herself badly, and in a most inconvenient place, and retired into the "rock cave of heaven"; whereupon the whole world was shrouded in impenetrable darkness.

Now the other gods, deeply concerned by this calamity, made and executed a plan calculated to exploit Amaterasu's feminine vanity. They dug up by the roots a five-hundred-branched sacred *sakaki* tree and hung on its higher branches strings of strange, comma-shaped jewels, on its middle branches a mirror, and pieces of cloth upon its lower branches. Then they approached the rock cave with the festooned tree. Before the closed door of the cave they uttered loud praises of Amaterasu in song, while Ame no Uzume, "the Dread Female of Heaven," danced an obscene dance which made all of the assembled gods shake with uproarious laughter.

Piqued that they should be in the mood for laughter while she was hidden and the world was in darkness, Amaterasu opened the door of the cave a crack and asked the reason for it. They replied that they were laughing because they had found that there was one who was fairer than herself. Then she came out—apparently to prove that they were liars—whereupon they presented her with the mirror and the jewels, and she stayed out.

This is the legendary origin of two of the three sacred treasures (the mirror, the jewels, and the sword) which have been handed down from generation to generation of Japanese emperors, and without the possession of which no emperor could occupy the throne. The sword was found later by Susa no Wo in the tail of a dragon during a visit of the problem-child god to earth.

Ninigi no Mikoto was a grandson of Amaterasu Omikami. Looking down upon the islands of Japan and speaking to Ninigi, Amaterasu said, "This country is a land over which my offspring shall rule. Do thou, Imperial Grandson, go and rule over it. And the prosperity of the imperial throne shall be as everlasting as heaven and earth." Giving him the three sacred treasures, she charged him to look upon the mirror as though it were herself. And thus did Ninigi no Mikoto, a god, and grandson of the most illustrious of goddesses, descend to claim for himself and his descendants the unswerving obedience and worship of Japanese subjects to the end of time.

In a charitable approach to this legend on which Shinto is based, W. G. Aston, most tolerant of Shinto scholars, says:

The chief ideas underlying Japanese mythology are, firstly, the conception—piecemeal, it is true, and inadequate—of the so-called inanimate universe as being really instinct with sentient life, and exercising a loving, providential, care of mankind; and secondly, the doctrine that honor and obedience are due the sovereign whose beneficent rule secures to the people blessings comparable to that of the sun's light and warmth. For such, I take it, is the real meaning of the story by which the Mikados are feigned to be descendants of the Sun Goddess. It is the Japanese version of the doctrine of the divine right of kings. Without these and similar vital elements Japanese mythology would be nothing more than what some writers have supposed it—a farrago of absurdities, and its examination would belong not to the physiology, but to the pathology of the human mind.[1]

In another evaluation, written at about the same time, Percival Lowell said:

Shinto is a combination by the Japanese of the worship of nature and of their own ancestors. But the character of the combination is ethnologically instructive. For a lack of psychic development has made of these seemingly diverse elements a homogeneous whole. Both, of course, are aboriginal instincts. Next to the fear of natural phenomena, in point of primitiveness, comes the fear of one's father, as children and savages show. But races, like individuals, tend to outgrow it as they develop. Now the suggestive thing about the Japanese people is that this passing phase of religion has been perpetuated. The Japanese have stayed boys. Filial respect continued, and, by very virtue of not becoming less, became more, till it filled not only the whole sphere of morals, but expanded into the sphere of cosmogony. To the Japanese eye the universe took on the paternal look. Parental awe, which these people understood, lent explanation to natural dread, which they did not. Quite simply to their minds the thunder and the wind, the sunshine and the shower, were the work not only of anthropomorphic beings but of beings ancestrally related to themselves. In short Shinto, their explanation of things in general, is nothing else than the patriarchal principle projected without perspective into the past, dilating with distance into deity.[2]

According to interpretations of modern State Shinto, the heavenly mission to which the emperor and his people were committed from the beginning was to conquer the world so that all peoples would be "blessed" by the rule of the divine emperor. Two passages, both from the *Nihongi,* are sufficient to evidence the classical authority cited for these interpretations.

Hiko-hoho-demi, son of Ninigi, and grandfather of Jimmu Tenno (who was to become the first emperor to sit upon the throne of the established Japanese state) said to his elder brother:

The remote regions do not yet enjoy the blessings of imperial rule. . . . Now I have heard from the Ancient of the Sea that in the East there is a fair land encircled on all sides by blue mountains. . . . I think that this land will undoubtedly be suitable for the extension of the heavenly task, so that its glory should fill the universe. It is doubtless the center of the world. . . . Why should we not proceed thither and make it the capital?

Two generations later, when Jimmu Tenno ascended the throne and founded the Japanese state, he made a sacred promise to Amaterasu Omikami to "foster righteousness, and extend the line of the imperial descendants. Thus, hereafter, the imperial rule [literally 'the capital'] shall be extended so as to embrace the entire world [literally 'the six quarters,' i.e., north, south, east, west, zenith, and nadir] and the universe shall be covered so as to form a single roof."

It is on these and similar passages, and interpretations of them by revered scholars of the past, that the modern Japanese slogan, *hakko ichi-u,* "the world under one roof," or "the world one family," is based. It is by such passages in a sacred book, part of an old and sacred legend, that the seizures of Formosa, of Korea, of Manchuria, of much of China, of the Philippines (attempted in the sixteenth century and accomplished in the twentieth)—indeed the whole early pattern of conquest and the objective of "the Greater East Asia Co-Prosperity Sphere"—have been justified to an essentially childlike and emotional people, the Japanese. But it has been made clear for many years that the "one roof" under which the Japanese plan that the world shall live as a single family is the domination by the Japanese imperial rule.

Three quotations and an architectural fact are enough to illustrate this contemporary official Japanese point of view:

"To enhance justice and make of the world one household is the great injunction, bequeathed by our Imperial Ancestors, which we lay to heart day and night."—Imperial Edict of Emperor Hirohito announcing adherence to the Rome-Berlin Axis, September 27, 1940.

"The principle of the whole world under one roof embodies the spirit under which the Empire was founded by Jimmu Tenno. My understanding is that this is the spirit of making the boundless virtues of the Emperor prevail throughout the whole world."—Statement of Admiral Yonai, upon his appointment as Premier of Japan, 1940.

"Japan's actions since the founding of the Empire have invariably been based upon the spirit of universal brotherhood."—Statement of Premier General Kuniaki Koiso to the Imperial Diet Budgetary Committee, January 1945.

On Hakko hill in the city of Miyazaki, Kyushu, a monument of ferro-concrete to the principle of *hakko ichi-u* was erected by the Japanese in 1940. Four human figures grouped about the central pillar symbolize the four instruments by which the Japanese plan to bring the whole world "under one roof." They are commerce and industry, fishing, agriculture, and war.

It is doubtful whether, when the *Kojiki* and *Nihongi* were written, an attempt at actual world conquest was contemplated. To a primitive people, as to a child, the world is confined by narrow limits. The task of the Japanese during the first millennium of the Christian Era was to consolidate and unify the mixed peoples then dwelling on the islands which they had occupied. These islands were their world. While not only the conquered, but even the invaders themselves, were split into many rival factions, the position of the state was insecure. Only by unifying their own people and amalgamating those who remained alive of the aboriginals could stability be achieved. Then, indeed, could it be said that "the imperial rule would extend so as to embrace the entire world." Then, indeed, would the universe seem to be covered "so as to form a single roof." It was not until centuries later, when the rule of the emperor had been succeeded by that of the shogun, that the idea of actual world domination emerged clearly in the teachings of the Pure Shinto Revival.

Shinto ideologists seem to have had a genius for taking the political and social concepts of others and distorting them into directly antagonistic doctrines. We have seen how the basically exalted Chinese concept of the "Son of Heaven"—a deification of social government rather than of an individual—became in Japan a means to deprive the people of all rights to self-government, through exalting an individual as absolute ruler.

Similarly the Shinto concept of *hakko ichi-u* is a distortion and utter degradation of one of the greatest social concepts ever to arise in the mind of man. The great-hearted love of country which marked early Chinese philosophy was always essentially a love of mankind, a sense of universal brotherhood. It was never a narrow nationalism or a sense of racial superiority. "The world one family" or "the world under one roof," as it would be interpreted by a classical Chinese scholar, is a concept thoroughly Confucian and Taoist. It is also Hinduist, Buddhist, later Old Testament, Zoroastrian, and Christian.

But the Japanese concept of *hakko ichi-u,* which may be translated into English by either of the above quoted phrases, is the direct antithesis of everything Confucian, Taoist, Hinduist, Buddhist, Judaist, and Christian, for it sets at naught the doctrine of universal brotherhood, asserts the superiority of one race (the Japanese) over all other races on earth, and attempts to establish as the absolute ruler of all mankind a single potentate—the divine emperor of Japan.

4. Ritual and Ethics of Early Shinto

OTHER basic books of Shinto are the *Kiujiki*, compiled in A.D. 720, which contains little not in the *Kojiki* and the *Nihongi;* the *Kogoshui*, of A.D. 807, another repetition of the basic material of the *Kojiki* and *Nihongi;* the *Idzumo Fudoki*, A.D. 733, a topography of the Province of Idzumo, which contains some mythology; the *Shojiroku*, a peerage of Japan, in which the descent of many noble families is traced to deities in the Shinto pantheon; the *Engi Shiki*, or "Institutes of the Period of Engi," A.D. 901–923, which contains a collection of twenty-six *norito,* or prayers, to be used in rituals; and the *Manyoshu*, or "Collection of One Thousand Leaves," an anthology of poetry, probably compiled between the middle of the eighth century and the beginning of the tenth.

Examination of these books reveals much, but not all, of the structure of early Shinto, and basic concepts which survive in every modification of it to the present day. The theology has been briefly discussed above. The ritual consisted in making offerings of praise and appeasement (mirrors, food, shields, spears, pieces of cloth, etc.). Prayers consisted of praise and requests for material advantages in return for offerings which had been made or which would be made if the pleas were granted. There were no prayers for righteousness, for greater enlightenment, even that the will of the gods should be clear so that it could be followed by men, or for a state of blessedness after death. Indeed in early Shinto there is nowhere revealed any conception of the state of man's soul after death. That was to come later, first in Buddhism, and again when Shinto was molded to the purposes of the almighty state and deification was assured all soldiers of the empire who died in battle, regardless of the worthiness or unworthiness of their lives.

Although the early Japanese had simple ideas of morality, little

26

consciousness of this is reflected in their earliest books. There is evidence that theft, lying, and adultery were condemned by them. The *Nihongi* records some early imperial edicts of a social nature. But, in comparison with the sacred books of other religions, there is little direct moral teaching or ethical code, and no conception of sin in the Western sense of the word, in the sacred books of early Shinto. A schedule of offenses against the gods included incest, bestiality, wounding, witchcraft, and certain interferences with the processes of agriculture.

From the time of the Pure Shinto Revival to the present, Japanese commentators have presented this lack of a moral code in Shinto as a virtue rather than an inadequacy. Inazo Nitobe states this apologia well:

A "Naturfolk" learns by intimate contact with nature that there is a healing power in the flower and the grass, in the mountains and streams, in the rain and the clouds. He comes to see gods working in these phenomena, and if they are of divine origin do they not contain goodly qualities? Why seek afar for the divine? It is even in the objects around you. They are good and just. Why seek elsewhere for justice and goodness? So, to live a natural life is to be just and good. There is no evil in nature. What seems to be evil is the tipping of the balance scale. Evil is immoderation. All natural appetites are good and they become evil only when indulged in to excess. This is Shinto, the Way of the Gods, naïve primitive teaching aboriginal to the soil of Japan.[1]

There were no priests in the earliest days. Later, family and tribal leaders developed a priesthood in four classes: the ritualists, who read the *norito* and directed the ceremonies; the diviners, who sought the intent of the gods through divination; the abstainers, who warded off evil influences through ritualistic abstention; and the musicians and dancers. The earliest of these last were women whose designation contains the same root name as that given to phallic deities, which suggests that they may have had some part in temple sexual rites.

Much of the ritual was directed toward purification, for in Shinto the conception of uncleanliness is the nearest approach to the Western conception of sin. To be dirty was to show disrespect for the gods. One could be contaminated by contact with filth, by sickness, or by ordinary physical functions. Because the consummation of marriage was a defilement, special houses were constructed in which brides and grooms spent their wedding night, so that the regular dwellings would not be contaminated. The modern Japanese custom of dousing with buckets of water on New Year's Day all men who have been married during the year is a survival from this belief. Childbirth, the death of a relative, touching a dead body, and many other things produced contamination.

Early Japanese funeral rites were elaborate and filled with a sense of awe and fear. The bodies of the dead were placed in "mourning houses" and left there for periods which varied from a week or more to over a year (as in the cases of some emperors) before burial. Houses in which death had occurred were sometimes abandoned and never lived in again. During the period in which the body of the dead lay in the mourning house, friends and relatives gathered daily to utter laudations, to wail, and to play musical instruments which perhaps they believed might tempt the spirit of the dead to return to the body, as it had once tempted the divine ancestress, Amaterasu Omikami, to emerge from her sulking in the rock cave of heaven. In earliest times, when one in a high position died, servants of the dead—sometimes to a rather large number—were buried alive up to the neck in the earth, forming a human hedge around the burial place, and left to die, thus giving the spirit of the dead companionship, protection, and attendance. Later the practice was discontinued and clay effigies were substituted for living persons. Material objects buried with the dead were so many and costly that they constituted a serious economic drain and frequently impoverished the families of the deceased. Funerals were often held at night with as much secrecy as possible, as though an effort was being made to conceal a shameful and fearful fact.

All evidence points to the fact that the early Japanese felt an almost pathological repugnance for and fear of death. Thus they were willing subjects to submit themselves to the doctrines of Mahayana Buddhism which gave them a goal beyond death and a conviction of the undesirability of life, to the code of the Buddhist-influenced Samurai, which glorified death in battle, and to the later doctrines of State Shinto which made death in the service of the emperor the infallible formula for a glorious existence as *kami*. These were psychological routes over which the Japanese mind was enabled to escape from its early horror of death which found no relief in the sterile cult of primitive Shinto.

5. The Coming of Buddhism

WITH the advent of Buddhism to Japan (about the middle of the sixth century A.D.) Shinto entered its second period. Skillful Buddhist priests made the most of the colorful and profound philosophy and mysticism of their faith to lure converts. With the new religion came also an importation of culture from the Asiatic continent. The Japanese people were taught how to weave better cloth, grow better grain, raise tea, brew better beer, build better roads and bridges, dig better canals, make better pottery. Buddhism brought books with it and began to teach more than the doctrines of Karma and Nirvana. Education improved in all its branches. Principles of compassion, of benevolence, and of human brotherhood were inculcated. Buddhist monasteries and almshouses were established, free clothing was distributed to the needy and medicine to the sick. For the first time the Japanese were systematically offered an ethical code and a goal to seek beyond death.

It is necessary to bear in mind the fact that Buddhism—over a thousand years old before it reached Japan—had itself gone through many modifications since its founding, and that the Mahayana doctrine that the monks taught to the Japanese differed radically from the combination of abstruse philosophical training and exalted moral code that Gautama had preached to his bhikkhus. It had acquired a pantheon, made up largely of gods of India and Central Asia, with the Buddha the supreme deity, a ritual of prayer, and a paradise, which were, indeed, directly contrary to the teachings of the founder, but which offered rewards the Japanese could never have found in either the austere doctrines of Gautama or the sterile superstitions of old Shinto.

The processes of amalgamation were similar to those which have marked syncretism in all religions. The methods are familiar to anyone who knows how many of the holy festivals of the Christian church are but pagan festivals adapted by early Christian missionaries, how even pre-Christian classic art in some cases was given new Christian interpretations, or who has read Bible history as taught to American children in parochial schools and noted how early Jewish tradition and ritual has been given Christian meaning. In such teaching the pillar of cloud by day and of fire by night which led the Children of Israel after they had escaped from Egypt is represented as the spirit of Jesus; Jewish blood sacrifices are tokens of Christ's crucifixion, etc. Such were the methods used also by Buddhism in its task of assimilating Shinto.

The most influential early priest of this broad syncretism was Kukai, better known by his posthumous title of Kobo Daishi, founder of the Shingon, or "true word" sect. Born in 774, Kobo Daishi turned in his youth from a study of the Confucian classics to Buddhism. In the great shrine of Tse he received a revelation from the Food-Possessing Goddess which showed him the way to reconciliation of Shinto with Buddhism.

Emerging from the shrine after a week's seclusion, Kobo announced that all the deities of the Shinto pantheon were but avatars, or manifestations, of the Buddha, and that it was the same Buddha spirit which appeared as a *kami* to Shintoists, as a sage to Confucianists, or as a Buddha to Buddhists. With this basic principle established, it was a fairly simple matter to set up a catalogue of correspondence between Shinto *kami* and Mahayana Buddhist gods, and between Shinto and Mahayana festivals and liturgies. Then, with a band of disciples who formed the Shingon, or "true word" sect, he set out to give his system to Japan.

Beginning boldly at the top, Kobo announced that Amaterasu Omikami, or Ten-Sho-Dai-Jiu, was in truth Dai Nichi Niorai or Amida Buddha. Oijui, the God of War, became Hachiman Dai Bosatsu, or the great Bodhisattva of the Eight Banners. Hundreds of Shinto *kami,* including heroes of local tradition as well as the deified forces of nature, such as wind and fire, were catalogued as manifestations of Buddha, and the process was characterized by the phrase *Ichi-jitzu,* or "one reality."

Phallic deities, represented by undisguised phallic shapes, were given little caps and gowns, faces, arms, and legs, and renamed as Buddhist deities. Sometimes the two were combined. At the entrance to the Buddhist temple in Sakabe village in Harihara-Gun, Shizuoka Prefecture, Genchi Kato reports an erect phallic pillar of stone around which have been carved six figures of Jizo, the Mahayana god of children. A similar amalgamation occurs in a stone phallic emblem at Takasago village in the same neighborhood, which has been changed into a Jizo and is worshiped as a divine guardian angel for women who desire easy childbirth. In other instances the phallic deity Dosojin was changed into two figures of Jizo, called Doraku-Jizu and plainly shown in an amorous embrace.

Ancient blood sacrifices to the god Takeminakata-no-Kami were reconciled to the Buddhist doctrine which forbade the killing of animals by an elaborate casuistry. The divine will of the Buddha, it was said, arranged that there would be selected for the sacrifice only such animals as were about to die anyway through sickness or old age. Their death as sacrificial offerings assured them of a more advantageous reincarnation.

A vital and searching creed, the religion of the Buddha had acquired much from other systems of thought during its thousand years of traveling. In it were the influences of the ever active philosophy of India and Persia, the creative spirit of Grecian art, the speculation of the gnostics, and an accretion of ideas from some of the lesser-known sects of Christianity. Up to this time art in Japan had been a meager feast, but now Buddhist artists from Korea and China filled the temples with a blaze of gold, black, and color which excited the imagination and stirred the emotions. Magnificent altar pieces in which gold was lavishly applied on a black background, paintings in which the whole body of the Buddha shone forth in gold or a golden lake lay calmly resplendent in a scene in which the most lavish colors were beautifully distributed, greeted the eyes of those who had formerly worshiped in bare Shinto shrines. The artistic souls of the Japanese, scarcely knowing that they had been starved until now, stirred with life as a racial artistic consciousness was awakened. Perhaps visual beauty was even a more powerful weapon in Buddhism's near conquest of Japan than religion and philosophy.

Japanese swarmed to the foreign faith; the government, seeing here elements which might strengthen the state, encouraged it. Emperors and high government officials became adherents, several emperors abdicating in order to enter Buddhist monasteries. Buddhist texts were read in the imperial palace and to the people under government direction. Imperial decrees regulated Buddhist affairs and Buddhist festivals became ceremonies of state. Buddhist rites were performed in Shinto shrines.

"Kobo finding a Chinese worm, made a Japanese dragon able to swallow a national religion," writes W. E. Griffis. "In the act of deglutition and the long process of the digestion of Shinto, Japanese Buddhism became something different from every other form of the faith in Asia." [1]

It is interesting to note that Shinto's most prolific literary period was during the time when Buddhism was gaining the ascendancy—that is, from the beginning of the Nara Era, A.D. 710, to the early part of the tenth century. During this time all the important books of Old Shinto were compiled—the *Kojiki,* or "Record of Ancient Matters," in A.D. 712, the *Nihongi,* or "Chronicles of Japan," in 720, the *Idzumo Fudoki* in 733, the *Kogoshui* in 807, the *Manyoshu,* or "Collection of One Thousand Leaves" sometime between 750 and 900, the *Engi Shiki,* or "Rituals of Engi," about 923. Thus it seems evident not only that Buddhism was a powerful stimulant to religious thought and literary effort, but that actually the earliest records of Shinto may have shown some of the influence of the faith that originated in India. Indeed the *Nihongi* is replete with evidences of Buddhist influence at court. Buddhist priests were early welcomed at the imperial palace, and were instrumental in the Taikwa Reform.

Chief rival of Kobo Daishi's Shingon sect was the Tendai sect, founded by Dengyo Daishi in 788, which grew rapidly, until it supported about three thousand temples and an organized military force which warred with the military forces established by Kobo Daishi. But though the two sects were in constant conflict with each other, both contributed materially to the growing power of Buddhism, which year by year seemed more influential in obscuring the ancient faith.

And yet that there is still a reasonable doubt as to whether Buddhism had the greater effect on Shinto, or Shinto on the formation of Japanese Buddhism, is evidenced by the fact that the resulting syncretism is called Ryobu, or "dual," Shinto by some, and Ryobu, or "mixed," Buddhism by others, and that all forms of Japanese Buddhism today are interlaced with Shinto concepts. If phallic symbols were turned into Buddhist gods by the Buddhists, it is certain that in some Japanese monuments still extant Buddhist gods are represented as phallic deities by the Shintoists. Buddhists priests officiated at Shinto shrines; Shintoists worshiped at Buddhist temples. The philosophical and ethical strength of Buddhism pushed on in seemingly irresistible conquest, but underneath there remained the strength of Shinto.

Selections from one of the late Ryobu books, *Wa Rongo,* or "Japanese Analects" (included in the texts which follow this discussion), evidence how large a part of the doctrine was Buddhism, the absorption of certain Confucian ideas, and the high degree of spiritual aspiration which the older religion had brought to the younger by 1669, the year in which the *Wa Rongo* was published. Yet they show, too, that the core of Shinto remained intact. Year by year and century by century the processes of syncretism, rather than the conquest of either by the other, continued. After the end of the ninth century it was almost impossible to find anywhere in Japan the simple unmixed doctrines of the *Kojiki* and *Nihongi,* or to recognize in Japanese Buddhism even the adulterated Mahayana which had entered Japan in the sixth century.

6. Decline of the Emperor

IN ORDER to understand the political significance of the reestablishment of Shinto in Japan nearly a millennium after the beginnings of Kobo Daishi's successful Ryobu, it is necessary now to examine a phase of Japan's secular history.

During the early centuries of the Buddhist conquest the Japanese military establishment was continuously engaged in its unceasing, and never completely successful, attempts to subdue the aboriginal

Ainu, while the emperor and his court seemed lost in a maze of ever more complex ceremonials. Solemn edicts established every detail of dress and deportment for court officials—from the colors of the robes which must be worn on specific occasions, to the exact method in which each rank must pay homage to the emperor. Many days of every year were fully occupied with the most elaborate official rites, which left little time for the pressing political and economic questions crowding for answers. The system of taxation was not functioning well, and the treasury was in a perpetual state of depletion. Domestic disorders and raids by the Ainu were many. But the official records of the period are cluttered with such entries as these: "The Emperor gave a winding water banquet and caused scholars to compose verses"; and "A great wind broke down two trees in the Southern Park. They turned into pheasants." [1]

And while the court was engaged in its winding water banquets and watching trees fall down and turn into pheasants, military and civil authorities in the eastern part of the country (that which includes the present capital, Tokyo) were cheating the government by using military supplies and taxes for their own purposes and making the soldiers do farm labor. When the government learned of this state of affairs, it ordered the formation of permanent defense forces made up of levies from the families of the district chiefs. It was not a large force at the outset—consisting altogether of only about four thousand combatant troops—but it is important in the history of Japan, for it formed the beginning of the privileged class of hereditary soldiery, the class which later so shaped the feudal period of Japan, and still later produced the High Command that opened the Pandora box of the Pacific.

In 784 Otomo Yakamochi, a high court official, was styled Seito Shogun, or "General for Subduing the East." But Otomo's skill in diplomacy and in ways of gaining honorable appointments was apparently greater than his military ability, for his troops were roundly defeated by the aborigines. A new commander was selected—also by reason of court favor rather than military ability—and his failure was as great as had been Otomo's.

In 794 the title Seii-Tai-Shogun, or "Barbarian-Subduing-Generalissimo," was first conferred on Otomo Otomaro, and with his success the Japanese were well on the road to the eventual subjugation of the Ainu. Here was first established a title which was later to designate the real rulers of Japan for several centuries—from 1185 to 1867.

One by-product of the joint influences of Buddhism and the difficulties of government which accompanied the subjugation of the Ainu and the consolidation of the conquering Japanese peoples was the practice of abdication and retirement to Buddhist monasteries which, under the encouragement of Buddhist priests, became common among Japanese emperors. From 782 to 1185 Japan had a total of over thirty emperors, and government was still further complicated, not only by the unwillingness of the titular head of the state to assume the responsibilities of his office, and by frequent shifts in government, but also by the fact that while one Son of Heaven sat on the throne there was always at least one—and sometimes more than one—ex-emperor and older Son of Heaven in a near-by monastery whose word, when he chose to speak, carried even greater divine sanction than did that of the ruling emperor. The situation was one which made for a weak central government. Now the large landholding military clans, which had lost out in the earlier contest for supreme power which had resulted in the Taikwa Reform and the establishment of the imperial family as supreme rulers, indulged their desire to increase their holdings of land and their power by engaging in widespread military conflict with one another.

Some landholding clans were themselves of noble origin— often of such exalted rank that they formed a constant challenge to imperial authority. In the ascendancy were three great clans, the Taira (or Heike, subjects of the classic *Heike Monogatari*), the Minamoto (or Genji, subject of the classic *Genji Monogatari*), and the Fujiwara—the first two military groups, the last the great family of statesmen whose standing at court arose from the facts that they claimed descent from a god only a little lower in the Shinto pantheon than Amaterasu, and that they supplied wives to the emperors. The history of centuries in Japan is closely wrapped up in the history of families which were descended from these—the Ashikaga, the Nitta, the Satake, and the Tokugawa, which issued from the Minamotos; the Miura and the Hojo from the Taira; the Kikuchi and the Utsunomiya from the Fujiwara.

While the landholding clans warred with one another for supremacy, disorder, crime, and misery increased among the people. Even the Buddhists, protestants of a religion of peace and love, joined in the melee of fighting for acquisition of land and power. Irritated by the government's attempt to check increases in their tax-free lands, abbots of the great Buddhist temples formed, equipped, and trained armies of Buddhist priests who not only waged battles between the temples, but often attacked the capital in sanguinary raids which the government was powerless to stop.

By 1100 the imperial government's influence was largely confined to the capital itself, while in the provinces, force applied by the land-owning clans constituted the real law of Japan. Within the warring clans a new military caste had arisen, which was to have a profound influence upon the thought and the history of Japan, and upon world events of the twentieth century.

It was inevitable that rivalry between the Tairas and the Mina-motos—the two most powerful of the many warring clans—should eventually produce a supreme contest for dominance between them. The first stage of the critical test came in a series of battles waged between 1156 and 1160 in which the power of the Minamotos was eclipsed by that of the Tairas, who thereupon assumed a position of unquestioned authority over the emperor and the affairs of gov-ernment, superseding the court influence of the Fujiwaras as well as the military power of the Minamotos.

But the beaten Minamotos quietly gathered their strength and in 1185 under Yoritomo they subjected the Tairas to utter defeat. In the final battle of Dannoura in 1185, the child emperor, who had been kidnaped by the Tairas, died.

Yoritomo now established himself at Kamakura, set up an ad-ministration called the *Bakufu* (or "tent administration," signifying that the seat of authority is in army headquarters in the field, with the army ready for instant combat), and began to petition the throne for a commission as Seii-Tai-Shogun, meanwhile strengthening his position by adding constantly to his landholdings and to the num-ber of feudal sub-chieftains who owed allegiance to him. In a few years the emperor acceded to his demands, and Yoritomo became the first of a succession of military dictators who (with brief exception) were the actual rulers of Japan from 1185 to 1867, while the powerless emperors lived in seclusion—mere figureheads and symbols of Japanese divinity.

It is not difficult to see how control of the emperors by the shoguns was established and maintained when the ages of the emperors during the early years of the shogunate are examined. From 1198 to 1318 Japan had fourteen emperors. Of these one was two years old when he ascended the throne and twelve when he abdicated. One was three years old when he began his "reign" and left the throne the same year. Two occupied the throne from the ages of four to sixteen and seventeen respectively. Only three were over twenty-one when they ascended the throne. The oldest at the time of his accession was thirty-two. The average age of the fourteen at accession was twelve and a half.

But obviously the number of years during which a god incarnate had occupied a mortal body had little significance in his importance as an object of worship, and it was the very sacredness of the emperor's person which made it possible for the shoguns to rationalize removal of the Son of Heaven from the defiling influence of military and governmental affairs. In effect he was put into a niche to be worshiped, but not to be soiled by the conflicts of everyday life.

During the era of the shoguns both Shinto and Buddhism were in process of development. The period of feudal strife saw the rise of four Buddhist sects which are still leaders of Japanese Buddhists, chief and most influential of which are the Jodo, or "pure land" sect, founded by Honen Shonin, a monk of the Tendai sect, and Zen, which had been introduced without success in the seventh century, and was again propagated by the monk Eisai in 1191.

Jodo emphasized the burden and worthlessness of life and the glories of the Buddhist heaven which could be attained after death. The way to gain this reward as explained by Honen, the founder, was easy:

The method of salvation which I have taught is neither a sort of meditation such as that practiced by many scholars in China and Japan in the past, nor is it a repetition of the Buddha's name by those who have studied and understood the deep meaning of it. It is nothing but the mere repetition of the name of Buddha Amida, without a doubt of his mercy, whereby one may be born into the happiest land of the Buddha.[2]

In Zen rigorous physical training and privation were stressed. "Honest poverty" was a mark of distinction. Dignity of manner, which often amounted to rudeness, was encouraged. Wordiness was considered as emptiness and a mere device which obscured meanings. When Yoh Shan, a Zen priest, sat silent for a long time before his monks who were waiting for him to preach, one of them finally asked why he did not speak. "Sutras are taught by the sutra teachers," answered the master. "Shastras are taught by the shastra teachers. No wonder that I say nothing." In other words, Zen, unlike other creeds, has no fixed doctrine which can be fitted into words, but is a matter of inner conviction, purpose, and conduct. Another Zen priest, about to preach a sermon out of doors, heard a swallow singing. "Listen," said he. "That small bird preaches the essential doctrine and proclaims the eternal truth." Then he went indoors, refusing to speak further. Purity, peace, perseverance, strength, enlightenment—all are found in nature. Truth cannot go beyond such statements as "The cloud is in the sky. The sun rises." A seemingly dead clod of earth is imbued with divine life. Vegetables are the children of earth, animals which feed on vegetables earth's grandchildren; men who feed on animals, her great-grandchildren. Life is transitory and must be faced with courage. Death is the one human certainty. Ambition, fame, pleasure, all are vain. In the court of death the high and the low, the rich and the poor, are one, tranquil and at ease, with greater enjoyments than those of any earthly king. Death sweeps away the decaying organisms which obstruct life. It is only through death that life may push onward and renew itself. Hope therefore is possible—through death.[3]

There were several movements against the Buddhist sects. Of these one of the most influential in the early centuries of shogun domination was Yiu-itsu or Yoshida Shinto, founded by the Urabe family of priests who presided over Kasuga shrine from 1192 to 1333. Their doctrine attempted to offset Buddhism with the declaration that not the Buddhist deities but the gods of the Shinto pantheon were the original manifestations of universal life, and that the Buddhist gods were but manifestations of them—thus reversing the syncretic doctrine of Buddhism. Proceeding from this basic premise, the doctrine stated arbitrarily that, because the Life of the Universe has been revealed through the creative activity of Japanese gods, Japan is the divine country and her emperor, directly descended from the sun goddess, is a god incarnate. Here is the nationalistic base on which the Pure Shinto Revival was later to build, and on which modern State Shinto rests.

There were other attempts to preserve Shinto against the on-slaughts of Buddhism during this period: Watarai Shinto, which repudiated both Buddhism and Confucianism, though it included much doctrine from both, and which placed the basic authority for government in the Old Shinto doctrine; Suiga Shinto, which leaned heavily toward Confucianism; and other movements. Kitabatake Chicafusa (1293–1354) enunciated the theory that the imperial insignia represented unique virtues of the Japanese—veracity, symbolized by the mirror, mercy, represented by the jewels, and justice, represented by the sword—and that, since the imperial dynasty was of divine origin, the land of Japan was itself divine. In his *History of the True Succession of Divine Monarchs* he wrote:

> Great Yamato is a divine country; it alone has been transmitted by the Sun-Goddess to a long line of her descendants. . . . It is the duty of every man born on imperial soil to yield devoted loyalty to his Sovereign, even to the sacrifice of his life.[4]

Two other important contributors to the religious thought of the middle ages were Imibe Masamichi, whose doctrine (promulgated in 1367) contained Confucian and Buddhist elements, but to whom the main tenets of Shinto constituted the correct path for the Japanese people, and Tchijo Kaneyoshi (1402–1481), to whom the imperial insignia represented the divine virtue of Buddhahood.

So the amalgamation went on, with alternate conflict and reconciliation between the faiths of Old Shinto and those of Buddhism and Confucianism, until, with the founding of the Fukko, or "Ancient Learning," school in the eighteenth century "Pure" Shinto began to return to its earlier importance in Japanese life.

Let us now see how Japan's religious history during these years went hand in hand with political development, each depending on the other, even in that early day.

From Old Shinto the Japanese had acquired the conception of reverence for the divine emperor and the Confucian concept of filial piety and absolute obedience to superior authority. But early Shinto had been a sterile creed as regards compensation for the calamity of death. Now, however, Shinto was almost completely superseded in influence by Mahayana Buddhism, which, with its accent on the undesirability of life on the one hand, and its paradise after death on the other ("To live is to die," said Jodo; "To die is to live," said Zen), not merely robbed death of its terrors but actually made it seem a more advantageous state than life.

The military leaders were quick to take advantage of this indoctrination and to encourage Buddhist adherence among their followers. During the struggle of the Minamoto and Taira clans for supremacy (a period which was marked also by constant fighting among smaller, less important clans) a special code of behavior and a new morality developed, marked by supreme courage on the field of battle, complete and undying fidelity to leaders, self-sacrifice to a cause, and an utter disregard for death. It was at this time that the Samurai caste was formed, and the Samurai code of fidelity and contempt for death became the highest morality in Japan. So many of the feudal retainers became adherents of Zen that it has been called "the religion of the Samurai." Death in battle for a chieftain became the sought for seal of success upon life. Among the sacred shibboleths of the Samurai were the words attributed to ancestors who had been bodyguards to emperors: "We will not die peacefully, but will die by the side of our sovereign. If we go to the sea, our bodies shall steep in the water. If we go to the hills, on our bodies the grass shall grow."

The word Samurai meant literally "guards" or "attendants." They were also known by a Sinico-Japanese word *Bu-ke* or *Bu-shi* (fighting knights), from which the term *Bushido,* or "Code of the Warrior," came.

It is not difficult to find the sources of Bushido in both Shinto and Buddhism—Buddhism's calm fatalism, its disdain of life and welcoming of death, its acceptance of inevitability, its attempt to find union with the absolute, and Shinto's reverence for and loyalty to the sovereign, the absence of a conception of sin within it, and its concept of the divinity of the very soil of the Japanese islands, for which the Samurai theoretically fought.

Proverbs and legends upon which the Samurai raised their children are legion: "Rectitude is the power of deciding upon a certain course of conduct in accordance with reason, without wavering; to die when it is right to die, to strike when to strike is right." "It is true courage to live when it is right to live, and to die only when it is right to die." A child crying because of some small pain is scolded by his mother in these words: "What a coward to cry for this little pain, what will you do when your arm is cut off in battle? What when you are called on to commit hara-kiri?" A picture is drawn of small sparrows in the nest crying for food. "But for a Samurai," the story ends, "it is a disgrace to feel hunger when the stomach is empty." * Children were hardened by periods in which food and sleep were denied them, by exposure to cold, and by being made to attend executions and touch the heads of the decapitated.[5]

Boys of seven or eight were asked by their Samurai fathers, without any explanation, "Are you ready to die for your lord or for your father?" If they were quick to answer "I am ready to die," all was well. If they were not, they were beaten until they were ready to take the pledge.[6]

There was a grim reminder of this indoctrination in a story issued by the Japanese Domei news agency concerning the fighting on Aka Island near Okinawa in World War II. Here, according to the Japanese report, school children formed suicide squads to help repel the American invasion, running into the midst of the American troops holding hand grenades about to explode. The Tokyo *Mainichi* printed a poem about it which, it said, had been written by a Japanese soldier:

> Clutching tightly in their tiny palms
> Real fire-belching hand grenades,
> Charging into enemy tanks,

> [A detailed account of the banzai charge,
> said to have been here in the original, was
> omitted from the English translation.]

---

* An echo of this proverb was heard in the Japanese-occupied Philippines in January 1943, when a propaganda booklet called "The Flowering of the Racial Spirit" was issued in English. In it the propagandist tells of the contempt he felt when an American officer, having been taken prisoner, asked to be taught to say in Japanese, "I am hungry" and "I am thirsty." The Japanese writer sums up his scorn in the words, "I wanted to spit at him, seeing such a shameless attitude."

They carried shells too weighty for their hands.
Even in childhood they fell admirably,
Like petals on a cherry blossom.
The pitter-patter of their small shoes
Keeps pounding on my breast incessantly.
None can help shedding a tear for,
None can help but follow in the wake of
These children of Aka-Jima.[7]

Common sayings of the Samurai were: "All sins, great and small, may be forgiven on repentance and no scars remain, except two— the flight of a Samurai from the post where he should die, and theft. These leave a lifelong wound which never heals. All born as Samurai, men and women, are taught in childhood that fidelity must never be forgotten." "A faithful wife never seeks another husband; a loyal servant never seeks a second master." "The warrior should act not only with thought for himself but also for his generation and the long future. He should not taint his name forever with cowardice, to save his life which is of short duration. He should regard it as the highest object of desire to die for the sake of his sovereign or sacrifice his life upon any great occasion on the battlefield." "A man lives but one generation, his name lives unto all generations." "The superior man sacrificing his life does a truly human deed." "Life I desire, but justice also I desire. If I cannot have both I take justice and cast my life away." * "To see justice and to fail to do it is an act of cowardice." "Who is he uncorrupted by riches and high rank, unmoved by poverty and misery, unawed by authority and power? He is a man, the truly manly man." [8]

It was during the Middle Ages, under the influence of the Samurai, that the practice of hara-kiri, or ritualistic suicide, developed. It was not simply suicide, an escape from life, but a ritualistic performance, subject to the most detailed rules, by which one could expiate a crime, apologize for error, avoid disgrace, merely prove his sincerity, or follow his master in death. An example of the latter application of the ritual became world famous in 1921. When the Emperor Meiji

---

* "I like fish and I also like bears' paws. If I cannot have the two together, I will let the fish go and take the bears' paws. So, I like life, and I also like righteousness. If I cannot keep the two together, I will let life go and choose righteousness."—*The Works of Mencius*, the great Chinese exponent of the doctrines of Confucius.

died, General Nogi and his wife purified themselves by Shinto rites, and, kneeling before their household shrine in the manner established during the Middle Ages, plunged ceremonial hara-kiri swords into their viscera at the left, drew them across to the right and slightly upward in the prescribed manner, and died. Contemporary Japanese soldiers engaged in banzai charges, lacking the opportunity to follow the prescribed ritual, are permitted to substitute hand grenades for hara-kiri swords. *Kami-kaze* pilots, taken alive in the Pacific, are reported to have worn ceremonial hara-kiri robes under their flying suits.

During this early medieval period the vitalizing core of Shinto remained intact against the assaults of Buddhism, and was used as justification for medieval attempts toward expansion, as is reflected in stories which have an unhappily familiar sound to twentieth-century ears.

When Hideyoshi became regent near the end of the sixteenth century, almost constant clan warfare had raged in the country for a century. Through a series of brilliant military victories, and an efficiently stern control in peace, he overcame the various rebellions and ambitious chieftains, established securely his own rule as military dictator, and cast greedy eyes abroad. His forces invaded Korea and China (though ineffectively), and he announced the intentions which even then Japan had in regard to the Philippines in the following remarkable letter which he sent to the Spanish governor of the Islands:

For more than a hundred years, military leaders in all the provinces had fought with one another and had been continuously engaged in warfare. Our country had thereby lost its national unity, having been split into innumerable separate units. It had also lost communication and traffic facilities. My birth was accompanied by miraculous omens which were interpreted by physiognomists to mean that I was destined to rule nations. This prediction has been fulfilled. Even in my youth, to control national affairs became my duty, within less than ten years the unification of the nation was effected, not even an inch of land being left unconquered. Our national authority has been extended far beyond our borders. Korea, Liu Chiu,* and other nations that are far away have sent their tribute-bearing envoys and paid homage to us. We are now undertaking the con-

---

* Loo Choo, former name of a group of islands (the Ryukus) of which Bloody Okinawa, of World War II fame, is a part.

quest of Tai-Min [China]. This step, however, is not actuated by our own inclinations, but is taken in pursuance of a heavenly command. As for your own country, we have not yet received either homage or tribute. Accordingly we have decided to send our military forces to your country to mete out due punishment. Our vessels are ready to sail to your shores. . . .[9]

Korea, China, the Philippines! Long before the sixteenth century the rites and temples of Buddhism had gone far toward superseding the ceremonials and shrines of Shinto, but Amaterasu Omikami's heavenly command to Jimmu Tenno that he extend the imperial rule so as to embrace the world was still vivid to a military overlord of the time—or at least seemed to him to put an excellent face upon his aggressive ambitions.

In a small outline *History of Japan* issued by the Japanese government in 1939, considerable attention and unstinted praise is given to Hideyoshi. He is praised for his acts of social welfare and his reverence for the gods. Much is made of his campaign against Korea. There then follows this quaint sentence, containing that which for the non-Japanese is a *non sequitur,* but which is completely logical to the mind conditioned by the concept of *hakko ichi-u:*

Hideyoshi was a very great-hearted man with an international outlook, and sent messages to the viceroy of the Philippines and to the head of Kosan-Koku (as Formosa or Taiwan was then called) urging them to despatch envoys with tributes.[10]

7. Return of the Native

BY THE end of the seventeenth century the Samurai, now among the true elite of Japan, not only had established leadership in their code of ethics and etiquette—Bushido—but also, through setting an intellectual example in their own pursuit of Chinese and Japanese studies, had turned the minds of the intelligentsia more and more away from Buddhist literature. With the rise of Confucian and

Taoist studies, there came a decline in Buddhism, which was losing strength in high places and becoming more and more the religion of the masses.

In opposition to all religions and systems of thought originating in foreign lands, there now arose (in the eighteenth century) the *Fukko,* or "Restoration of Antiquity," school of "pure" or "ancient learning" Shinto which attempted to offset the effect of Chinese and Indian ideological infiltrations and restore to the Japanese the Shinto of the *Kojiki* and *Nihongi,* centered in a passionate nationalism. It is not necessary to the purpose of this discussion to analyze the various sects which arose under this movement, but only to mention the principles of its most effective leaders and teachers, Kamo-no-Mabuchi (1697–1769), Motoöri Norinaga (1730–1801), and Hirata Atsutane (1776–1843), and a lesser one, Hatori Nakatsune, whose writings contain the doctrine of the Pure Shinto Revival, and whose influence did a great deal to prepare Japan for the fourth period of Shinto in which the state was to use the old religion as a political weapon of almost inconceivable power.

Descended from a long line of Shinto priests, Mabuchi was thoroughly familiar not only with the classical Shinto texts, but also with Chinese philosophy. Thus he was able to speak with authority when he began a series of attacks on Chinese institutions, setting forth specifically the superiority of the Japanese imperial lineage.

Mabuchi, viewing with horror the fact that the rule of the Son of Heaven had been brushed aside by that of the shogun, charged this degradation of the emperor to the influence of the Chinese, and reviled China and all her works. Yet in his statement of this thesis there is a persistent echo of the Chinese Lao Tze's doctrine of simplicity and of the Confucian theory of government:

In ancient times when men's dispositions were straightforward, a complicated system of morals was unnecessary. . . . But the Chinese, being bad at heart, in spite of the teaching which they got, were only good on the outside. The Japanese, being straightforward, could do without teaching. . . . So long as the sovereign maintains a simple style of living, the people are contented with their own hard lot. Their wants are few and they are easily ruled. But if the sovereign has a magnificent palace, gorgeous clothing, and crowds of finely dressed women to wait on him, the sight of these must cause in others a desire to possess the same luxuries;

or if they are not strong enough to take them by force, it excites their envy. If the Mikado had continued to live in a house roofed with shingles, and whose walls were mud, to wear hempen clothes, to carry his sword in a scabbard wound round the tendrils of some creeping plant, and to go to the chase carrying his bows and arrows, as was the ancient custom, the present state of things would never have come about. But since the introduction of Chinese manners, the sovereign, while occupying a highly dignified place, has been degraded to the intellectual level of a woman. The power fell into the hands of servants, and although they never actually assumed the title, they were sovereigns in fact, while the Mikado became an utter nullity.[1]

Following Mabuchi was his student Motoöri Norinaga, ranked among the greatest scholars that Japan has produced. Motoöri carried Mabuchi's attacks on China to the point of bitter and constant vilification, utterly repudiating the teaching of Lao Tze, which he said was merely a "way of nature" while the true Shinto was "a Way of the Gods." And, like Mabuchi, far from making any apology for the lack of moral teaching in the *Kojiki* and *Nihongi,* he makes capital of this fact as a peculiar and essential virtue in Japanese religion.

The Japanese state, he reasoned, was instituted by Amaterasu Omikami, and is thus superior to every other country in the world. No other nation is entitled to believe itself equal to her, and all are obligated to do homage and pay tribute to the Japanese emperor who is a direct descendant of Amaterasu Omikami. Since the Mikado is a god and vicar of all the gods, the highest duty of a Japanese subject is reverence for and unquestioning obedience to him. Government and religion are the same. Indeed the word *Matsurigoto* means either to govern or to worship. Thus, he wrote:

To the end of time each Mikado is a goddess' son. His mind is in perfect harmony of thought and feeling with hers. He does not seek out new inventions, but rules in accordance with precedents which date from the age of the gods. And if he is ever in doubt he has resort to divination, which reveals to him the mind of the great goddess. Not only the Mikado, but his ministers and people also act up to the traditions of the divine age. Hence in ancient times the idea of *Michi,* or way, ethics, was never broached. In ancient times, although there was no prosy system of doctrine in Japan, there were no popular disturbances and the empire was peacefully ruled. It is because the Japanese were truly moral in their practise that they required no theory of morals. And the fuss made by the Chinese about theoretical morals is owing to their laxity in practice.[2]

One of his most spirited attacks was made against the Confucian doctrine that proclaimed that the emperor was worthy of reverence only while he ruled well, and that revolution against a bad emperor was the inalienable right of the people. Those who proclaimed this doctrine, he said, were merely rebels, for:

The Mikado is the sovereign appointed by the pair of deities Izanagi and Izanami who created this country. The sun goddess never said "disobey the Mikado if he is bad," and therefore, whether he is good or bad, no one attempts to deprive him of his authority. He is the immovable ruler who must endure to the end of time, as long as the sun and moon continue to shine. In ancient language the Mikado was called a god, and that is his real character. Duty therefore consists in obeying him implicitly without questioning his acts. During the middle ages, such men as How-den . . . and others violated this duty and took up arms against him. Their disobedience to the Mikado is attributable to the influence of Chinese learning.[3]

It is interesting and hopeful to find that, in this era of reaction, there were rationalist voices in Japan to challenge the extreme assertions of the Pure Shinto school. One of the most important protests came from a scholar named Ichikawa Tatsumaro who, in a fifty-four page pamphlet, took exception to the extremity of Motoöri's doctrines.

Unwritten traditions, he said, had always to be examined with skepticism, because of the obvious difficulties which stood in the way of handing them down accurately, and the fact that, because of human nature's gullibility, the most fantastic stories were the ones which were the most likely to be preserved. Far from being divine and absolute truth, he declared boldly, the stories which had been handed down as the base of the Shinto tradition were probably invented by the Mikados, and the name of Amaterasu herself probably but a posthumous title conferred long after the age of the gods had passed. If the sun goddess were, indeed, the sun herself, the universe must have been in total darkness before she was born, yet the tradition relates that there were trees and plants, clothing, weapons, boats, and buildings before this time—things which could not have grown or been made and used in darkness. Either these things did exist—and thus were proof that the existence of the sun preceded the time when Amaterasu was said to have been born—or they did not exist at that early date, as it was said they did. In either case the record was thus proved erroneous. Following this argument, he flatly stated the bold heresy that, in his opinion, the entire claim that the sun was born in Japan was invented by the early Mikados as support for the assertion that Japan is the root and all other countries but the branches. And then there follows what is, from the point of view of Western thought, one of the most interesting statements in Japanese religious literature, for it shows conclusively that in the desert of Shinto primitivism there were cases of enlightened thought which promised the possibility of an eventual harmony between matured religious thought in Japan and that of the good-will religions of China, India, Persia, and the West. He wrote:

The gods in heaven make no difference between races of mankind, who are formed into separate nations by the seas and mountain ranges which divide them off from each other, and the sun shines equally over all.

In the first and last part of that sentence there is a pure universalism which is the basic stuff of social thought in all the good-will religions and the direct antagonist of old Shinto, the Pure Shinto Revival, and the state doctrine which flowed from it; and the middle part of the sentence exhibits the healthiest kind of realistic rationalism which is the foe of religious superstition and bigotry anywhere in the world.

Following through in his clear rational thought, Ichikawa continues to say flatly that the ancestors of the Mikados were not gods, but men, and if they were worthy of reverence it was for their virtue alone, not for their ancestry. None of their acts was miraculous or supernatural. If the ancestors of living human beings were not men, they were more likely to have been birds or beasts than gods.[4]

Motoöri responded in a book called *Kuzuhana,* written in 1780, reiterating with greater force than ever his fundamentalist creed, and the enlightenment of Ichikawa and other rationalists of the period was submerged by the dark and mighty wave of reaction. But the record of their thought stands as evidence that not all was retrogression in Japan's great reactionary period, and as a hopeful sign for the potentialities of the Japanese mind once the national polity of Japan is purged of aggressive militarism and totalitarianism.

The third important scholar of this period to turn the tide of thought back to an extremely nationalistic, emperor-worshiping Shinto was Hirata Atsutane, whose father was a Samurai of the Satake family, and who traced his own ancestry to Amaterasu Omikami through Kuammu Tenno, the fiftieth Mikado after Jimmu Tenno. A devoted student of Motoöri, Atsutane made a vow at the latter's grave to become his disciple, and spent the rest of his life working to strengthen Pure Shinto.

At the base of Hirata's teaching was his doctrine of the peculiar and innate virtue of the Japanese people, between whom and others, he wrote, there existed a difference in kind rather than in degree:

We who have been brought into existence through the creative spirits of the sacred ancestral *kami* are, each and every one, in spontaneous possession of the Way of the Gods. This means that we are equipped by nature with the virtues of reverences for the gods, for rulers and parents, with kindness toward wife and children, with the moral qualities which, in Confucianism, are called the five great ethical relationships (i.e., those of ruler and subjects, parent and child, husband and wife, older and younger brothers, and friend with friend) and also with the five virtues (i.e., benevolence, justice, propriety, wisdom, and faith), and to follow this nature just as it is, without bending or turning aside, is to conform to the teachings of the *kami*.[5]

He emphasized, to an extent neither of his predecessors had done, the virtue of Shinto as pure knowledge. Indeed, he said, it was the chief of all knowledge, the wisest and most inclusive of all that had ever come to human minds. By a naïve bit of false logic he justified his statement that it included everything which it was necessary for mankind to know, for, he reasoned, whatever there was of foreign science or technique that could be turned to use by the Japanese was thereby absorbed by Shinto and became Shinto knowledge. This is because (though Japan was the first of all lands, born of the gods, and others were made later of a mixture of sea-foam and mud) all countries owe their origin to the creative activity of Japanese gods and goddesses, and are therefore subservient to Japan. As to Shinto, its obviously superior merits make every other religion not only super-

fluous but actually harmful. Therefore let the people do away with
Buddhism and all other faiths and return to the religion of the *Kojiki*
and *Nihongi*.

A less frequently quoted scholar of the Pure Shinto Revival was
Hatori Nakatsune, Motoöri's favorite pupil, whose name appeared in
1791 as author of a book called the *Sandaiko,* which forms a supplement to Motoöri's *Kojiki-den.* Satow says that the *Sandaiko* may
actually have been written by Motoöri himself, who had perhaps
changed some details of his own theory by this time, yet did not want
to say so openly, and so adopted this device to express his changing
thought through words ascribed to another. But there is no certainty
of this, and the book remains as the product of Hatori.

The central thought of the *Sandaiko* doctrines reiterated and
strengthened the bases of the Pure Shinto Revival. How is it possible
for men born in other countries hundreds of thousands of years after
the formation of the universe to know how it happened, he asks, in
refuting all foreign theories of creation. But the Japanese, whose
country was begotten by Izanagi and Izanami, was the birthplace of
Amaterasu Omikami, and was ruled by the divine descendants forever and ever, were in spontaneous possession of the truth. Japan was
thus infinitely superior to all other countries, whose chief and head it
was; the Japanese people were honest and upright of heart and not
given to useless theorizing and falsehoods, as were the peoples of all
other countries, and were in possession of true and correct information which had descended to them unaltered from the age of the
gods, and unmixed in the slightest degree with the unsupported notions of individuals. (He conveniently ignores such "individual notions" as those of Ichikawa, which, if they had become as widespread
in Japan as those of the Pure Shinto Revivalists, might have materially
changed the course of twentieth-century world history.)

During this period of the revival of Pure Shinto, Christianity,
which had entered Japan about the middle of the sixteenth century,
became the object of violent persecution. Laws of the state, written on
wooden tablets and placed under tiny roofs along the highways, at
bridges, and in cities and villages, named Christianity "an accursed
sect" and offered monetary rewards to those who would reveal the
names of practicing Christians. Strangely enough, Buddhist priests,
perhaps too strongly entrenched in high places and leaders of a relig-

ion too widely spread among the people to make immediate opposition practical, were assigned the task of seeing that no Christian received burial in an ancestral cemetery. Thousands of Christians were put to death by beheading and crucifixion.* Japanese were instructed in ritualistic defilement of the cross. The rite of *fumiita* was instituted, in which large groups of people were made to trample upon a copper plate bearing the image of Christ and the cross, thus proving their scorn for the despised faith and their determination to eradicate it. Now small crucifixes found their way into objects of worship in Shinto shrines where, hidden with the *Shintai* which not even the priests dared uncover, they received the secret obeisance of Christians who outwardly followed the routine of Shinto ritual. And when one bowed low before a representation of Jizo, the Buddhist god of children, who was to know if the yearning of the heart was to that other gentle god of the children whose name sounded so much the same? Thus Christianity went underground, while Shinto—which had been sleeping perhaps, but never dead—woke and faced forward to its modern destiny.

---

* This was not the first time that Christians had been crucified in Japan. In 1587 Hideyoshi, the "great-hearted" regent who invited the Philippines to pay tribute to the emperor, believing that European Catholic missionaries were spies, ordered them to leave the country. When they did not leave, nothing was done about it for ten years. In 1597, however, Hideyoshi's suspicions were again aroused, and he ordered crucifixion of twenty-six. The sentence was executed after the prisoners were subjected to a "horror march" somewhat similar to that forced upon the American prisoners from Bataan in 1942. The Christian prisoners are reported in a contemporary account as having rejoiced and given thanks for having had bestowed upon them the highest privilege possible to man—to die for Christ. One may perhaps be forgiven if he sees here something like an emotional parallel to the modern phenomenon of Japanese soldiers who seek death for the divine emperor as the highest blessing which may be granted to them.

8. Restoration of the Emperor

PERHAPS the most important effect of the teachings of the Fukko school of Shinto was a widespread loyalist movement which swayed not only religious thought, but also became, first, a powerful contributing cause of political change, and later, a political tool. But before examining the dramatic events which, in the last third of the nineteenth century, so changed the political face of Japan, let us look briefly at slow changes which were taking place during the last two centuries of Japanese feudalism.

For more than two hundred years (1615–1868) the powerful Tokugawa shoguns (members of a branch of the Minamoto family) gave Japan an era of peace achieved by an iron rule and the enforcement of the most stringent and detailed regulations, which provided a place for everyone, and kept everyone in his place.

Nominally at the top of the social and political structure was, of course, the sacred emperor, who lived in the court city of Kyoto. But his position was purely nominal. The real government was at Yedo (now Tokyo) at the headquarters of the Tokugawas. The country was split up into feudal fiefs, each with a feudal lord, or *daimyo,* who had absolute authority in his district, but along with it the responsibility to collect taxes and to keep order. The only difference between any one of these feudal lords and the Tokugawas, was that the Tokugawas had more land, more soldiers, more wealth—were, in short, more powerful—and so could hold their authority over the whole country. Under the feudal lords were the Samurai, who regulated the common people, most of whom were farmers, each giving fealty and paying taxes to a local *daimyo.*

There was a rigid system of social classes, each with its prescribed dress, occupation, and laws, which included different penalties for members of different classes who committed the same offenses. Socially the emperor, his family, and his court were, of course, at the top of the scale. But this had little bearing in the large part of the country

52

ruled by the Tokugawa shoguns, where the Tokugawa lords and their families headed the social list. Under them were the other feudal lords, and even they were ranked; those who had always supported the Tokugawas being superior to those who had reluctantly given their fealty after they had been conquered in battle. Next to the lords were the Samurai, who, now that there were no more wars, devoted themselves to collecting taxes, reading and commenting on the Chinese and Japanese classics, and such graceful social accomplishments as the tea ceremony and attendance at the "No" plays. For the Samurai there were very special laws indeed, most resented of which by the common people was that which gave the Samurai the privilege of *Kiri-sute-gomen,* that is, the right of killing a commoner without ever being called to account for it.

Under the Samurai were the farmers, the economic backbone of Japanese feudalism. During the centuries of Japan's isolation she was almost entirely an agricultural nation. The wealth of the feudal lords consisted in the sacks of rice grown by the farmers and collected by the Samurai for the lords.

The fact of the farmer's essentiality to the feudal system helped to place him in a somewhat favored position in medieval Japanese life. Indeed there are some apologists for Japanese feudalism on the grounds of the security and essential dignity which it is asserted were its gifts to the common man. One such, Arthur May Knapp, says:

The leading and most natural result of the situation was the exaltation of the farmer class. The cultivation of the soil was raised to the dignity of a profession, nay, even of a fine art, especially in the provinces under the direct control of the Shogunate. Every effort was made by the government, not only to improve the condition, but also to cultivate the self-respect of the agricultural class. . . .

The fostering of the spirit of independence and self-respect among the farming population led to the formation of village communities as highly organized and as independent and democratic in the conduct of their municipal affairs as those of New England. The iron hand of the central government was indeed everywhere seen, but hardly ever felt. "The laws," says Dr. Simmons, "under which the people lived came out and up from them instead of down and upon them. They were mainly local customs matured by centuries of growth and experience, the general principle of their enactment being that any custom of the rural districts

which had existed for fifty years or more should be recognized and respected as laws." . . . There was a Kyoto saying, "government-made
laws are but three-day laws." [1]

But these, it must be said, are the words of an enthusiastic Japanophile. More objective students have characterized the situation in
far different terms. E. Herbert Norman, for instance (in *Japan's
Emergence as a Modern State,* published in 1940 by the Institute of
Pacific Relations), quotes a well-known saying which characterized
Tokugawa agrarian policy: "To impose taxes upon farmers to such
an extent that they could neither live nor die." And Sir George Sansom
sums up the situation by saying that the Tokugawas thought highly
of agriculture but not of agriculturists. According to a statement of
Matsudaira Sadanobu, a Tokugawa councilor, the direct taxes upon
a farmer's produce ate up from fifty to seventy per cent of the fruits of
his labor. Other taxes—on his doors, on his windows, on female
children, on cloth, on *sake,* on hazel trees, on beans, on hemp, on a
room added to his hut—took much of the meager subsistence allowance which was left to him. Requisitions for his person or/and
horses for such government service as was required for the postal
system added further drains. Even in good years the peasant's lot
was almost intolerable; in lean years it became almost exterminative.

As money economy penetrated the villages the peasant was no
longer able to live by barter alone. Needing money for fertilizer and
agricultural implements, the prices of which were constantly rising
though his income never increased, he was driven to usurers whose
oppression was added to that of the *daimyo*-controlled Samurai.

Even so enthusiastic a Japanophile as Arthur May Knapp reports
details which scarcely fit into the idyllic picture of pastoral bliss,
horny-handed dignity, and essential democracy which he has otherwise painted of the Japanese farmer:

In a democracy in many regards well-nigh idyllic, there ruled a despotism which made itself felt in every corner of every home. Independent
in the conduct and administration of their municipal affairs, in their
domestic concerns the villagers were practically deprived of their freedom. With the general laws of the empire they had little or nothing to
do save to meet their annual taxes. But the sumptuary laws imposed upon
them regulated almost every item of household and even of personal

economy. Every farmer was restricted in his expenditures by prescribed rules. So minute were these rules that any but a literal transcription would fail to give an idea of the scope and extent of the paternal supervision of the homes of the Japanese people by the government in the interests of economy.[2]

There follows a list of regulations limiting (to a minimum below which bearable existence would seem impossible) the size and style of a farmer's house (which must not, for instance, be roofed with tile); the value of gifts which may be made when a son or daughter is married; the food which may be served on the occasion of the marriage; the clothes which may be worn (silk is forbidden); the number of people who may be invited to a wedding; the food which may be served on other occasions (when a visit of condolence is made in the case of death, for instance, wine is forbidden); the presents which may be given on the birth of a child; the ornaments which may be worn in the hair, footwear, etc. It is explained that these regulations were made so that persons may live contentedly in their own stations without exceeding their incomes and aspiring to higher states.

Next below the farmers in the social scale were the merchants. But if respect (or, if you like, a paternalistic condescension and opportunistic humoring) was shown the farmers by the government officials and the Samurai—all of whom depended for their living and their power upon the farmers' rice—scorn and social ostracism were the lot of the medieval Japanese merchant. This was partly an outgrowth of the code of the Samurai, which despised both the processes of making money and its inevitable result in a departure from the simple and unostentatious life recommended by Zen and forced upon both the Samurai and the farmer—on the former by both his code and his modest financial circumstance, on the latter by the government's system of depriving him in taxes of all but the barest essentials of living, and its far-reaching restrictions on his personal habits. But it is impossible to escape the implications of danger to an agricultural feudal regime which the rise of a merchant class threatened. Perhaps this danger was the reason for placing the merchant in a social class below which there were only laborers who dealt with such unpleasant tasks as slaughtering animals and tanning hides.

Within the frame of this closely knit social and economic scheme the Tokugawas developed checks to incipient revolution which were simple, ruthless, and, for centuries, effective. Every *daimyo* (or feudal lord) was compelled to spend a part of each year in Tokyo, and while he was at home to leave his wife and children at Tokyo as hostages. Social intercourse between the fiefs was discouraged. Rigid passport regulations were enforced to see that a *daimyo's* armies and armaments were not increased. New buildings or remodeling of old could not be made without first submitting the plans to the shogun's government. Marriages between the families of the *daimyos* had to be approved by the shogun. Functions of officials were rotated, in a way to prevent a monopoly of an office—a plan which to some extent is in operation in Japan today.

Meanwhile Europe had left its period of feudalism behind it, and the spirit of human freedom and initiative—archenemy of feudalism —was sweeping the Western world. Seeing the danger which the Western ideas constituted, the Tokugawas sought to quarantine Japan in utter isolation—and for two centuries succeeded amazingly well. Christians in Japan were persecuted and Christian missionaries and teachers were expelled. All foreign trade, save for a closely regulated small traffic with the Dutch and the Chinese, was prohibited. The building of ships capable of going to sea was forbidden, and every Japanese was strictly enjoined against leaving the islands against pain of death if he returned.

But generations of peaceful isolation, with their accompanying increase in population and exploitation of the farmer, tended to undo the best-laid plans of the Tokugawas. The Samurai, no longer stimulated by war, failed to maintain their former position of prestige and power, and merchants, under the beneficent atmosphere of peaceful internal trade, were able to increase their holding and influence, and, with their rising power, resented more and more the authority exercised over them by the Samurai and the feudal lords.

Other related factors contributed to the growing pattern of the dissolution of the shogunate. In their hideously submerged state the farmers had long been exercising certain forms of passive resistance, chief of which were infanticide (which they called *mabiki,* or "thinning"), an almost inevitable outcome of a situation in which subsistence was barely possible, and leaving their farms for the cities, especially during the years of famine. In addition there were more and more frequent active revolts, which toward the end of the period of the shoguns became commonplace.

With diminishing support from the farmers, and the rise of money economy, the financial condition of the *daimyos* became acute, and there was widespread bankruptcy, which in turn made it impossible for the lesser *daimyos* to support their Samurai, who left their lords in increasing numbers and became *ronin,* wandering independent adventurers, frequently brigands, and often, in their angry frustration, outspoken enemies of the *Bakufu,* or shogun's government. There were frequent intermarriages between the families of Samurai and merchants, still further breaking into the rigid class system which was already toppling under economic pressure.

G. B. Sansom summarizes the economic situation in this concise paragraph:

The peasants were heavily oppressed by members of the knightly order, who soon, in their turn, were exploited by the rising class of merchants. Then as the daimyo and the samurai tried to transfer their burden of debt to the already overladen shoulders of the farmers, the agricultural economy broke down, and was replaced by a mercantile economy which Japan was unable to support without calling upon the outside world.[3]

Such was Japan's situation when, in 1853 and 1854, Commodore Perry, disregarding the inhospitality of the reigning shogun, made his historic calls upon Japan with an invitation to trade with the United States. That the shogunate seemed unable to prevent his visit further weakened its prestige.

The shogunate tried to bolster its position in consenting to trade with the United States and European countries by pointing out how foreign intercourse could be made to advance the divinely ordained destiny of the emperor to rule the world. In a remarkable memorandum to the throne in 1858 Lord Hotta, last of the Tokugawa premiers, called the emperor's attention to "the power and authority deputed to us [the Japanese] by the Spirit of Heaven," and pointed out that national resources should be developed, the military establishment built up, and that, in all relations with foreign countries, it should constantly be borne in mind that Japan's objective was eventual sovereignty over them. When all the nations of the world were made to accept the authority of the divine emperor of Japan, he wrote, then "the Ruler of Japan will have accomplished a deed commensurate with the great responsibilities he owes to Heaven and Earth." [4]

But impoverished Samurai, resenting the shogunate because under it they had lost their position, and seizing upon the weakness of the shogun in admitting the Westerners, turned to the basic doctrines of Old Shinto, now strengthened by the Pure Shinto Revival, and adopted as their slogans, Son-no—"Revere the Emperor!" and Jo-i—"Expel the barbarians!"

Soon their revolt against the shogunate drew within its circle a class of pre-feudal court nobility, the kuge—also reduced by the Tokugawas to poverty and ineffectiveness—who in turn established a secret alliance with determined members of the opposition to the shogunate in the Chosu clan. Around these rallied other discontented lords of the Choshu, Satsuma, Tosa, and Hizen clans, and an anti-Bakufu league was formed.

Meanwhile Perry had opened the gates which admitted the West, and Europe began to take a renewed interest in Japanese affairs. During the early 1860's, when the Bakufu was continually losing strength before its opponents, France and Britain carried on their ancient rivalry in a struggle for predominant influence in Japan—France backing the Bakufu, Britain the anti-Bakufu clans, further confusing the Japanese political situation.

All of these influences paved the way for the revolution of 1867–68, in which the last of the shoguns was forced to resign, and the emperor (Meiji) was restored to the throne as the actual as well as the titular head of the Japanese government. The revolution was accomplished by a combination of warlike clans (who thus regained an influence which they had lost through submergence by the Tokugawas and preceding shoguns), by a lower rank of Samurai (who, impoverished by the financial collapse of their lords, gained through the restoration of the emperor a higher rank than even the Tokugawa Samurai), by a wealthy merchant class (who thus gained social, political, and economic power through the elevation of the political group which they backed, with the emperor at their head), by kuge (who thus regained their lost influence at court), and by revolting peasants who had been forced to the point of desperation by taxes which drove them to starvation. And as a background of strength supporting the movement was the ancient conception of the sacredness of the emperor, first enunciated by the *Kojiki,* and used seven centuries before as a justification for removing him from the mundane influences of government.

It is well to remember these things in evaluating the significance of the Restoration of 1868 and the reforms which followed it. It is necessary to bear in mind the fact that, although the struggle of 1867–68 was in the nature of a revolution, it was a revolution of autocrats against autocrats—a contest for power on the upper economic, political, and social levels rather than a revolt of people against their rulers. To be sure, there were included in the revolting groups many oppressed peasants, but their interest was in relief from the unbearable burden of taxation and in local affairs; their interest in the national government was meager or nonexistent and what little they had was sternly discouraged by the nobles.

Throughout Japan's history, with but minor exceptions, contests for authority in the national government have always been waged at the top of the political and social scale. In a people who had been taught from the beginnings of their history that their emperor was divine and destined to rule not only over themselves but also over all peoples, and who for seven centuries had been subject to powerful military rule, there had been little tendency to popular revolution as the Western world knows the phenomenon, and no widespread consideration of the doctrine of the rightness and desirability of self-government such as that which swept Europe and America during the seventeenth and eighteenth centuries. Just as the Taikwa Reform of the seventh century, which set up Japan's first centralized government, firmly established the right of the nobly born to rule the humbly born, just as the long struggles for supremacy among the feudal lords during the Middle Ages but shifted authority from one high-born group to another as their relative powers shifted and constantly confirmed the existence of a ruling class and the subjugation of the people, so did the 1868 Restoration go even a step further in this confirmation. Though the reign of the Emperor Meiji was one of reform and modernization, led by the most imaginative group of men in Japan, which included some liberals, every improvement of conditions offered to the Japanese was in the nature of a *gift from the Son of Heaven to his trusting children* rather than something which was their inherent right, and careful provisions left no loophole for slow entry of popular authority. The absolute authority of the emperor, and the duty of submission of the subjects, was confirmed more strongly than ever. The conception that the people were capable of determining what their government should be, and controlling it, though it was voiced by a tiny minority group, did not enter the thinking of the Restoration leaders.

Indeed there was but little change in the actual character of a basic feature of the government. During the early stages of the pacification of the Japanese islands the way of life of the conquering clans was the way of the warrior, the strongest clans seeking, by force of arms, to gain the right to govern. The Taikwa Reform, born in war, established the imperial family as the rulers, but they never showed themselves capable of maintaining a strong central government. From the twelfth-century days of the reign of Minamoto Yoritomo, the first of the ruler shoguns, Japan had been governed by families of warriors. Now the powerful warrior families, who—in a struggle not dissimilar to those which had marked the entire feudal era—had overthrown the Tokugawa rule, quietly exercised their influence as they had always wished to do—their identity somewhat obscured by the emperor whom their "revolution" had pushed once more into the political foreground.

9. The Devil Quotes Scripture

A FEW weeks after the re-establishment of the imperial authority, there was issued in the name of the sixteen-year-old Emperor Meiji a declaration pledging the emperor to "call councils and rule the nation according to public opinion," to unite in all enterprises "men of upper and lower classes," to treat civil officials and military authorities so "that they can attain their aims and feel no discontent," to "destroy old unworthy ways and customs" so that "the people shall walk along the highways of heaven and earth," and to "seek knowledge among the nations of the world" so that "the Empire shall be led up to the zenith of prosperity." This last was to bring in its train an influx of Western culture, including Christianity, and the faint breath of democratic idealism, which created such wholesale, if often ununderstanding, ardor among the Japanese that it was soon to bring about a reaction in a renewed and bitter hatred for all foreign ways.* But it also fathered among Japanese intellectuals a liberal movement which has proved a frequent embarrassment to the Japanese militarists of the twentieth century.

Less than a year later, in March 1869, the lords of the Satsuma, Choshu, Hizen, and Tosa—those clans which had been primarily responsible for the overthrow of the Tokugawas—sent a remarkable memorandum to the emperor (quoted in the texts which follow this discussion). With it they included a list of all of their holdings and men, returning, they said, the emperor's property to him. The government replied briefly and to the point: "The proposal of the western lords is highly approved by the Court." The example of these leading clans was soon followed by the rest of the feudal lords.

Actually this seeming bit of patriotic generosity was as much as anything a political gesture on a grand scale. By overthrowing the ruling Tokugawas, and elevating the position of the emperor in every way possible, they made their own position as a power behind the throne secure. Thus, though these military leaders of the great clans who engineered the restoration of the emperor were willing to sacrifice some of the special rights and privileges which they had enjoyed under feudalism, they never sacrificed the basic idea of military government which had made feudalism secure. Japan, born in military conquest, unified by sanguinary might, and governed in peace by warriors with the political ambitions of soldiers and an international outlook completely in harmony with Amaterasu Omikami's heavenly command to extend the imperial rule over the entire world, was still in the hands of a group in which military influence predominated.

The position of the small peasant was not noticeably bettered by

---

* "The Western civilization, generally speaking, intoxicated our Japanese minds like strong drink; and as a matter of course we often found ourselves, when we awoke from that intoxication, sadder, and even inclined to despise ourselves."—Yone Noguchi, *Japan and America* (Tokyo: Keio University Press; New York: Orientalia, 1921).

the Meiji restoration. To be sure, he had a certain amount of theoretical freedom which he had not enjoyed under the shoguns. And while the principle of his taxation was changed so that it was no longer a matter of plan to take from him all of his produce save a bare minimum necessary to his subsistence, the actual taxes were not reduced and were now payable in money, which meant that he was forced to sell his crops as soon as he harvested them, in order to acquire money for his taxes, and thus was compelled to sell on a glutted market at a low price. Since his misery was unalleviated, he felt that he had been sold out by the revolution to which he had contributed, and peasant revolts increased to a point at which the success of the Restoration was endangered.

The government, needing desperately to bolster the re-established authority of the Mikado, was quick to take advantage of the nationalism and renewed reverence for the emperor which the revival of Pure Shinto and the Samurai slogan, "Revere the Emperor," had emphasized. The teachings of Mabuchi, Motoöri, and Hirata were at once seized upon to bring about unification of the state and support of the emperor through a heightened reverence for his sacred person, and a renewed affirmation of his divine mission to rule.

An imperial edict was issued during the first year of Meiji which announced that:

The worship of the gods and regard for ceremonies [Shinto] are the great properties of the Empire and the fundamental principles of national polity and education. . . . On this occasion of the restoration [of direct imperial rule] Tokyo has been made the new capital and the Emperor shall reign in person. First of all, rituals shall be initiated and the initiation of law and order shall be established. Thus the way of the unity of religion and government [*saisei itchi*] shall be revived.[1]

During the same year a Department of Shinto was set up within the government, ranking ahead of all other governmental departments, and Shinto was made the state religion. Buddhism was refused recognition by the state and a great many Buddhist properties confiscated. (Though the department was abolished three years later, it was supplanted by a Department of Religion, which gave Buddhism privileges under a certain amount of jurisdiction, but the prin-

ciple of governmental regulation of religion had been firmly established and through several variations, including the theoretical "freedom of religion" granted by the constitution of 1889, has remained
operative to this day.) Regulations for preaching were established in
which Shinto priests (and later Buddhist, when they were again
allowed to preach) were required to combine political indoctrination
with religious precepts.

In 1870 another imperial rescript called attention to the antiquity
of the principle of *saisei itchi:*

From the very beginning of the establishment of the affairs of government by the Great Ancestress [Amaterasu Omikami] she worshipped the
gods and cherished the people with tender affection. The origin of the
unity of religion and the state [*saisei itchi*] is long ago.

On the same day another edict was issued:

We solemnly announce: The Heavenly Deities and the Great Ancestress established the throne and made the succession secure. The line of
Emperors in unbroken succession entered into possession thereof and
handed it on. Religious ceremonies and government were one and the
same [*saisei itchi*] and the innumerable subjects were united. Government and education were clear to those above, while below them the
manners and customs of the people were beautiful. Beginning with the
Middle Ages, however, there were sometimes seasons of decay alternat-
ing with seasons of progress. Sometimes the Way was plain, sometimes,
darkened: and the period in which government and education failed to
flourish was long.

Now, in the cycle of fate, all things have become new. Polity and
education must be made clear to the nation and the Great Way of obedience to the gods must be promulgated. Therefore we newly appoint
propagandists to proclaim this to the nation. Do you, our subjects, keep
this commandment in mind.[2]

It need scarcely be pointed out that "obedience to the gods," in
the meaning of this edict, was synonymous with obedience to the
emperor-god and the warrior politicians whose counsels were so
accurately reflected in the decisions announced in his name.

Regulations of the law adopted in 1872 required that all religious
instructors were to embody in their teachings these principles: "To
make plain the laws of Heaven and the way to Humanity, to lead

the people to respect the Emperor and be obedient to his will, and to embody the principles of reverence and patriotism." The principle of *saisei itchi* (unity of Shinto and state) was instituted in public education and has increasingly dominated it ever since.

In 1881, as a measure against growing dissatisfaction throughout Japan, an imperial rescript signified to the people the emperor's intention to establish a parliamentary form of government. But the very wording of the rescript reaffirmed the glory of the emperor and his responsibility to the gods rather than any right of the people to self-government.

During this period the Japanese government obviously saw clearly that, on the one hand, it had ready for its use in a plan of intensified nationalism the tremendous emotional power of a religion which had been laying a base for nationalism over a period of nearly nineteen centuries, but that, on the other hand, an ethic had been superimposed upon the ancient religion (chiefly through the influences of Buddhism, Confucianism, and, to a much lesser extent, even Christianity) which, through having injected a strain of universalism and love for peace, however faint, worked directly against the aggressive, ready-for-war nationalism which was to be intensified. Wisely it did not attempt the probably impossible task of suppressing the doctrines in the Shinto sects that held within them elements of danger to the nationalistic program, nor did it attempt to unite the sects as such in one body to back the government's plan for aggressive unification.

Instead it devised a thoroughly workable and startlingly effective plan. In 1882 all Shinto organizations were divided into two classes: (1) institutions of the state, that is, shrines, and (2) institutions of sectarian Shinto, that is, churches. All government support was withdrawn from the sectarian bodies, who were now (as are our churches) compelled to depend upon private support, while the shrines, under government supervision, were given partial financial support by the government.

Never has a more unbeatable plan been devised to unify a people for possible future war. The patterns devised by Fascist Italy and Nazi Germany are but pale imitations in which it was impossible to achieve the almost total indoctrination which the Japanese sought— and attained. For here were the basic tenets of a religion nearly two thousand years old—the divinity of the emperor, the sacredness of the

Japanese homeland, the divine superiority of Japan and the Japanese, and the heavenly command to spread the imperial glory throughout the world. By this separation the leaders of the sectarian churches were left free (under the watchful eye of the state) to increase religious emotion in the people (which included reverence for Amaterasu Omikami, and her divine descendant, the emperor), while the state stood by to emphasize the divinity of the emperor and the heavenly command and to build layer upon layer of nationalistic indoctrination upon the bases which the sects were continually laying and relaying. The facts of this separation must be constantly kept in mind while considering the meaning of Shinto from 1882 onward.

Actually today the word "Shinto" designates three distinct though overlapping forces: (1) "popular" Shinto, (2) sectarian Shinto, and (3) State Shinto.

Popular Shinto is a composite of folk beliefs and practices, some of which are common to all Japan and some of which are indigenous to specific localities. It includes the cult of Inari, the fox god, worshiped as the spirit of the rice and as the deity of the geisha and the prostitutes, who make offerings at Inari shrines in the hope of getting many patrons. There is black magic in it, healing by talismans and folk rituals, worship of the sun, etc. Every village has a local shrine which is an edifice of neither sectarian nor State Shinto, but merely the habitation of the local god who protects the village. Soldiers going into battle are wont to carry with them a bit of earth from the village shrine to protect them. Tree worship, phallicism, worship of the mountain and forest gods, are all parts of popular Shinto, to some or many features of which almost all Japanese, whether they are members of Shinto sects, Buddhists, or even Japanese Christians, subscribe. The practice of keeping "god shelves" for the spirits of ancestors in every Japanese home, and making offerings to them, is within the realm of popular Shinto. It is popular Shinto which accounts for the sacred talismans against evil and sickness which may be found pasted at the front gate of a home or in the kitchen, even though the main room of the house may contain a sacred Buddhist alcove for the ancestral tablets. It is popular Shinto which explains the sacred talisman which is hidden in the rafters when a house is built, and the practice prevalent in some rural areas of spilling some of the first drink of the evening into the fire pit to appease the spirits which frequent the house. Popular Shinto has no organization or unified church body. While it is filled with religious tradition and implications, it may be likened more readily to a powerful folklore than to a religion.

The Shinto sects constitute a genuine religious force, inadequate and immature, to be sure, by comparison with any of the good-will religions in their contemporary forms, containing much primitivism, much seemingly empty ritual and superstition, yet with the potential values of enlightenment, peace, civilization, and universalism which mark all religions that have a sincerely felt theology and ethic. Hindered in their normal development by the peculiar circumstances of Japan's political, economic, and social history, they could not, in their present forms, constitute an adequate faith for an enlightened people. Yet their movement has been definitely in the direction of enlightenment.

State Shinto, on the other hand, is the most reactionary and most powerful doctrine of aggressive nationalism and conquest which has ever been forced upon any people—a doctrine which has exploited with almost inconceivable success the religious fervor of a nation. It will be well if we of the United Nations remember this distinction clearly in our regulation of Japan now that we have won through military victory the opportunity to influence Japanese thought. The government of Japan has done the most thorough job of scrambling religion and political indoctrination in history. One of the most difficult—and necessary—tasks which now faces the United Nations is that of helping the Japanese people to unscramble them.

From 1882 to the present the separation between state-supervised shrines and the churches of sectarian Shinto has continued. The sects carry on religious indoctrination, usually centering about the precepts of the sect founders or other important religious teachers of the past. There are regular church services, with instruction, prayer, and ritualistic observances. The church bodies supervise a certain amount of social welfare work and publish religious literature. The state shrines, on the other hand, confine themselves to formal ceremonials and festivals calculated to increase the spirit of nationalism and loyalty to the emperor and to the government program.

During the decade immediately following the Restoration, government leaders, impressed by the wealth and power of the Western nations, studied European and American political principles for ideas that might be used in the reformation and strengthening of the Japanese government. The philosophies of Rousseau, John Stuart Mill, Adam Smith, and Thomas Jefferson were all examined, but were rejected as being too dangerously democratic. A delegation sent to Europe, headed by Hirobumi Ito, found the Prussian oligarchic government best suited to their needs, and, with certain modifications to Japonize it, the German form was adopted as a model in the establishment of the Japanese Constitution of 1889. The Japanese modification carefully centralized authority in the emperor, which is to say, in the oligarchy. The cabinet was made responsible not to the Diet but to the emperor himself, and every possible loophole for democratic government was sealed up.

The first article of the Constitution states that "The Empire of Japan shall be reigned over and governed by a line of Emperors unbroken for ages eternal." The third article says, "The Emperor is sacred and inviolable." Article XXVIII declares, "Japanese subjects shall, within limits of law, not prejudicial to peace and order, and not antagonistic to their duties as subjects, enjoy freedom of religious belief." But interpretation of the limiting clauses and the enforced indoctrination of the tenets of State Shinto have operated to make the freedom of the Japanese in religion comparable to that of a railroad engine confined by its two narrow ribbons of steel and the controlling hand of the engineer.

Perhaps the true purpose of the Constitution is best expressed in a paragraph written by Prince Ito in 1889:

The Sacred Throne was established at the time when the heavens and the earth became separated. The Emperor is Heaven descended, divine and sacred; He is pre-eminent above all his subjects. He must be reverenced and is inviolable. He has indeed to pay due respect to the law, but the law has no power to hold him accountable to it. Not only shall there be no irreverence for the Emperor's person, but also He shall not be made a topic of derogatory comment nor one of discussion.[3]

The "freedom of religous belief," limited though it was by the qualifying phrases and assailed by state indoctrination, nevertheless encouraged the spread of Buddhism, Christianity, Confucianism, and the doctrines of the Shinto sects, all of which by now included the admixture of foreign faith, while the state, through its shrines and religiously based propaganda, concentrated on the barest and simplest of the nationalistic doctrines of Old Shinto, interpreting them in ways which would furnish the strongest support for its policies.

On October 30, 1890, there was issued an Imperial Rescript on Education which has become so important in the religious and cultural history of modern Japan that it must be quoted in full:

Know ye, Our Subjects:
Our Imperial Ancestors have founded our Empire on a basis broad and everlasting, and have deeply and firmly implanted virtue; Our subjects, ever united in loyalty and filial piety, have from generation to generation illustrated the beauty thereof. This is the glory of the fundamental character of Our Empire, and herein also lies the source of our education. Ye, Our subjects, be filial to your parents, affectionate to your brothers and sisters; as husbands and wives be harmonious, as friends true; bear yourselves in modesty and moderation; extend your benevolence to all; pursue learning and cultivate arts, and thereby cultivate intellectual faculties and perfect moral powers; furthermore advance public good and promote common interests; always respect the Constitution and observe the laws; should emergency arise, offer yourselves courageously to the State; and thus guard and maintain the prosperity of Our Imperial Throne coeval with heaven and earth. So shall ye be not only Our good and faithful subjects but render illustrious the best tradition of your forefathers.

The Way here set forth is indeed the teaching bequeathed by Our Imperial Ancestors, to be observed by Their Descendants and the subjects, infallible in all ages and true in all places. It is Our wish to lay it to heart in all reverence, in common with you, Our subjects, that we may attain to the same virtue.

It is interesting that this rescript, which has been quoted over and over as authority for the contempt of foreign religions, is almost pure Confucianism. Yet it may almost be called a "scripture" of State Shinto, so highly is it regarded as a guide by interpreters of the state religion.

On August 12, 1899, "Order Number Twelve" prohibited religious instruction in both public and private schools. But the rituals practiced in the state shrines, and the all-pervading doctrine of national divinity, national loyalty, and emperor-worship being taught under rigid state supervision in the schools, in other words, State Shinto, were considered not as a religion but as training in civic responsibility, so that enforced teaching of its doctrines would not seemingly conflict with the order.

The logic by which this position is supported is stated by an early twentieth-century writer:

In the case of a civilized country there must exist freedom of faith. If Shinto is a religion, however, the acceptance or refusal thereof must be left to personal choice. Yet for a Japanese subject to refuse to honor the ancestors of the Emperor is disloyal. Indeed a Japanese out of his duty as a subject must honor the ancestors of the Emperor. This cannot be a matter of choice. It is a duty. Therefore this cannot be regarded as a religion. It is a ritual. In this respect the government protects the shrines and does not expound doctrines. On the other hand, since it is possible to establish doctrines with regard to the Shinto deities, it is necessary to permit freedom of belief in Shinto considered as religion. Hence there has arisen the necessity of making a distinction between Shinto regarded as the functioning of national ritual and that Shinto which proclaims doctrines as a religion.[4]

There was no open hint of international aggression in any of these early measures which followed the Restoration, and so successful was Japan in convincing the world that her intentions were altogether peaceful and nonaggressive that statements such as the following from Western Japanophiles were not uncommon during the early years of the present century:

While there is no peril for the West to dread from the sudden and extraordinary development of the new power which has appeared in the Far East, the place which Japan is hereafter to hold among the nations becomes nevertheless a matter of profound interest. To her it may be said there now appertains a "sphere of influence" in a far wider sense than any which has heretofore attached to the well-worn phrase. In the development of international politics the "sphere of influence" of a great power . . . means practically the first step taken by a so-called civilized nation to grab the territory of some weaker power or people . . . and the establishment of an alien sovereignty.

It is not at all surprising, therefore, that this being the confirmed habit of the Western powers, the advent of Japan among the greatest and most puissant of them all should be interpreted by them as a fearsome indication that an Asiatic nation, having learned their game, is about to play it in an alarming fashion and become the dominating influence over the regions of the earth not yet fully appropriated by them. It is only recently that intelligent American fools have put forward the belief that Japan means to take the Philippines as soon as she is done with Russia, just as some French fools have started the myth that she means to take Indo-China from France. Still greater, of course, is the fear that Korea and Manchuria . . . will, in the very near future, become component parts of the Japanese Empire.[5]

Yet it is perhaps not without significance that, in a militaristically indoctrinated nation, even the popular appellations for newly born infants have military origins. A newly born boy is called *taiho* (cannon), a newly born girl *gunkan* (warship).

In the years immediately preceding and during World War II state indoctrination, through the medium of State Shinto, rose in a progressive crescendo. From the day of birth the child's progress in life was clearly directed toward service to the state. When a month old (thirty-one days if a boy, thirty-two days if a girl), the child was taken to the local shrine to be presented to the local deities, where his life was dedicated to service to the god-emperor. At three or four the child's education began with rudimentary lessons in the superiority of the male over the female. Save that a rigid cleanliness was forced upon him (in accordance with Shinto doctrines of purity), the boy's least whim was granted, and the mother was not permitted to use physical force against him in discipline. His sisters were made to walk behind him when they went out together. At six formal education began when the local Shinto priest gave the child his first book of nationalist ethics and patriotism. During his first year in school emphasis was upon emotional, dramatic songs glorifying the soldier and inculcating the lessons of filial obedience, co-operativeness, reverence for the emperor, and gratitude for the blessing which had been conferred on him through being born in the divine land. He joined in many celebrations of a nature to increase his reverence for the state, the emperor, and the soldiers who died in battle for their country. After 1932 one of these special celebrations was regularly held on February 22 in honor of the three human bombs who, on February 22, 1932, took a bomb with lighted fuse into a stubborn patch of barbed wire in the Chinese lines near Shanghai, blowing themselves to bits and clearing a path through the wire. He was taught to reverence the statue erected to these men in Tokyo. On December 14 he honored the classic Forty-seven Ronin who waited several years to revenge the death of their lord and then committed hara-kiri en masse.

The doctrines of the divine origin of the Japanese people, the especial divinity of the emperors, and the inferiority of all other peoples were injected into school textbooks and oral instruction, especially in history, geography, reading, and ethics (for, in spite of the doctrine that the Japanese, by nature pure, need no system of morals, courses in ethics in the public schools have existed since the beginning of the State Shinto program for the purpose of instilling the principles of national loyalty). The *Kojiki* myth, including the story of Izanagi and Izanami, the birth of the islands of Japan and Amaterasu Omikami, the descent of Ninigi-no-Mikoto from heaven, the birth of Jimmu Tenno and his ascent to the throne—all were taught not as myth or religion but as factual history. To these teachings were added statements that the Japanese are themselves descendants of the gods and therefore *kami,* and that all other peoples are inferior. Every morning, at the beginning of classes, all children were compelled to make obeisance in the direction of the imperial palace at Tokyo, reverencing the emperor. Children were marched in large bodies from the schools to State Shinto shrines for rituals of ancestor- and emperor-worship. Even the prayers (*norito*) were regulated by the government and constantly reiterated the theme of the divine emperor and the reverence due him. Workers in factories were given lectures in their duty to the emperor and compelled to bow in the direction of the imperial palace every morning. Soldiers gathered periodically for "worship of the throne." Hillis Lory [6] records the case of a lieutenant who, when reading a rescript of the Emperor Meiji at such an occasion, misread one word and, though he had not thereby changed the meaning in any particular, he committed hara-kiri as the only way he felt that he could atone for his sacrilege. Soldiers were taught that when they died in battle for the emperor they became *kami* and their souls returned to protect the homeland. Solemn ceremonies were held periodically at the Yasukuni shrine, attended by thousands of persons, to deify all soldiers who had died since the last ceremony. Their names were inscribed in a record of the shrine itself and thereafter they were considered gods, regardless of their former conduct in civil life. A common farewell of a soldier leaving for the front was, "I'll meet you at the Yasukuni shrine."

How thoroughly State Shinto ideology penetrated the mind of Japan may be judged by statements of some of its modern intellectuals:

He [the Emperor] is to the Japanese mind the Supreme Being in the Cosmos of Japan, as God is in the universe of the pantheistic philosopher. From him everything emanates, in him everything subsists. . . . He is supreme in all temporal matters of the state as well as in all spiritual matters.[7]

Subjects have no will apart from the will of the Emperor. Their individual selves are merged with the Emperor. If they act according to the mind of the Emperor, they can realize their true nature and attain the moral ideal. . . . The organizing will resides inherently in the Emperor and apart from the Imperial mind there exists no organizing will.[8]

The Japanese conception of political origin lies in the very law of nature in conformity with Divine Will. . . . We are proud to look upon our Emperor as the fountain-head of our national life. In this respect our Empire rests upon the foundation of blood relationship which far transcends mere morality, and our ruler is viewed in the light of a super-moral being.[9]

The position occupied by *Ten* and *Jotei* among the Chinese or by Jehovah among the Jews has been held in Japan from ancient days by the Emperor.[10]

Shinto has culminated in Mikadoism or the worship of the Mikado or Japanese Emperor as a divinity, during his lifetime as well as after his death. . . . Japanese patriotism or loyalty, as you might call it, really is not simple patriotism or mere loyalty as understood in the ordinary sense of the word, that is, the mere ethical sense of the term. It is more— it is the lofty, self-denying, enthusiastic sentiment of the Japanese people toward their august Ruler, believed to be something divine, rendering them capable of offering up anything and everything, all dearest to them, willingly, that is, of their own free will; of sacrificing not only their wealth or property, but their own life itself, for the sake of their divinely gracious sovereign. . . . All this is nothing but the actual manifestation of the religious consciousness of the Japanese people.[11]

Rigid restrictions were designed to make lapses from reverence of the emperor impossible. No one was allowed to look down upon his sacred person from a higher level. Thus, when the emperor was about to pass along the street the police saw that blinds were drawn in the windows of all upper stories along the way. When it was discovered that the tower of a recently erected police building was higher than the imperial palace, the tower was at once pulled down. When, in 1932, the American news weekly *Time* carried a picture of Hirohito on its front cover, the Japanese government made the following request: "Let copies of the present issue lie face upwards on all tables; let no object be placed on the likeness of the Emperor." [12] Similarly when, on October 22, 1942, newspapers in Japanese-occupied Manila published a photograph of the Emperor, a large legend under the picture warned all Filipinos to treat the paper with reverence, and forbade them to leave it lying about carelessly, to wrap anything in it, or to throw it into a wastebasket.

Not only in the primary and middle public schools, in which only texts chosen by the state department of education could be used, but also in the public press, over the radio, and from the lecture platform, were the themes of Japanese superiority and the divinity of the emperor, the Japanese people, and the islands of Japan, constantly reiterated. John Morris reports articles claiming that the airplane is a Japanese invention, that a long list of European scientific developments were the product of Japan, and that Christ was born in northern Japan. "The Myth of divinity," he writes, "has been built up by methods similar to those employed by advertising agents, that is to say, it has constantly been brought to the notice of the people. It is the method adopted by Mr. Goebbels for misleading the German people, also that employed by the manufacturers of soap and tooth paste, but the Japanese thought of it first." [13]

H. J. Timperley [14] relates a modern Japanese legend which tells of the years Jesus spent in Japan studying Shinto between the time when he appeared in the Temple and the beginning of his public ministry. Another recent "discovery" in Japan, according to Japanese sources, consists of the original tablets bearing the Ten Commandments given by God to Moses.

For those who may have leanings toward Christianity, the state-inspired commentators made statements like this:

Christianity advocates universalism and a love that knows no distinctions, and consequently it cannot be harmonized with the purport of the Imperial Rescript on Education which is nationalistic. Moreover Christianity places its Heavenly Father and its Christ above the Emperor and therein it contradicts the principles of loyalty and filial piety of the Imperial Rescript on Education.[15]

The doctrines of Christianity are quite irreconcilable with the Imperial Rescript on Education. In the Imperial Rescript on Education there is not a single word about the Heavenly Father who is the object of absolute reverence in Christianity. The rescript speaks only of the Imperial Ancestors. For this reason they [the Christians] cannot have it in their hearts at all to read the rescript acceptably. They must practice deception. . . .

Sovereignty in Japan is vested in a single Race-father, a form of government without peer among all the nations of the world. It is, therefore, not to be tolerated that a sovereign should be accepted who receives reverence above and beyond the Emperor and the Imperial Ancestress. Our national structure makes it impossible to permit the acceptance of a "One True God" above the Emperor.[16]

This point of view may have some bearing on the murder of Christian missionaries in Japanese-occupied territory during World War II.

Though the encouragement of ancestor worship cannot be regarded as part of the essential teaching of Christianity it [Christianity] is not opposed to the notion that, when the Japanese Empire was founded its early rulers were in communication with the Great Spirit that rules the universe. Christians, according to this theory, without doing violence to their creed, may acknowledge that the Japanese nation has a divine origin. It is only when we realize that the Imperial Ancestors were in close communication with God [the gods] that we understand how sacred is the country in which we live.[17]

And yet, with a marvelous agility, a Japanese mind, trained in the tenets of both Shinto and Christianity, can bring forth such a statement as this:

What then is the plan for the long-term reconstruction of East Asia? Its purpose is that of realizing the vision emblazoned on the banner, "The World One Family." And that purpose we must recognize afresh, coincides spontaneously with the fundamental faith of Christianity. The

policy of extending even to the continent our family principle which finds
its center in the Imperial House so that all may bathe in its holy benevolence—this policy, can we not see is none other than the concrete realization on earth of the spirtual family principle of Christianity which looks
up to God as the Father of mankind and regards all men as brethren.
This is the Christian conception of the Kingdom of God. The basis of
the Japanese spirit also consists in this: and thus, wonderful to relate, is
one with Christianity.[18]

Karl Lowith [19] tells of a Japanese philosopher, thoroughly indoctrinated with the tenets of modern Shinto, who, in 1940, solemnly
interpreted the *Analects* of Confucius by Hitler's *Mein Kampf,* holding that the political wisdom of Confucius had much in common
with that of Hitler.

10. The Ray of Hope

CONSIDERABLE space has been given here to a discussion of
and commentary on State Shinto, which dominates the education of every school child of Japan and the daily indoctrination of
every adult—and which, according to the latest available count (1930),
supports over 110,000 religious shrines where the people worship—
for the interpretations which have made its effect so important to
the Western world will not be found in the classic books of Shinto.
Yet it is in those interpretations that the most far-reaching implications of Japan's national religion today are to be discovered.

Fortunately there is a somewhat brighter aspect to the over-all
picture of Shinto. While the state was tightening its hold on the
minds of the people through the medium of their indigenous religion,
the measure of religious freedom allowed to the Shinto sects by the
Constitution made possible for them a certain amount of normal development in the direction of religious idealism. To be sure, this
development has been inevitably hampered by the indoctrination of
State Shinto, and doctrines of all the sects include the basic tenets of

the state, belief in the divinity of, and therefore reverence for, the emperor, and teaching that the first duty of every Japanese is unquestioning loyalty to the government. There are also, within the sect practices, a large number of esoteric rites which can seem only like degrading and primitive hocus-pocus to a Western mind—ritualistic showering with boiling water, walking barefoot on a bed of live coals, regulated breathing, ritualistic twisting of fingers, induced trances, magic, divination, worship of actual mountains, etc. Yet the doctrines of some of the sects reveal also a high degree of ethical and spiritual content.

Sectarian Shinto has approximately 17,000,000 adherents in Japan, divided into thirteen sects which may be classified in five groups as follows: [1]

(1) Pure Shinto sects
Shinto Honkyoku
Shinri Kyo
Taisha Kyo
(2) The Confucian sects
Shusei Ha
Taisei Kyo
(3) The Mountain sects
Jikko Kyo
Fuso Kyo
Mitake Kyo
(4) The Purification sects
Shinshu Kyo
Misogi Kyo
(5) The Faith Healing sects
Kurozumi Kyo
Konko Kyo
Tenri Kyo

The names designating the groups in a measure reveal the directions taken by the sects represented. The "Pure" sects, building on the base of the Pure Shinto Revival, have attempted to free themselves from foreign religious ideas and to re-establish the Shinto of early Japan. Yet even in these there are traces of an ethical idealism which far transcends any statement in the *Kojiki,* the *Nihongi,* the *Engi Shiki,* or the doctrines of State Shinto.

The Confucian sects frankly admit the value of, and elaborate upon, Confucian tradition, and attempt to amalgamate the teachings of the Chinese sage with the tenets of Shinto.

The Mountain sects are a natural outgrowth of early belief that mountains are the abode of the gods and themselves often gods. The sects emphasize purity, religious faith, and the worship of mountains. To the devout of *Jikko Kyo* and *Fuso Kyo,* Mount Fuji is "the soul of the earth," and pilgrims who in great numbers ascend its slopes believe that they are there closer to the gods than they can be in any other spot of earth. The central object of worship for adherents to Mitake Kyo is Mount Ontake, in the north central part of the island of Hondo.

The Purification sects place great emphasis upon physical and spiritual purity, and teach doctrines reminiscent of (and undoubtedly arising from) the exalted philosophy of Buddhism.

The Faith Healing sects, as their name indicates, believe in the power of religious attitudes and ceremonies to cure disease, and tend, in one direction, toward monotheism, and, in another, toward pantheism, in their worship. There is a considerable element of ancient magic in their rites.

It may be profitable in closing to consider Shinto in comparison with those religious forces which have shaped the ethical concepts of the Western world, and to examine specifically its pertinence to our relations with postwar Japan.

During the great religious era which extended roughly from 800 to 400 B.C., religions in India, China, Persia, Greece, and Israel were shaping the moral and social concepts which form the basis of the social idealism proclaimed by the greater part of the civilized world today. Theologically this period was marked by a falling away from polytheism; morally it was distinguished by the amalgamation with theology of codes of ethics dominated by the principle of universal brotherhood, and thus, "peace on earth, good will to men."

Such has been the course of the emergence of religions from the primitive into the enlightened social stage throughout the world. Actually there is little or nothing in primitive Shinto which is unique among primitive religions. Elements of polytheistic nature worship, of ritualistic propitiation of exacting deities without pertinence to a social or ethical consciousness, of a distinctive sense of racial superiority so useful in tribal survival—all are common attributes of the dawning religious consciousness of mankind. In the "good-will" religions of China, India, Persia, and the Western world, morality, social ethics, and their extension in the concept of world brotherhood and the equality of peoples developed as natural outgrowths overlying the more primitive beliefs. In Japan the normal process of development was interrupted in its early stages, perpetuating a religion which contains an abnormal number of primitive elements.

Yet in no religion has the process of enlightenment ever reached its perfect and ideal development. There are obvious survivals of primitive polytheism, the formalisms of magic, and nature worship in some forms of Christian ritual today. One of the curses of the Judeo-Christian Western world is the persistence of a consciousness of racial, tribal, or ideological superiority (marked in the discrimination against, and the persecution of, minority groups such as Negroes, Jews, Orientals, and followers of heterodox religious faiths) similar to that which distinguished many primitive religions and which is a basic factor of State Shinto. And the phenomenon of the churchman who rigorously carries out the rituals of his church on holy days and habitually engages in unethical, antisocial conduct on other days (thereby following the pattern of early religions which contained a superstitious theology but no social code) is notorious to objective observers of church bodies all over the world.

Thus the difference between State Shinto and the good-will religions may almost be said to be one of degree rather than of kind. Almost, but not quite. For there are these two marked and important differences: the official doctrines of Hinduism, Buddhism, Confucianism, Taoism, Zoroastrianism, modern Mohammedanism, Judaism, and Christianity proclaim the equality of mankind the world over and urge upon all men the ideals of world brotherhood, peace, and good will, while the failure to realize these ideals among the adherents to these religions is a failure to "practice what they preach." But the official doctrine of State Shinto reiterates the divine superiority of the Japanese over all other peoples and the rightful place of their emperor as ruler of the world.

Further, in nations whose people adhere to the good-will religions, there is, to a very large degree, a separation of church and state, and a true freedom of religion. Though the religious beliefs of the people may be used by the state as arguments for the acceptance of state policies (as has been true notably in both England and America during World War II), state doctrines have not, in these countries, as in Japan, been forced upon the people as a religion which they are compelled to accept and forbidden to refute.

Because of these facts and their cataclysmic consequences, State Shinto becomes a peculiar religious phenomenon which must be regarded outside the field of pure religion and within that of international relations, and therefore of the utmost concern to the Western as well as the Eastern world. It is but a logical and objective statement to say that the objectives of the good-will religions (and thus of the world's freedom-loving peoples) and those of State Shinto are diametrically and irreconcilably opposed to each other. One group of concepts, in order to obtain its objectives, must wipe out the other group. They are mutually exclusive. We dare not adopt toward Shinto's contemporary manifestations as a doctrine of state that religious tolerance which is dictated by our belief in religious freedom. State Shinto must be approached not as a religion but as a political creed which is an enemy of civilization, with the same intelligent and righteous intolerance and angry resolve to exterminate it as that which marked the ideological strength of the democratic nations' union against Nazism.

Yet in that angry denunciation and resolve to exterminate it, we must not make the mistake of including among our objectives for extermination those who may be among our best allies—members of the Shinto sects.

In the religion of the Japanese a normal process of emergence from primitivism, such as that which marked other religions, was begun with the advent of Confucianism, carried a long step forward through Buddhism and Ryobu Shinto, and has survived as a living force in certain elements of the Shinto sects. But through a strange phenomenon only partly explained by the continuance of feudalism into modern times, centuries of isolation from the rest of the world, the poverty and lack of enlightenment which these circumstances forced upon the masses, and the desperate struggle for quick modernization after the Restoration, the natural and healthy course of Japan's religious development has been distorted, and a vast reservoir of religious power, harnessed for political rather than ethical service, has been driven into activities which can only label the doctrine that has provided Japan with ideological strength in World War II as the enemy of all peace- and freedom-loving people.

Why this has been possible may be explained (outside of social and economic influences) only by a peculiar capacity for unity and fidelity to an idea which is characteristic of the Japanese people. (An examination of centuries-old Japanese customs of child training, and other psychological factors, which have no real place in this book, would be pertinent to this explanation.) That capacity, properly directed, can make as great a contribution toward the progress of civilization as, in this century, it has made to retrogression. The strength which is inherent in the ancient doctrines of Shinto is obviously as powerful a potential for a peaceful and progressive world of good will as it has been proved to be a frighteningly strong base for a nation united in a war of aggression. As regards the Japanese themselves, in relation to one another and their government, it has produced one of the most unified, friendly, peaceful, orderly, home-loving, hard-working peoples on earth—quick to devote their individual lives to what they believe to be the good of the whole nation, quick to lay down their lives in service to a cause.

Not only is this a force which has been unconquered for two thousand years and which is probably as unconquerable as is Christianity or the democratic spirit, but is it not one which may be made more valuable in its properly directed use than in its submergence? Cannot this power for unification in service be utilized in a world dedicated to the ways of peace?

What is needed, perhaps, is a new political and religious syncretism, in which the Japanese have proved themselves to be so very adept. Is it not possible for us to take a leaf out of their own book, and perhaps from that of the unmourned Nazis?

When Buddhism made its deep and powerful penetration of Japan, it did not attempt to suppress Shinto, or even to deny its doctrines. Rather it achieved its foothold by syncretism, by reconciling the doctrines of Shinto with those of Buddhism, matching gods with gods, doctrines with doctrines, and rituals with rituals. When National Socialism started on its program of indoctrinating German youth, and used emotional and dramatic songs as a part of its indoctrination, it did not write new tunes, but put new words to old familiar melodies which for years had held meaning for the German people.

Now that the Japanese military might has been finally overthrown by the United Nations, it is as necessary to see that the indoctrinations of State Shinto are discontinued as it has been necessary and wise to exclude rigidly from Germany expression of the ideologies of Nazism. But if, in Japan, our zeal includes an effort to suppress true Shinto worship, as expressed in the Shinto sects, and the conceptions of the Shinto classics because of their ancient doctrine of the divinity of the emperor and the rest of the *Kojiki* mythology (which is not, in the light of objective analysis, one whit more naïve or fantastic than the mythology of the Old Testament or even some of the New), if, in short, we set out to discredit, or even to ignore, the whole complex structure of ancient Shinto, we shall be making one of our gravest mistakes in postwar Pacific relations. Further, if we ignore these factors, we shall miss one of our greatest opportunities.

The truth is a comparatively simple fact: In Japan the devil has quoted scriptures to suit his purposes. The same scriptures—the sacred authorities which the Japanese have recognized for over a thousand years—can be quoted in at least equal length and with equal positiveness to controvert the doctrines of international evil which have been built on Shinto texts.

If we are wise, our propagandists will make the most minute study of all Shinto literature from A.D. 712 (the *Kojiki*) to the present day, and enlist the co-operation of the Shinto sects to the end that the unifying strength of the ancient religion may be preserved as a base on which to build new interpretations in which the official state doctrine of *hakko ichi-u* may be superseded in Japan by an enlightened universalism such as that which distinguishes the ethical doctrines of the good-will religions, and which has already been faintly enunciated in the precepts of sectarian Shinto.

We have no quarrel with the assertion that the world is one family. Indeed, one of our own stated objectives in World War II has been to preserve our interpretation of this statement of principle. Are we of the United Nations poorer indoctrinators than were the Buddhist priests of ancient Japan? We have been; must we always be? Do we care enough about peace in the Pacific to give to building it one-tenth of the effort and ingenuity we have devoted to the war? Is it impossible for us to bring about a political syncretism which will demonstrate that Amaterasu Omikami's heavenly dictum actually enjoined the emperor and the people of Japan to live according to the nonaggressive principle of world brotherhood enunciated by the good-will religions, and that this principle, rather than the forceful domination of a militaristic imperial rule, is what the "good Japanese" must help to spread to "the six quarters"? Are we not capable of stimulating again the healthy development of a true religious consciousness in the Japanese to the end that sectarian Shinto may become the full well-rounded religion into which it has never developed under the "divine emperor," and thus of deep social meaning and of value to the Japanese and the world at large?

If we are capable of achieving this tremendous task, we shall enlist the most powerful ideological force in Japan in the service of peace and civilization, and make of Shinto a strong and trustworthy friend instead of the enemy which it now is.

It has frequently been stated in contemporary commentaries on Japan that it would be futile to hope to find any Japanese liberal elements whatever to help in the postwar task of ideological reconstruction. If this is so it constitutes a refutation of history. Liberals have always been even a smaller minority in Japan than in most countries. Since the Middle Ages their doctrines have always been effectively submerged by the forces of reaction and the widely and effectively stated doctrines of authoritarianism, nationalism, and racial superiority. Yet it is necessary to call attention to only a few of the names and documents of the past (some of which are cited in this book) to show that a flame of progressive liberal enlightenment in both religion and politics has always burned in Japan, however dimly.

The first citation is from a most influential source—the sacred *Nihongi,* compiled A.D. 720, and one of the two most important books of Shinto. It is an imperial edict issued A.D. 604, containing imperial laws. (*See* pp. 104–107 for text.) Examine for a moment some of the social principles enunciated here. It enjoins upon Japanese subjects most of the old social virtues—harmony, sincerity, obedience to duly constituted authority, decorous behavior and responsibility among officials, justice and not the desire for gain among judges, chastisement of crime and state encouragement of civic virtue, the choosing of wise men for public office, good faith and tolerance in the relations of the authorities with the people, care lest the people be overburdened with taxation and laws, abandonment of private interests for the public good, the basing of decisions in important matters of government upon their discussion with advisers, and *even a hint that the divine emperor myth is a lot of nonsense:*

We [the imperial government] are not all sages nor are they [the people] unquestionably fools. *Both of us are simply ordinary men.* [No italics in original.] How then can anyone lay down a rule by which to distinguish right and wrong? For we are all, one with another, wise and foolish, like a ring which has no end.

Actually the whole doctrine of emperor divinity, racial superiority, and the mission to conquer the world is founded (so far as the *Kojiki* and *Nihongi* are concerned) on little, if any, more evidence than that which may be deduced to controvert such doctrine from the above quoted *Nihongi* paragraph and the whole edict of which it is a part. The vicious, world-disturbing strength of the doctrine of aggression has grown from the emphasis of later interpretations.

The second example is that of the eighteenth-century Ichikawa Tatsumaru (*see* p. 47) whose rationalism sought in vain to refute the doctrines of the Pure Shinto Revival. To Ichikawa the Japanese did not constitute a special, superior race, commanded by heaven to rule the world. "The gods in heaven make no difference between different races of mankind . . . and the sun shines equally over all." One could wish that Ichikawa were living in Japan today, but it would only be a man in the depths of pessimism who could believe that he has no spiritual descendants.

The third historical example consists of a group of liberals who in the early years of the Restoration agitated for a form of popular government for Japan. The Constitution of 1889 was partially a gesture of appeasement to them, but it fell far short of the ideas embodied in their demands. On January 17, 1874, a memorial was sent to the government signed by nine men, eight of whom were Samurai, calling attention to the turbulence of the empire and ascribing it to the fact that government officials were not alive to their responsibility to the people, who were of right entitled to a share in their own government. "Administration," they wrote, "is conducted in an arbitrary manner, rewards and punishments are prompted by partiality, the channel by which the people should communicate with the government is blocked up and they cannot state their grievances. Is it to be hoped that the empire can be perfectly ruled in this manner? An infant knows that it cannot be done. We fear, therefore, that if a reform is not affected, the state will be ruined."

Their remedy was a representative government; as did the American colonists a century earlier, they complained against "taxation without representation":

The people whose duty it is to pay taxes to the government possess the right of sharing in their government's affairs and of approving or condemning. This being a principle universally acknowledged it is not necessary to waste words in discussing it. We therefore humbly pray that the officials will not resist this great truth. Those who just now oppose the establishment of a council-chamber chosen by the people say: "Our people are wanting in culture and intelligence, and have not yet advanced into the region of enlightenment. It is too early yet to establish a council-chamber elected by the people." If it really be as they say, then the way to give the people culture and intelligence and to cause them to advance swiftly into the region of enlightenment is to establish a council-chamber chosen by the people. For in order to give our people culture and intelligence and to cause them to advance into the region of enlightenment, they must in the first place be induced to protect their rights, to respect and value themselves, and be inspired by a spirit of sympathy with the griefs and joys of the empire, which can only be done by giving them a voice in its concerns. It has never happened that under such circumstances the people have been content to remain in backward condition or have been satisfied with want of culture and intelligence. . . . The worst argument they put forward is that to establish a council-chamber at once would be simply to assemble all the blockheads in the empire. What shocking self-conceit and arrogant contempt for the people this indicates! No doubt there are among the officials men who surpass others in intelligence and ingenuity, but how do they know that society does not contain men who surpass them in intelligence and knowledge? . . . The duty of a government and the object which it ought to promote in the fulfillment of that duty is to enable the people to make progress.[2]

That is a paragraph which might have been written in eighteenth-century England or America.

Finally, there are such modern scholars as Inazo Nitobe and Genchi

Kato whose work was always directed toward a true meeting of East and West, and an exciting note of liberalist revolt which marked some utterances from Tokyo during the week of Japan's surrender (week of August 12, 1945) to bring the record of the liberalist leaven down to the present. In the cautious statement of Reickichi Tada, president of the Japanese Board of Technology (made on August 15, 1945, and cancelled by Domei an hour after Tada made it) there is evidence of an eagerness on the part of some of Japan's leading thinkers to abandon completely Japan's doctrines of emperor worship and world conquest in favor of rationalism and peaceful co-operation. (*See* p. 195 for text.) And some puzzling editorials in Tokyo's newspapers during that week of catastrophe (or new birth?) for Japan evidence the possibility of an exciting trend toward democratic thought reminiscent of the memorial of the nineteenth-century samurai.

It is necessary to remember constantly that in Japan religious and political thought have always gone hand in hand and will continue, at least in the immediate future, to do so. And it is essential to keep in mind in deciding upon an approach to the people of postwar Japan both such elements of political thought as are represented by these documents, and the comparative religious enlightenment of the iconoclasts of history and the Shinto sects of today.

How should such an approach be made? It should enlist immediately the aid of a panel of Western, Chinese, and Japanese scholars. These scholars should be asked to search Japanese literature from the *Kojiki* and the *Nihongi* to that of the immediate prewar years for authority to support the concepts of the equality of man, peace, and international co-operation. Much of the pertinent material is not available in translation and would have to be sought in the original Japanese in documents which exist (if they have not been destroyed) only in Japan. Some of these, withheld in the past from Western scholars, can now be made available through United Nations occupation of Japan. Especial attention should be given to such passages as the imperial edict of A.D. 604, quoted above, the interpretations of such men as Ichikawa Tatsumaru, the writings of Ryobu Shinto, and the most enlightened teachings of the Shinto sects and should examine carefully the points of view of such contemporaries as Reickichi Tada to determine whether, and if so, how, they may be used in the re-education of Japan. Once the program is decided upon it should be pushed with the thorough intensity which has marked Japanese state indoctrination and through the same media.

It is folly to discredit the gods of a people whose co-operation is sought, and nowhere greater folly than in Japan, where state doctrine has injected religious concepts into every aspect of life, so that the task of approaching the minds of the Japanese, save through these concepts, seems a hopeless one. But with the material furnished by such a group of scholars as that suggested above, it should be possible to demonstrate to the Japanese people that the meaning and will of their gods have been misinterpreted by mortals, by leaders who through a combination of misunderstanding and willful ambition have misrepresented the heavenly commands and thus betrayed both gods and men.

Meanwhile a decision as to the permanent form of the Japanese government may well be left in abeyance for the moment, and finally entrusted to the Japanese people—the only group who, by our own political philosophy could establish an effective Japanese government. As to whether the government takes the form of a constitutional monarchy, a republic, or a socialist state, and whether the imperial succession plays any part in it—these matters are perhaps less important than the people's attitude toward the function of government and its head. The "Son of Heaven" concept, as originally enunciated by the Chinese, was basically an enlightened doctrine which conceded a measure of sacredness to the function and the representative of good government because of its profound influence upon the happiness and well-being of the people. The Chinese emperor, so long as he ruled well, was a spiritual descendant of heaven.

This concept of spiritual heritage is not by any means unfamiliar to the Japanese. It is in the teachings of Mahayana Buddhism, Ryobu, and some sectarian Shinto. It has been intimated in the imperial succession when emperors, having no male issue, have adopted sons to make the succession secure, thus passing on the throne to successors who were not their direct physiological descendants.

Could we not, backed by carefully selected authority out of sacred and secular literature and history, demonstrate to the Japanese that when Amaterasu Omikami said that her descendants would rule over Japan for ages eternal she meant her spiritual descendants who would gain the right to that title by ruling in righteousness? Could we not even go a step further and, using the carefully built up doctrine that the people themselves are the descendants of the gods, demonstrate that, when the sun goddess sent the three sacred treasures and symbols of authority, the mirror, the jewels, and the sword, to earth, she was sending them to her children, the people?

This whole approach may seem fantastic, but one has only to examine the statements made by State Shinto indoctrinators to see how steeped in fantasy the contemporary Japanese mind is, and how futile a purely factual, realistic approach would seem.

The price of such a program, carried on for a quarter of a century, with a corps of the best scholars available in the world and a large and efficient staff, would be a small fraction of the cost of modern warfare for a single month. Dare we, through niggardliness or lack of interest, refuse to accept this responsibility for leadership which has been thrust upon us by military victory? Or are we really unmoved by and indifferent to the millions who, during this generation, have been slaughtered by human stupidity?

One of the most powerful slogans of America's eighteenth-century revolt was *"Vox populi, vox Dei."* The voice of the people is the voice of God. Would it be difficult to demonstrate that the voice of the Japanese people is the voice of Amaterasu Omikami?

The United Nations, as trustees of the future of Japan and of the world, can go far toward such a demonstration if they have the wisdom, the patience, the tolerance—not of State Shinto, not of the militarists, not of the doctrines of racial superiority and world conquest, but of the people who have been their dupes.

With such wisdom and patience it should be possible to make the ethical seeds already planted by Buddhism, Ryobu, the Shinto sects, and wise liberal secular leaders of the past blossom into a doctrine which would make *hakko ichi-u* and our concept of world brotherhood and the Golden Rule mean the same thing.

"Though at the foot of the hill the ways are far apart," wrote the late Inazo Nitobe, one of the wisest of all modern Japanese philosophers, "as we ascend higher and higher, the nearer approach our paths, until they meet at the summit, to share the view of the plains below from the height of the same divine wisdom. On this height, in the fulness of time, may be brought into common brotherhood, the philosophers of the North and the seers of the South, the thinkers of the West, and the wisemen of the East, and God shall be glorified by all his children. The hour is coming when neither on the mountains of Samaria nor in the city of Jerusalem, neither in the Orient nor in the Occident, but in spirit and truth, wherever men come together in brotherly love, shall they worship the same Father." [3]

Part II

SELECTIONS FROM JAPANESE TEXTS

1. Old Shinto Period
(A.D. 712–925)

From the Kojiki [1]
or "Records of Ancient Matters"
(A.D. 712)

Creation
(*Kojiki*, Preface)

Now when chaos had begun to condense, but force and form were not yet manifest, and there was nought named, nought done, who could know its shape? Nevertheless Heaven and Earth first parted, and the three deities performed the commencement of creation; the passive and active Essences then developed, and the Two Spirits became the ancestors of all things. Therefore did he enter obscurity and emerge into light, and the Sun and Moon were revealed by the washing of his eyes; he floated on and plunged into the sea-water, and Heavenly and Earthly Deities appeared through the ablution of his person. So, in the dimness of the great commencement, we, by relying on the original teaching, learn the time of the completion of the earth and of the birth of islands; in the remoteness of the original beginning, we, by trusting the former sages, perceive the era of the genesis of deities and of the establishment of men.

Creation of the First Island
(*Kojiki*, Section III)

Hereupon all the Heavenly Deities commanded the two Deities His Augustness the Male-Who-Invites [i.e., Izanagi] and Her Augustness the Female-Who-Invites [i.e., Izanami] ordering them to "make, consolidate, and give birth to this drifting land." Granting to them a heavenly jewelled spear, they thus deigned to charge them. So the two Deities, standing upon the Floating Bridge of Heaven, pushed down the jewelled spear and stirred with it, whereupon, when they had stirred the brine till it went curdlecurdle, and drew the spear up, the brine that dripped down from the end of the spear was piled up and became an island. This is the island of Onogoro.

The Union of Izanagi and Izanami [2]
(*Kojiki,* Section IV)

The two Deities, having descended on Onogoro-jima, erected there an eight fathom house with an august central pillar. Then Izanagi addressed Izanami, saying: "How is thy body formed?" Izanami replied, "My body is completely formed except one part which is incomplete." Then Izanagi said, "My body is completely formed and there is one part which is superfluous. Suppose that we supplement that which is incomplete in thee with that which is superfluous in me, and thereby procreate lands." Izanami replied, "It is well." Then Izanagi said, "Let me and thee go round the heavenly august pillar and, having met at the other side, let us become united in wedlock." This being agreed to, he said, "Do thou go around from the left and I will go around from the right." When they had gone around Izanami spoke first and exclaimed, "How delightful! I have met a lovely youth!" Izanagi then said, "How delightful! I have met a lovely maiden." Afterwards he said, "It was unlucky for the woman to speak first." The child which was the first offspring of their union was the Hiruko (leech child) which at the age of three was unable to stand upright, and was therefore placed in a reed-boat and sent adrift.

Birth of the Eight Islands
(*Kojiki,* Section V)

Hereupon the two Deities took counsel, saying: "The children to whom we have now given birth are not good. It will be best to announce this in the august place of the Heavenly Deities." They ascended forthwith to Heaven and enquired of Their Augustness the Heavenly Deities. Then the Heavenly Deities commanded and found out by grand divination, and ordered them, saying: "They were not good because the woman spoke first. Descend back again and amend your words." So thereupon descending back, they again went around the heavenly august pillar as before. Thereupon His Augustness Izanagi spoke first: "Ah! What a fair and lovely maiden!" Afterwards his younger sister Her Augustness Izanami spoke: "Ah! What a fair and lovely youth!" When they had finished speaking in this manner, they cohabited augustly and produced a child, the Island of Ahaji, Ho-no-sa-wake. Next they gave birth to the Island of Futa-no in Iyo. . . . Next [after several other islands had been born] they gave birth to Great-Yamato-the-Luxuriant-Island-of-the-Dragon-Fly, another name for which is Heavenly-August-Sky-Luxuriant-Dragon-Fly-Lord-Youth. The name of Land-of-the-Eight-Great-Islands therefore originated in these eight islands having been born first.

The Birth of Various Deities
(*Kojiki*, Sections VI–X)

When they had finished giving birth to countries, they began afresh giving birth to Deities. So the name of the Deity they gave birth to was the Deity Great-Male-of-the-Great-Thing. . . . Next [after many other deities have been born] they gave birth to the Fire-Burning-Swift-Male-Deity, another name for whom is the Deity Fire-Shining-Elder.

Through giving birth to this child her august private parts were burnt, and she sickened and lay down. The names of the Deities born from her vomit were the Deity Metal-Mountain-Prince and Metal-Mountain-Princess. The names of the Deities that were born from her faeces were Clay-Viscid-Prince and Clay-Viscid-Princess. The Deities that were born from her urine were Mitsuhanome and the Young-Wondrous-Producing-Deity. . . . So Izanami at length divinely retired. . . . So Izanagi buried Izanami on Mount Hiba at the boundary of the Land of Idzumo and the Land of Hahki. . . . Then Izanagi, drawing the ten-grasp sabre that was augustly girdled on him, cut off the head of his child the Deity Shining-Elder. Hereupon the Deities that were born from the blood that stuck to the point of the august sword and bespattered the multitudinous rock masses were: the Deity Rock-Splitter, the Deity Root-Splitter, and the Rock-Possessing-Male-Deity. . . . [Many other Deities were born in this episode from other drops of blood and from the various parts of the body of the slain Deity Shining-Elder.]

Thereupon Izanagi, wishing to meet and see his younger sister Izanami, followed after her to the Land of Hades. . . . Having taken and broken off one of the end-teeth of the multitudinous and close-toothed comb in the left bunch of his hair, he lit a light and went in and looked. Maggots were swarming and she was rotting, and in her head dwelt the Great Thunder, in her breast dwelt the Fire-Thunder, in her left hand dwelt the Young-Thunder, in her right hand dwelt the Earth-Thunder, in her left foot dwelt the Rumbling-Thunder, in her right foot dwelt the Couchant-Thunder—altogether eight Thunder Deities had been born and dwelt there. Hereupon Izanagi, overawed at the sight, fled back, whereupon his sister Izanami said, "Thou hast put me to shame," and at once sent the Ugly-Female-of-Hades to pursue him. So Izanagi took his black headdress and cast it down, and it instantly turned into grapes. While she picked them up and ate them, he fled on; but as she still pursued him, he took and broke the multitudinous and close-toothed comb which was in the right bunch of his hair and cast it down, and it instantly turned into bamboo sprouts. While she pulled them up and ate them, he fled on. Again later Izanami sent the eight Thunder-Deities with a thousand and five hundred warriors of Hades to pursue him. So he, drawing the ten-grasp sabre . . . fled forward brandishing it in his back hand; and as they still pursued him, he took, on reaching the base of the Even Pass of Hades, three peaches that were growing at its base, and waited and smote his pursuers with them, so that they all fled back. Then Izanagi announced to the peaches: "As ye have helped me, so must ye help all living people in the Central Land of Reed Plains when they fall into troublous circumstances and be harassed!" And he gave to the peaches the designation of Their Augustness Divine Fruit.

Last of all Izanami herself came out in pursuit. So he drew a thousand draught rock and blocked up the Even Pass of Hades, and placed the rock in the middle, and they stood opposite one another and exchanged leave-takings, and Izanami said, "My lovely elder-brother, Thine Augustness! If thou do like this, I will in one day strangle to death a thousand of the folks of thy land." The Izanagi replied: "My lovely younger sister, Thine Augustness! If thou do this, I will in one day set up a thousand and five hundred parturition houses. In this manner each day a thousand people would surely be born!" . . .

Therefore Izanagi said, "Nay! Hideous! I have come to a hideous and polluted land, I have! So I will perform the purification of my person." So he went to a plain at a small river mouth and purified and cleansed himself. [Twelve Deities were born as he disrobed, one from each of his garments, from his staff, from his bracelet, etc. Others were born from the filth which he washed from his body, and others to rectify the evil of these.]

The name of the Deity that was born as he washed his left august eye was the Heaven-Shining-Great-August-Deity [Amaterasu Omikami]. The name of the Deity that was next born as he washed his right august eye was His Augustness Moon-Night-Possessor. The name of the Deity that was next born as he washed his august nose was His Brave-Swift-Impetuous-Male-Augustness [Susa no Wo].

Investiture of the Three Deities
(*Kojiki,* Section XI)

Now Izanagi rejoiced, saying, "I, begetting child after child, have at my final begetting gotten three illustrious children." At once, taking off and shaking the jewel-string forming his august necklace, he bestowed it on Amaterasu Omikami (the Heaven-Shining-Great-August-Deity) saying, "Do Thine Augustness rule the Plain-of-High-Heaven." . . . Next he said to His Augustness Moon-Night-Possessor: "Do Thine Augustness rule the Dominion of the Night." . . . Next he said to His-Brave-Swift-Impetuous-Male-Augustness (Susa no Wo), "Do Thine Augustness rule the Sea-Plain."

Revolt of Susa no Wo
(*Kojiki,* Sections XII-XVI)

So while the other two Deities each assumed the rule according to the command with which Izanagi had charged them, Susa no Wo did not, but cried and wept till his eight-grasp beard reached the pit of his stomach. . . . So Izanagi said to Susa no Wo, "How is it . . . thou dost wail and weep?" He replied, "I wail because I wish to depart to my deceased mother's land. . . ." Then Izanagi was very angry and said, "If that be so, thou shall not dwell in this land," and forthwith expelled him with a divine expulsion. . . .

So Susa no Wo forthwith went up to Heaven, whereupon all the mountains and rivers shook, and every land and country quaked. Amaterasu Omikami . . . asked, "Wherefore ascendest thou hither?" Susa no Wo replied, saying, "I have no evil intent. . . . It is solely with the thought of taking leave of thee that I have ascended hither."

[Amaterasu then asked him to give proof of his good intentions, and Susa no Wo suggested that each of them give oath, and that they produce children. They then produced eight Deities.]

Then Susa no Wo said to Amaterasu Omikami, "Owing to the sincerity of my intentions I have, in begetting children, gotten delicate females. Judging from this I have undoubtedly gained the victory." With these words, and impetuous with victory, he broke down the divisions of the rice fields, laid out by Amaterasu Omikami, filled up the ditches, and moreover strewed excrements in the palace where she partook of the great food. . . . As Amaterasu Omikami sat in her awful weaving hall, seeing to the weaving of the august garments of the Deities, he broke a hole in the top of the weaving hall, and through it let fall a heavenly piebald horse which he had flayed with a backward flaying. . . .

Amaterasu Omikami, terrified at the sight, closed the door of the Heavenly Rock-Dwelling, made it fast, and retired. Then the whole plain of High Heaven darkened. Owing to this eternal night prevailed.

[Thereupon "the eight hundred myriad Deities" assembled and considered what was to be done to restore the light. First they made a mirror and a string of jewels eight feet long. They then indulged in various divinations. They laid various offerings before the door of the Heavenly Rock-Dwelling. The "Heavenly-Alarming Female" did an obscene dance before the door of the cave. Then the eight hundred myriad Deities laughed in concert.]

Hereupon Amaterasu Omikami was amazed, and slightly opening the door of the Heavenly Rock-Dwelling, asked . . . "How is it that the . . . eight hundred myriad Deities all laugh?" Then the Heavenly-Alarming Female spoke, saying: "We rejoice and are glad because there is a Deity more illustrious than Thine Augustness." While she was thus speaking His Augustness Heavenly-Beckoning-Ancestor-Lord and His Augustness Grand-Jewel pushed forward the mirror and respectfully showed it to Amaterasu Omikami, whereupon she gradually came forth from the door and gazed upon it. . . . So . . . both the Plain of High Heaven and the Central-Land-of-Reed-Plains again became light.

The Origin of Foods
(*Kojiki,* Section XVII)

Thereupon the eight hundred myriad Deities took counsel together and imposed on Susa no Wo a fine of a thousand tables, and likewise cut his beard, and even caused the nails of his fingers and toes to be pulled out, and expelled him with a divine expulsion. Again he begged food of the Deity Princess-of-Great-Food. Then the Princess-of-Great-Food took out all sorts of dainty things from her nose, her mouth, and her fundament, and made them up into all sorts of dishes which she offered to him. But Susa no Wo watched her proceedings, considered that she was offering him filth, and at once killed her. So the things that were born in the body of the Deity who had been killed were: in her head were born silkworms, in her two eyes were born rice seeds, in her two ears was born millet, in her nose were born small beans, in her private parts was born barley, in her fundament were born large beans. So His Augustness the Deity-Producing-Wondrous-Ancestor caused them to be taken and used as seeds.

Descent of the First Emperor
(*Kojiki*, Section XXXIII)

Then Amaterasu Omikami and the High Integrity Deity commanded and charged the Heir Apparent, His Augustness Truly-Conquer-I-Conquer-Swift-Heavenly-Great-Great-Ears: "The Brave-Awful-Possessing-Male-Deity says that he has now finished pacifying the Central-Land-of-Reed-Plains. So do thou, in accordance with our gracious charge, descend to and dwell in and rule over it."

Then the Heir Apparent replied: "While I have been getting ready to descend there has been born to me a child whose name is His Augustness Heaven-Plenty-Earth-Plenty-Heaven's-Sun-Height-Prince-Rice-Ear-Ruddy-Plenty. This child should be sent down." . . . Therefore, in accordance with these words, they laid their command on his Augustness Prince Rice-Ear-Ruddy-Plenty, deigning to charge him with these words: "This luxuriant Reed-Plain-Land-of-Fresh-Rice-Ears is the land over which thou shalt rule." So he replied: "I will descend from Heaven according to your commands." . . . Thereupon they joined to him the eight-foot curved jewels and mirror that had lured Amaterasu Omikami from the Rock Dwelling, and also the Herb-Quelling-Great-Sword . . . and charged him thus: "Regard the mirror exactly as if it were our august spirit, and reverence it as if reverencing us."

Two Drinking Songs
(*Kojiki*, Section CII)

This august liquor is not my august liquor;
Oh! It is august liquor respectfully brought
As a divine congratulation,
A bountiful congratulation,
A reiterated congratulation,
By the Small August Deity who dwells eternally,
    firmly standing.
Partake not shallowly!
Go on! Go on!

Whatever person distilled this august liquor
Must surely have distilled it singing the while
With that drum on the mortar—
Must surely have distilled it dancing the while,
For this august liquor, august liquor,
To be ever more and more joyful.
Go on! Go on!

Lament for Childlessness
(*Kojiki*, Section CXXV)

Will the one sedge-stem of Yata,
Having no children, wither as it stands?
Poor Sedge-moor!
Sedge-moor indeed is what I may say—
Poor Pure girl!

From the Nihongi [3]
(A.D. 720)

The Emperor Plans to Extend His Glory
(*Nihongi*, Book III)

The Emperor Kami Yamato Ihare-hiko's personal name was Hiko-hoho-demi. . . . When he reached the age of forty-five he addressed his elder brothers and his children, saying: "Of old our Heavenly Deities, . . . pointing to this land of fair rice ears of the fertile reed plain, gave it to our Heavenly Ancestor, Hiko-ho no ninigi no Mikoto. Thereupon Hiko-ho no ninigi no Mikoto, throwing open the barrier of Heaven and clearing a cloud path, urged on his superhuman course until he came to rest. At this time the world was given over to widespread desolation. It was an age of darkness and disorder. In this gloom, therefore, he fostered justice and so governed this western border. Our Imperial Ancestors and Imperial Parent, like gods, like sages, accumulated happiness and amassed glory. Many years elapsed.

From the date when our Heavenly Ancestor descended until now it is over 1,792,470 years. But the remote regions do not yet enjoy the blessings of Imperial rule. Every town has always been allowed to have its lord, and every village its chief, who, each one for himself, makes divisions of territory and practices mutual aggression and conflict.

"Now I have heard from the Ancient of the Sea that in the East there is a fair land encircled on all sides by blue mountains. Moreover there is there one who flew down riding in a Heavenly Rockboat. I think that this land will undoubtedly be suitable for the extension of the Heavenly task, so that its glory should fill the universe. It is doubtless the center of the world . . . why should we not proceed thither and make it the capital?"

All the Imperial Princes answered and said: "The truth of this is manifest. This thought is constantly present to our minds also. Let us go thither quickly."

To Form a Single Roof
(*Nihongi*, Book III)

The Emperor made an order, saying: "Owing to my reliance on the Majesty of Imperial Heaven, the wicked bands have met death. It is true that the frontier lands are still unpurified, and that a remnant of evil is still refractory. But in the region of the Central Land there is no more wind and dust. Truly we should make a vast and spacious capital and plan it great and strong.

"At present things are in a crude and obscure position, and the people's minds are unsophisticated. They roost in nests or dwell in caves. Their manners are simply what is customary. Now if a great man were to establish laws, justice could not fail to flourish. And even if some gain should accrue to the people, in what way would this interfere with the sage's action? Moreover, it will be well to open up and clear the mountains and forests and to construct a palace. Then I may reverently assume the Precious Dignity and so give peace to my good subjects. Above I should then respond to the kindness of the Heavenly Powers in granting me the kingdom, and below I should extend the line of the Imperial descendants and foster right-mindedness. Thereafter the capital may be extended so as to embrace the six cardinal points, and the eight cords may be covered so as to form a roof. Will this not be well?"

The Emperor as Diviner
(*Nihongi,* Book IV)

7th year, Spring, 2nd month, 15th day. The Emperor decreed as follows: "Of old our Imperial Ancestors greatly extended the vast foundation, and under the later Emperors the institution became more and more exalted. The royal influence spread and flourished. But now that it has devolved upon Us, numerous calamities have unexpectedly befallen it. It is to be feared that from the absence of good Government in the Court, We have incurred the blame of the Gods of Heaven and Earth. Would it not be well to commit the matter to the Sacred Tortoise and thereby ascertain the cause of the calamity?"

Accordingly, the Emperor hereupon proceeded to the plain of Kami-asachi, where he assembled the eighty myriads of Deities, and inquired of them by means of divination. At this time the Gods inspired Yamato-to-to-hi-momoso-hime no Mikoto to say as follows: "Why is the Emperor grieved at the disordered state of the country? If he duly did us reverent worship it would assuredly become pacified of itself." The Emperor inquired, saying: "What God is it that thus instructs me?" The answer was: "I am the God who dwells within the borders of the land of Yamato and my name is Oho-mono-nushi no Kami."

Now, having obtained this divine message, the Emperor worshipped as he was told, but without effect. Then, having bathed and practised abstinence, and purified the interior of the Hall, he prayed, saying: "Is Our observance of due ceremonies toward the Gods not yet complete? This non-acceptance is cruel. We pray that We may be further instructed in a dream, and the divine favour thereby consummated."

That night he had a dream. A man of noble appearance stood opposite to him in the door of the hall, and, announcing himself as Oho-mono-nushi no Kami said: "Let the Emperor grieve no more for the disorder of the country. This is my will. If thou wilt cause me to be worshipped by my child, Oho-tata-neko, then will there be peace at once. Moreover the lands beyond the sea will of their own accord render submission."

Autumn, 8th month, 7th day. Yamato-to-to-kami-asachi-hara-ma-guhashi-hime, Oho-mina-kuchi-no Sukune, the ancestor of the Hod-zumi no Omi, and the Kimi of Wo-umi in Ise had all three the same dream, which they reported to the Emperor, saying: "Last night we had a dream in which there appeared a man of noble aspect, who admonished us, saying: 'Let Oho-tato-neko no Mikoto be appointed master of the worship of Oho-mono-nushi-no-oho-kami, and let Ichi-shi no Nagaochi be appointed master of the worship of Yamato no Oho-kuni-dama no Kami. Then assuredly the Empire will have profound peace.'"

The Emperor, when he learned the words of the dream, was more and more delighted in his heart. By a proclamation to the Empire he sought for Oho-tata-neko, who was accordingly found in the village of Suye, in the district of Chinu, and sent to the Emperor, who forthwith proceeded in person to the plain of Kami-asachi, and assembled all the Princes and Ministers, and the eighty Be. He then inquired of Oho-tata-neko, saying: "Whose child art thou?" He answered and said: "My father's name is Oho-mono-nushi no Oho-kami. My mother's name is Ikudama-yori-bime, daughter of Suye-tsu mimi."

Also called Kushi-hi-kata-ame-hi-kata, daughter of Take-chinu-tsumi.

The Emperor said: "Now we shall be prosperous." So he ascertained by divination that it would be lucky to send Ika-shiko-wo to distribute offerings to the Gods. He also divined that it would be unlucky to take advantage of this opportunity to worship other Gods.

11th month, 8th day. The Emperor took the articles for the worship of the Gods which he ordered Ika-shiko-wo to have made by the hands of the eighty Mononobe, and appointed Oho-tata-neko Master of the worship of Oho-mono-nushi no Oho-kami. Moreover he made Nagaochi Master of the worship of Yamato no Oho-kuni-dama no Kami.

After that, he divined that it would be lucky to worship the other Gods. So he took the opportunity of separately worshipping the assemblage of eighty myriads of Deities. He also settled which were to be Heavenly shrines and which Earthly shrines, and allotted land and houses for the service of the Gods. Thereupon the pestilence first ceased; the country at length had peace, the five kinds of grain were produced, and the peasantry enjoyed abundance.

Establishment of the Shrine at Ise
(Nihongi, Book VI)

Now Amaterasu Omikami instructed Yamato-hime no Mikoto saying, "The Province of Ise, of the divine wind, is the land whither repair the waves from the eternal world. . . . It is a secluded and pleasant land. In this land I wish to dwell." In compliance therefore, with the instruction of the great goddess, a shrine was erected to her in the province of Ise. . . . It was there that Amaterasu Omikami first descended from heaven.

Following the Dead
(Nihongi, Book VI)

Yamato-hiko no Mikoto, the Emperor's younger brother . . . died [and] . . . was buried. . . . Thereupon his personal attendants were assembled and all were buried alive upright in the precinct of the Misasagi. For several days they died not, but wept and wailed night and day. At last they died and rotted. Dogs and crows gathered and ate them.

The Emperor, hearing the sound of their weeping and wailing, was grieved in heart and commanded his high officers, saying, "It is a very painful thing to force those whom one has loved in life to follow him in death. Though it be an ancient custom, why follow it, if it is bad? From this time forward take counsel so as to put a stop to the following of the dead." . . .

Nomi no Sukune came forward and said, . . . "I beg leave to propose an expedient which I will submit to your Majesty." . . . He himself directed men of the clay-workers Be to take clay and form therewith shapes of men, horses, and various objects, which he pre-

sented to the Emperor. . . . Then the Emperor greatly rejoiced. . . .
A decree was issued saying, "Henceforth these clay figures must be
set up at tumuli; let not men be harmed."

The Prince Prepares Laws
(*Nihongi*, Book XXII)

A.D. 604. The Prince Imperial in person prepared for the first time
laws. There were seventeen clauses, as follows:

I. Harmony is to be valued, and an avoidance of wanton opposition to be honoured. All men are influenced by class-feelings, and
there are few who are intelligent. Hence there are some who disobey
their lords and fathers, or who maintain feuds with the neighbouring
villages. But when those above are harmonious and those below are
friendly, and there is concord in the discussion of business, right
views of things spontaneously gain acceptance. Then what is there
which cannot be accomplished!

II. Sincerely reverence the three treasures. The three treasures, viz.
Buddha, the Law and the Priesthood, are the final refuge of the four
generated beings, and are the supreme objects of faith in all countries.
What man in what age can fail to reverence this law? Few men are
utterly bad. They may be taught to follow it. But if they do not betake them to the three treasures, wherewithal shall their crookedness
be made straight?

III. When you receive the Imperial commands, fail not scrupulously
to obey them. The lord is Heaven, the vassal is Earth. Heaven over-
spreads and Earth upbears. When this is so, the four seasons follow
their due course, and the powers of Nature obtain their efficacy. If
the Earth attempted to overspread, Heaven would simply fall in ruin.
Therefore is it that when the lord speaks, the vassal listens; when the
superior acts, the inferior yields compliance. Consequently when you
receive the Imperial commands, fail not to carry them out scrupulously. Let there be a want of care in this matter, and ruin is the
natural consequence.

IV. The Ministers and functionaries should make decorous behaviour their leading principle, for the leading principle of the government of the people consists in decorous behaviour. If the superiors

do not behave with decorum, the inferiors are disorderly: if inferiors are wanting in proper behaviour, there must necessarily be offences. Therefore it is that when lord and vassal behave with propriety, the distinction of rank are not confused: when the people behave with propriety, the Government of the Commonwealth proceeds of itself.

V. Ceasing from gluttony and abandoning covetous desires, deal impartially with the suits which are submitted to you. Of complaints brought by the people there are a thousand in one day. If in one day there are so many, how many will there be in a series of years? If the man who is to decide suits at law makes gain his ordinary motive, and hears causes with a view to receiving bribes, then will the suits of the rich man be like a stone flung into water, while the plaints of the poor will resemble water cast upon a stone. Under these circumstances the poor man will not know whither to betake himself. Here too there is a deficiency in the duty of the Minister.

VI. Chastise that which is evil and encourage that which is good. This was the excellent rule of antiquity. Conceal not, therefore, the good qualities of others, and fail not to correct that which is wrong when you see it. Flatterers and deceivers are a sharp weapon for the overthrow of the State, and a pointed sword for the destruction of the people. Sycophants are also fond, when they meet, of dilating to their superiors on the errors of their inferiors; to their inferiors, they censure the faults of their superiors. Men of this kind are all wanting in fidelity to their lord, and in benevolence towards the people. From such an origin great civil disturbances arise.

VII. Let every man have his own charge, and let not the spheres of duty be confused. When wise men are entrusted with office, the sound of praise arises. If unprincipled men hold office, disasters and tumults are multiplied. In this world, few are born with knowledge: wisdom is the product of earnest meditation. In all things, whether great or small, find the right man, and they will surely be well managed: on all occasions, be they urgent or the reverse, meet but with a wise man, and they will of themselves be amenable. In this way will the State be lasting and Temples of the Earth and of Grain will be free from danger. Therefore did the wise sovereigns of antiquity seek the man to fill the office, and not the office for the sake of the man.

VIII. Let the Ministers and functionaries attend the Court early in the morning, and retire late. The business of the State does not admit of remissness, and the whole day is hardly enough for its accomplishment. If, therefore, the attendance at Court is late, emergencies cannot be met: if officials retire soon, the work cannot be completed.

IX. Good faith is the foundation of right. In everything let there be good faith, for in it there surely consists the good and the bad, success and failure. If the lord and the vassal observe good faith one with another, what is there which cannot be accomplished? If the lord and the vassal do not observe good faith towards one another, everything without exception ends in failure.

X. Let us cease from wrath, and refrain from angry looks. Nor let us be resentful when others differ from us. For all men have hearts, and each heart has its own leanings. Their right is our wrong, and our right is their wrong. We are not unquestionably sages, nor are they unquestionably fools. Both of us are simply ordinary men. How can any one lay down a rule by which to distinguish right from wrong? For we are all, one with another, wise and foolish, like a ring which has no end. Therefore, although others give way to anger, let us on the contrary dread our own faults, and though we alone may be in the right, let us follow the multitude and act like them.

XI. Give clear appreciation to merit and demerit, and deal out to each its sure reward or punishment. In these days, reward does not attend upon merit, nor punishment upon crime. Ye high functionaries who have charge of public affairs, let it be your task to make clear rewards and punishments.

XII. Let not the provincial authorities or the Juni no Miyakko levy exactions on the people. In a country there are not two lords; the people have not two masters. The sovereign is the master of the people of the whole country. The officials to whom he gives charge are all his vassals. How can they, as well as the Government, presume to levy taxes on the people?

XIII. Let all persons entrusted with office attend equally to their functions. Owing to their illness or to their being sent on missions, their work may sometimes be neglected. But whenever they become able to attend to business, let them be as accommodating as if they had had cognizance of it from before, and not hinder public affairs on the score of their not having had to do with them.

XIV. Ye ministers and functionaries! Be not envious. For if we envy others, they in turn will envy us. The evils of envy know no limit. If others excel us in intelligence, it gives us no pleasure; if they surpass us in ability, we are envious. Therefore it is not until after a lapse of five hundred years that we at last meet with a wise man, and even in a thousand years we hardly obtain one sage. But if we do not find wise men and sages, wherewithal shall the country be governed?

XV. To turn away from that which is private, and to set our faces towards that which is public—this is the path of a Minister. Now if a man is influenced by private motives, he will assuredly feel resentments, and if he is influenced by resentful feelings, he will assuredly fail to act harmoniously with others. If he fails to act harmoniously with others, he will assuredly sacrifice the public interests to his private feelings. When resentment arises, it interferes with order, and is subversive of law. Therefore in the first clause it was said, that superiors and inferiors should agree together. The purport is the same as this.

·XVI. Let the people be employed [in forced labour] at seasonable times. This is an ancient and excellent rule. Let them be employed, therefore, in the winter months, when they are at leisure. But from spring to autumn, when they are engaged in agriculture or with the mulberry trees, the people should not be so employed. For if they do not attend to agriculture, what will they have to eat? If they do not attend to the mulberry trees, what will they do for clothing?

XVII. Decisions on important matters should not be made by one person alone. They should be discussed with many. But small matters are of less consequence. It is unnecessary to consult a number of people. It is only in the case of the discussion of weighty affairs, when there is a suspicion that they may miscarry, that one should arrange matters in concert with others, so as to arrive at the right conclusion.

From the Manyoshu [4]
(Late Eighth Century?)

The Three Hills
By Emperor Tenji

Mount Kagu strove with Mount Miminashi
    For the love of Mount Unebi.
Such is love since the age of the gods;
As it was thus in the early days,
So people strive for spouses even now.

Envoy
When Mount Kagu and Mount Miminashi wrangled,
A god came over and saw it
Here—on this plain of Inami!

On the rich banner-like clouds
That rim the waste of waters
The evening sun is glowing,
And promises to-night
The moon in beauty!

Presented to the Emperor Tenji on the Occasion of His Majesty's Illness
By Empress Yamato-hime

I turn and gaze far
    Towards the heavenly plains.
Lo, blest is my Sovereign Lord—
His long life overspans
The vast blue firmament.

On the Occasion of the Death of the Emperor Tenji
By a Lady of the Court

Mortal creature as I am,
    Whom the gods suffer not on high,
Wide sundered,
Each morning I lament my Lord;
Far divided,
I long and languish after my Lord;
Oh, were he a jewel
That I might put about my arm and cherish!
Oh, were he a garment
That I might wear and not put off!
The Lord whom I love so,
I saw but last night—in dream.

An Elegy on the Death of Prince Iwata
By Prince Niu

My prince, graceful as the pliant bamboo,
    My lord, with beauteous ruddy face,
Was enshrined as a god
In the hills of secluded Hatsuse:
So a messenger has told me.
Is this a rumour that I hear?
Is it a mockery that I am told?
My greatest sorrow under heaven,
My wildest grief in this world,
Is that I failed to travel,
With my staff or without it,
Far as the clouds of heaven wander,
Far as the ends of heaven and earth,
To consult the evening oracle,
To consult the oracle of stones;

Whereupon to build a shrine at my home,
With a wine-jar at my pillow,
Stringing many a bamboo-ring,
With bands of mulberry-cloth hanging on my arms,
And in my hand a seven-jointed sedge
From the Sasara Field of Heaven,
To purify myself and pray
On the Heavenly River's shore.
Ah that I must leave him lying
Among the rocks of that lofty hill!

Envoy

It is nothing but a trick
And a mere mockery,
That he, my prince, is laid
Among the rocks of that lofty hill!

Unlike the growth of the *sugi,* the pass trees,
On Furu's hill at Isonokami,
He is no such prince
As will pass from my mind!

Our Great Sovereign
By Kakinomoto Hitomaro

Our great Sovereign, a goddess,
    Of her sacred will
Has reared a towering palace
On Yoshinu's shore,
Encircled by its rapids;
And, climbing, she surveys the land.

The overlapping mountains,
Rising like green walls,
Offer the blossoms in spring,
And with autumn, show their tinted leaves,
As godly tributes to the Throne.

The god of the Yu River, to provide the royal table,
Holds the cormorant-fishing
In its upper shallows,
And sinks the fishing-nets
In the lower stream.

Thus the mountains and the river
Serve our Sovereign, one in will;
It is truly the reign of a divinity.

Envoy

The mountains and the waters
Serve our Sovereign, one in will;
And she, a goddess, is out on her pleasure-barge
Upon the foaming rapids.

At the Time of the Temporary Enshrinement of the Crown Prince Hinamishi

By Kakinomoto Hitomaro

At the beginning of heaven and earth
    The eight hundred, the thousand myriads of gods,
Assembled in high council
On the shining beach of the Heavenly River,
Consigned the government of the Heavens
Unto the Goddess Hirume, the Heaven-Illumining One,
And the government for all time,
As long as heaven and earth endured,
Of the Rice-abounding Land of Reed Plains
Unto her divine offspring,
Who, parting the eightfold clouds of the sky,
Made his godly descent upon the earth.

Our noble Prince, child of the Bright One above,
Regarding this—the land over which
The gracious Sovereign reigns as a god

From the Kiyomi Palace of Asuka, stout-pillared,
Has ascended the Plain of Heaven,
Opening wide the gate of stone.

Alas, our mighty lord and prince,
On whom the folk everywhere in the land leaned,
Trustful as one riding a great ship,
And to whom they looked up as eagerly
As to heaven for rain, hoping
That if he came to rule the under-heaven
He would bring to his reign
A glory of the spring flowers
And such perfection as of the full moon!

Ah, how was he minded that he chose
To plant stout pillars
And build him a palace high
On mayumi's alien hill!
There we wait on him each morning,
But no word he speaks—
So have passed days on days,
Wherefore now the servitors of the Prince
Must go, but know not where.

Envoy

The stately palace of our Prince
To whom we looked up
As we look up to high heaven,
Alas, must fall into ruin!
Though the ruddy sun shines,
The fair moon, that sails
The darkness of night,
Is hidden for ever—alas!

The birds of the Island Palace,
　　Kept in the lake of Crescent Gem,
Will not dive under water,
Craving the sight of men.

On the Death of Prince Yuge
By Okisome Azumabito

Our lord and prince, ruling in peace,
    Child of the Bright One above,
God as he is, has taken
His divine seat in the Heavenly Palace
Far above. We, awe-stricken,
Lie prostrate and weep
Day after day, and night after night,
And to our weeping there is no end.

Envoy
Our lord and prince,
Because he is a god,
Has gone to dwell unseen
In the five-hundredfold clouds of heaven.

At the Palace Banquet on the Eighteenth Day of the Eleventh Month of the First Year of Tempyo-hoji (757)
By Emperor Junnin

Since thy reign is to endure
    With the sun and the moon
That illumine heaven and earth,
What could ever trouble our hearts?

Chanted at a Religious Service to Her Ancestral God
By Lady Otomo of Sakanoe

Oh, our heaven-born god,
    Descended from the heavenly plains—
With the *sakaki* branch

Fresh from the inmost hill.
Tied with white paper and mulberry cloth,
With a wine-jar set in the purified earth,
With a cord of many bamboo-rings .
Hanging from my neck,
With my knees bent like the deer's,
With my maiden's scarf flung over me,—
Thus I entreat thee, our god,
Yet can I not meet him?

Envoy

With folded mulberry cloth in my hands,
Thus I entreat thee, our god,
Yet can I not meet him?

Congratulatory Poem and Envoy on the Issuance of the Imperial Rescript Regarding the Production of Gold in Michinoku
By Otomo Yakamochi

Succeeding to the Celestial Throne
    Of the Imperial Ancestor divine,
Who came down from heaven to rule
The Rice-abounding Land of Reed Plains,
A long line of Emperors has reigned
From age to age over these provinces,
Which with their deep mountains and wide rivers
Yield countless tribute and inexhaustible treasures.
However, our great Lord and Sovereign,
On convoking the people and inaugurating
His auspicious work, was sorely troubled
For fear lest there should not be gold enough.
It was then reported to the Throne
That gold had been found in the Eastland—
In the hills of Oda of "Road's End"—

Setting the mind of our Sovereign at rest,
"The gods of heaven and earth," thought he—
Himself a god—"have approved
My enterprise, and the spirits of my ancestors
Have given aid that such a marvel
As might have been in the ancient days
Should be revealed under my reign,
Auguring prosperity for my realm."
So now he exhorts his vassals of many clans
To loyalty and devotion,
Extending at the same time his benevolence
To the old and to women and children
Till their hearts' desires are satisfied.
This overcomes me with awe and joy.
I ponder more deeply than ever
How to the Otomo clan belongs a great office
In which served our far-off divine ancestor
Who bore the title of Okume-nushi.
We are the sons of the fathers who sang,
         "At sea be my body water-soaked,
         On land be it with grass overgrown,
         Let me die by the side of my Sovereign!
         Never will I look back";
And who to this day from olden times
Have kept their warriors' name for ever clean.
Verily Otomo and Saheki are the clans
Pledged to the maxim, as pronounced
By their ancestors: "Extinguish not, sons,
The name of your fathers! Serve your Sovereign!"

O let us grip birchwood bows in our hands,
Wear on our loins double-edged swords,
And stand guard morning and evening!
There are no men but we to defend the imperial gate—
I exclaim with a fervent heart
When I hear His Majesty's gracious words,
That overwhelm me with awe.

Envoy

I feel within me a warrior's heart
When I hear my Sovereign's gracious words
That overcome me with awe.

Set a mark plainly over the grave
Of Otomo's far-off divine ancestor
To make it known to the world!

Among the hills of Michinoku in the Eastland
Gold has bloomed forth—an augury
That His Imperial Majesty's reign shall prosper.

Desiring to Pursue the Way of Buddha
while Lying in his Sick-bed and
Lamenting the Transience
of Life

By Otomo Yakamochi

Brief is this mortal life—
    Let me go and seek the Way,
Contemplating the hills and streams undefiled!

O let me seek the Pure Way,
Striving against the light of the heaven-coursing sun,
That I may find it again in after-life!

From the Engi-Shiki
(A.D. 923)

Prayer for a Blessing on the Harvest [5]

He says: [6] Hear all of you, assembled Kannushi and hafuri.
He says: I declare in the presence of the sovran gods, whose praises
by the words of the sovran's dear progenitor's Augustness and pro-

genitrix, who divinely remained in the plain of high heaven, are fulfilled as heavenly temples and country temples. I fulfill your praises by setting up the great offerings of the sovran Grandchild's Augustness, made with the intention of beginning the harvest in the second month of this year as the morning sun rises in glory.

He says: I declare in the presence of the sovran gods of the Harvest. If the sovran gods will bestow in many-bundled ears, and in luxuriant ears, the ripening harvest which will be produced by the dripping of foam from the arms and by drawing the mud together between the opposing thighs, then I will fulfill their praises by setting up the first fruits in a thousand ears and many hundred ears, raising high the beer jars, filling and ranging in rows the bellies of the beer jars. I will present them in juice and in ear, as to things which grow in the great field plain, sweet herbs and bitter herbs; as to things which dwell in the blue sea plain—things wide of fin and things narrow of fin, down to the weeds of the offing and weeds of the shore. And as to clothes—with bright cloth, glittering cloth, soft cloth, and coarse cloth, will I fulfill praises. And, having furnished a white horse, a white boar and a white cock, and the various kinds of things in the presence of the sovran God of the Harvest, I fulfill his praises by setting up the great offerings of the sovran Grandchild's Augustness. . . .

[The names of several of the gods being praised are here read.]

Because you praise the age of the sovran Grandchild's Augustness as a long age eternally and unchangingly, and bless it as a luxuriant age, I fulfill your praises as our sovran's dear progenitor's Augustness and progenitrix's Augustness by setting up the great offerings of the sovran Grandchild's Augustness. . . .

[Other gods' names are mentioned, and routine reasons for praising them cited.]

He says: Because the sovran Great Deity bestows on him the countries of the four quarters over which her glance extends as far as the limit where heaven stands up like a wall, as far as the bound where the blue clouds lie flat, as far as the bounds where the white clouds lie away fallen—the blue sea plain as far as the limit whither come the prows of the ships without letting their poles or paddles be dry, the ships which continuously crowd on the great sea plain—the road which men go by land, as far as the limit whither come the horses' hooves, with the baggage cords tied tightly, treading the uneven rocks and tree-roots and standing up continuously in a long path without a break, making the narrow countries wide, and the hilly countries plain, and, as it were, drawing the distant countries together by throwing many tans of ropes over them, because she does all this, he will pile up the first fruits like a range of hills in the great presence of the sovran Great Deity, and will tranquilly take for himself the remainder.

2. Second Period
(A.D. 925–1700)
(Including Texts of Ryobu Shinto)

From the Shoku Nihongi [1]
(Twelfth Century?)

The Priest Dosho [1]

The priest Dosho died. The Emperor was greatly grieved and sent a messenger to convey his condolences. He was a man from Tachibi in Kawachi. His family-name was Fune no Muraji. His father was Esaka, of Sho-kin-ge rank. His manner of preaching was faultless, he especially was an exponent of the virtue of patience. Once there had been a disciple who had wanted to put him to the test and secretly made a hole in the urinal so that the bedding became unclean. The priest only smiled and said: "Some naughty kozo has made my bedding unclean," and not a word more. . . .

Later, traveling all over the country, he made wells by the roadsides, placed ferry-boats at fords, built bridges. The Ujibashi in Yamashiro, for instance, has been built by this priest. For more than ten years the priest had been traveling in this way when he received an

Imperial request to come back. Coming back, he lived in a meditation-hall and practised Zen as before. Sometimes he did not rise once in three days, at other times not once in seven days. Suddenly there came a fragrance from his room. His disciples were frightened and went to see. The priest was in sitting posture and did not breathe.

At the time he was three score and twelve. His disciples, in conformity with instructions he left behind, incinerated him in Awahara. This is the origin of cremation in the Realm. It is said that after the cremation relatives and disciples were fighting for his bones, when suddenly a strong hurricane sprung up and took them away, so they disappeared entirely. The people at the time thought it strange. When afterwards the capital was moved to Nara, the priest's younger brothers and the disciples brought the meditation-hall to the new place and rebuilt it there. This is the Zen-temple in the district of the right in Nara. In this temple there are many sutras and sastras.

Imperial Penitence [1]

Summer, 4th month, 3rd day. In an Imperial Decree it was said: We, with insufficient qualifications, are nevertheless at the head of Princes and High Dignitaries. Our conduct is not approved of by Heaven, our benevolence does not reach the people. For this reason the seasonal changes are out of order, rain and drought do not come when due, the crops do not ripen, the people are suffering. Each time We think of this, We feel compassion in Our heart. To alleviate the sufferings of the population, We order the Konko Myokyo [Suvarna-prabhasa-sutra] to be read at the five Great Temples, the interest on loans [from the government] is not to be collected, the yo is reduced to half.

The Holder of the Mirror [1]

11th month, 3rd day. The King of Shiragi was granted an Imperial Message in which it was said: The Emperor respectfully informs the King of Shiragi that We, completely lacking virtue, nevertheless have received an exalted destiny. We are ashamed that, without the abilities of the polisher with stones, yet We have been entrusted with the holding of the mirror. Till evening We forget to partake of food,

Our worries whether Our acts have been good or bad gradually increasing; till deep in the night We do not sleep, the doubts about Our acts still increasing. We fervently hope that Our benevolence penetrates unto far-away realms. You, Sir, have been in your realm since generations, loving your subjects. Inspired by the greatest sincerity, for a long time your ships have been bringing tribute to Our court. We pray that by making rock-like foundations you will bring about that beautiful sounds penetrate unto the shy doe's retreat, that by strengthening the castle a beautiful model be provided for the goose-pond, so that peace and happiness prevail [in the State], and honest and quiet customs [among the population].

The cold season being at its severest, We wonder how you are nowadays.

Signs, Portents, Magic and Remedies [1]

9th month, 3rd day. Felicitous rice came from the house of Momotari, Omiwa no Oyosami no Miyatsuko, a man from the capital. Omi presented white turtles, Tamba white deer.

5th month, 1st day. Drought in all provinces, accordingly offerings of *heihaku* were made at all shrines.

5th day. Messengers were despatched to the Home provinces, to pray to famous mountains and great rivers for rain.

28th day. Horses were offered to several shrines; prayers for rain were said.

17th day. Shimodzuke and Bizen presented red crows, Iyo tin.

9th day. Kawachi presented a white dove. By an Imperial Decree the district of Nishigori was exempted from one year's land-tax and forced labour, besides, the family of the man who had captured the auspicious [bird], Inukai no Hiromaro, was exempted for three years; moreover [persons with] sentences of tozai and less in the [four] Home provinces were pardoned.

24th day. En no Kimi Otsunu was banished to the peninsula of Izu. Originally Otsunu had lived on Katsuragiyama and had been reputed as an adept in magic. Karakuni no Muraji, Hirotari, Gejugoige, took him as his professor. Later, jealous of his art, he slandered him that he led people astray by weird arts and therefore he was banished to a far-away place. It was said among the population that he often commanded spirits to draw water or to gather firewood for him. If they did not obey his orders, he bound them with magic.

21st day. Iyo presented a white swallow.

10th day. Nagato presented a white turtle.

28th day. A woman from the district of Katsuragi no kami in Yamato, Kamo no kimi, Nukame by name, gave birth to two boys and one girl. She was given . . . coarse silk, . . . cotton silk, . . . cloth, . . . rice, and a wet-nurse.

15th day. Mitegura [offerings] were made to all shrines, rain was prayed for from [the deities of] great mountains and broad rivers. Superintendents of Imperial estates were dismissed and officials of provinces were entrusted to make tours of inspection instead.

25th day. Since the seasonal rain did not fall, prayers for rain were ordered in the four Home provinces. This year's tribute was relinquished.

8th day. Hida presented a sacred horse. A general amnesty in the Realm was proclaimed, not including thieves. . . . The people were granted tax-exemption for three years, the priest Ryukwan who had obtained it was forgiven his crimes and made to enter the capital.

10th day. A man from Onogori in Mino, Miwahito Futo, presented an eight-legged horse. He was given one thousand soku of rice.

8th day. The grave of Yamato Takeru no Mikoto trembled. A messenger was despatched to worship.

11th day. Omi presented auspicious rice-ears, ears from different ridges, which had grown together.

6th day. Stars were seen by day-time.

5th month, 10th day. Bizen presented a sacred horse.

Above the western tower a felicitous cloud was seen. There was, by Imperial Decree, a general amnesty. The name of the period was changed to the first year of Keiun. Aged and infirm people were consoled, the collection of the main tax was remitted from the year Jinin [Taiho 2], the tribute of this year from the *gun* where the sacred horse came from was exempted. Imperial Princes, other Princes, the officials from tsukaibe upwards were given emoluments, in varying amounts. The governor of the province which had presented the sacred horse, Ina no Mabito Iwasaki, sho-go-i-ge, was raised one step in rank. The man who had first seen the felicitous cloud, an official of the third rank in the Ministry of Examinations, by name of One no Ason Umakai, ju-shichi-i-jo, was raised three steps in rank. He was given . . . coarse silk, . . . silk yarn, . . . hempspun cloth, . . . hoes.

15th day. Awa presented trees which had grown together.

22nd day. Offering nusa, prayers for rain were said at all shrines.

3rd day. The mayor of the left part of the capital presented a white swallow, Shimosa a white crow.

9th day. Since the seasonal rain did not come, messengers were despatched to the shrines to pray for rain.

8th month, 11th day. It was said in an Imperial Edict:

The seasonal changes have become irregular, it has been dry for a long time. The farmers are reduced to hunger and despair, or become criminals. [Therefore] granting a great amnesty in the realm, We ought to make a new start together with the people. Crimes, minor or major, from punishable by death downwards, are all pardoned; old and sick people, widows and widowers, people without families, who are unable to subsist alone, are all granted relief. Those who under ordinary amnesties are not pardoned on account of eight major crimes [this time] will not be pardoned either.

26th day. Echizen presented a red crow. The governor of the province, the head of the district from where the felicitous bird had come, and others, were raised one step in rank.

The farmers were exempted from taxes during a year; the man who had captured it, Shishibito no Omi Kunimochi, was given ju-hachi-i-ge and [together with the above-mentioned officials] coarse silk, floss silk, cloth and holes in varying quantities.

5th month, 15th day. A man from Ishikawa-gori in Kawachi, Kawabe no Ason Otsumaro, presented a white dove; he was given five hiki of coarse silk, ten ku of yarn, twenty tan of cloth, twenty hoes and three hundred sheaves of seed-rice.

4th day. The home provinces were ordered to pray for rain to famous mountain and great rivers.

24th day. There were forest fires in Tamba and Tajima. Messengers were despatched to offer mitegura to the divinities of Heaven and Earth. Immediately there was a thunderstorm and without beating it out, the fire went out by itself.

There was fire on the Samine-mountain in Uchi-gori, Yamato, this was beaten out.

9th day. This year many people in the realm died of contagious disease. For the first time evil spirits were driven out by making cows of clay.

Keiun Fourth year, Spring, 1st month, 6th day. There being contagious disease in various provinces, messengers were despatched to convey the order for performing the ceremonies of Great Purification.

A Manifest God [2]

He says: Hearken all ye assembled August Children, Princes, Nobles, Officials and People of the Realm-under-Heaven to the Word which He speaks *even* as the Word of the Sovereign that is a manifest God ruling over the Great Land of Many Islands.

He says: Hearken ye all to the Word of the Sovereign who proclaims thus: We have listened with reverence to the noble, high, broad, warm Words of the charge vouchsafed to Us by the Sovereign Prince of Yamato.

Who is a Manifest God ruling over the Great Land of Many Islands in performance of the Task of this High Throne of Heavenly Succession, in the same wise as the August Child of the God of Heaven, as it was decreed by the God which is in Heaven, that from the beginning in the High Plain of Heaven, through the reigns of our Distant Ancestors down to these days and onwards, Sovereign August Children should be born in succession for ever to succeed to the rule of the Great Land of many islands.

And, even as a God, it is Our wish to give Peace and Order to this Realm-under-Heaven and to deign to cherish and soothe its People.

He says: Hearken ye all to Word which the Sovereign proclaims, saying thus: And therefore all ye functionaries of every kind, even unto the officers appointed to govern the countries under our rule in the four quarters, do ye, neither mistaking nor violating the laws of the land which the Sovereign House has proclaimed and enforced, even striving, without delay or neglect, with bright, pure and true hearts, earnestly labour and serve.

He says: Hearken ye all to the Word which the Sovereign proclaims, saying thus: And all people who, hearing and understanding in this wise, shall serve Us faithfully, We will in divers ways reward, praising them and lifting them up.

A Great Sign [2]

He says: Hearken all ye August Children, Princes, etc., etc. He says: Hearken all to the Word which *He* proclaims, saying: Even as a God, We think that, in governing all the quarters of Heaven and Earth seated in this High Throne which began in the August Reign of the Sovereign who descended from the High Plain of Heaven, it is when, the Sovereign being a Sage and served by wise Ministers, the Realm under Heaven is at peace and the hundred officials are tranquil, that a Great Sign appears in Heaven and Earth. . . .

When We heard that the Governor of the Capital, the Minister of the Junior Third Rank Fujiwara no Asomi Maro had offered to the Throne a tortoise bearing writing [on its back] We were surprised and astounded, and when We saw it We were rejoiced and were glad. For We thought, "Is this a thing which has come to pass through the merit of Our Government? Nay, it is a great Sign which has appeared because of the high and noble conduct and under the warm and broad virtue of the Great Sovereign the Empress Dowager."

"We Will Die by Our King" [2]

He says: Hearken ye all to the Word of the Sovereign Prince of Yamato that is a Manifest God, saying:

A report has been made to Us that in the East of this land which We rule in the throne of Heavenly Sun Succession, etc., in the district of Oda in the country of Michinoku, Gold has been found. . . .

Therefore We have joyfully received it and reverently received it, and not knowing whether to go forward or backward night and day We have humbly reflected, thinking that whereas such a thing might come to pass in the reign of a King wise in the cherishing and soothing of the people, We are indeed ashamed and overcome with thankfulness because it has been manifested in Our time, who are unworthy and unskilled.

Shall we alone, therefore, receive this Great and Precious Sign? Nay, it is right that We should humbly receive it and accept it in rejoicing together with Our people. And inasmuch as We, even as a

God, do so consider, We will cherish and reward them All. . . .

Further, ye men of the house of Omoto and Saeki, as it is always said, in serving the Sovereign House have no regard for aught else, and We know that your forebears have always said, "We will not die peacefully, We will die by the side of our King. If we go to the sea our bodies shall steep in the water. If we go to the mountains over our corpses the grass shall grow." Wherefore We employ you, in our reign as in the reigns of Our Distant Sovereign Ancestors, to be Our bodyguard. Let the children then be children that do the will of their fathers. That ye may not neglect their will, but serve with bright pure hearts. We will reward some of ye, men and women together.

From Various Sources

Great Yamato, the Divine Country [3]
By Kitabatake Chicafusa (1293–1354)

Great Yamato is a divine country. It is only our land whose foundations were first laid by the divine ancestor. It alone has been transmitted by the Sun Goddess to a long line of her descendants. There is nothing of this kind in foreign countries. Therefore it is called the divine land.

It is only our country which, from the time that heaven and earth were first unfolded until this very day, has preserved the succession to the throne intact in one single family. Even when, as sometimes naturally happened, it descended to a lateral branch, it was held in accordance with just principles. This shows that the august oath of the gods [to preserve the succession] is ever renewed in a way which distinguishes Japan from all other countries. . . .

Of officials there are two classes—the civil and the military. The method of the civil official is to remain at home and reason upon the right way, wherein, if he attains to lucidity, he may rise to be a Minister of State. It is the business of the soldier, on the other hand, to render service in warlike expeditions, wherein, if he gains fame, he may become a general. Therefore these two professions ought not to be neglected for a moment. It has been said, "In times of civil dis-order, arms are placed to the right and letters to the left; in peace, letters are put to the right and arms to the left." . . .

It is the duty of every man born on the Imperial soil to yield de-voted loyalty to his sovereign, even to the sacrifice of his own life. Let no one suppose for a moment that there is any credit due to him for so doing. Nevertheless, in order to stimulate the zeal of those who come after, and in loving memory of the dead, it is the business of the ruler to grant rewards in such cases [to the children]. Those who are in an inferior position should not enter into rivalry with them. Still more should those who have done no specially meritorious service abstain from inordinate ambitions. It is a truly blessed prin-ciple to observe the rut of the chariot which has preceded, at whatever risk to our own safety [that is, a conservative policy should be main-tained at all hazards].

The Kami Kaze [4]
By a priest named Kojima (?–1374)

Since the Creation there have been seven invasions of Japan by foreign countries. The most notable of these attacks were in the periods Bunyei [1264–1275] and Koan [1278–1288]. At this time the Great Yuan Emperor [Kublai Khan] had conquered by force of arms the four hundred provinces of China. Heaven and earth were oppressed by his power. Hard would it have been for a small country like our own to repel him, and that it was able easily and without effort to destroy the armies of Great Yuan was due to naught else but the divine blessing. . . .

General Wan . . . set forth from the various ports and bays with his troops embarked in a fleet of more than 70,000 great ships [which] . . . arrived together at the port of Hakata on the third day of the eighth month of the second year of Bunyei [1265]. Their great vessels were lashed together, and gangways laid across from one to another. . . . On the bows of hostile ships, beams like those used for raising water from wells were set up to a height of several hundred feet, at the ends of which platforms were placed. Men seated on these were able to look down into the Japanese camp and count every hair's end. Moreover, they chained together planks forty or fifty feet wide so as to form a sort of rafts, which, when laid on the surface of the water, provided a number of level roads over the waves, like the three great thoroughfares or the twelve main streets [of Kyoto]. By these roads the enemy's cavalry appeared in many tens of thousands, and fought so desperately that our troops relaxed their ardour, and many of them had thoughts of retreat. When the drum was beaten, and a hand-to-hand contest was already engaged, iron balls, like footballs, were let fly from things called "cannon" [with a sound] like cartwheels rolling down a steep declivity, and accompanied by flashes like lightning. Two or three thousand of these were let go at once. Most of the Japanese troops were burnt to death, and their gates and turrets set fire to. There was no opportunity of putting out the flames. . . .

No further resistance was possible. All the men of Kiushiu fled to Shikoku and the provinces north of the Inland Sea. The whole Japanese nation was struck with panic, and knew not what to do. Visits to the shrines of the Shinto gods, and public and secret services in the Buddhist temples, bowed down the Imperial mind and crushed the Imperial liver and gall-bladder. Imperial messengers were despatched with offerings to all the gods of heaven and earth, and all the Buddhist temples of virtue to answer prayer, great and small alike, throughout the sixty provinces. On the seventh day, when the Imperial devotions were completed, from Lake Suwa there arose a cloud of many colours, in shape like a great serpent, which spread away towards the west. The doors of the Temple-treasury of Hachiman flew open, and the skies were filled with a sound of galloping horses and of ringing bits. In the twenty-one shrines of Yoshino the brocade-curtained mirrors moved, the swords in the Temple-treasury put on a sharp edge, and all the shoes offered to the god turned towards the west. At Sumiyoshi sweat poured from below the saddles of the four horses sacred to the deities, and the iron shields turned of themselves and faced the enemy in a line. . . .

Now General Wan of Great Yuan, having cast off the moorings of his 70,000 ships, at the hour of the dragon on the seventeenth day of the eighth month started for Nagato and Suwo by way of Moji and Akamagaseki [Shimonoseki]. His fleet were midway on their course when the weather, which had been windless, with the clouds at rest, changed abruptly. A mass of black clouds arising from the north-east covered the sky, the wind blew fiercely, the tumultuous billows surged up to heaven, the thunder rolled and the lightning dashed against the ground so abundantly that it seemed as if great mountains were crumbling down and high heaven falling to the earth. The 70,000 warships of the foreign pirates either struck upon cragged reefs and were broken to atoms, or whirling round in the surging eddies, went down with all hands.

Nevertheless, General Wan alone was neither driven off by the storm nor buried beneath the waves, but flew aloft and stood in the calm seclusion of the middle heaven. Here he was met by a sage named Ryo To-bin, who came soaring from the west. He addressed General Wan as follows: "The gods of heaven and the gods of earth of the entire country of Japan, 3700 shrines or more, have raised this evil wind and made the angry billows surge aloft. Human power cannot cope with them. I advise you to embark at once in your one shattered ship and return to your own country." General Wan was persuaded. He embarked in the one shattered ship which remained, braved all alone the waves of 10,000 ri of ocean, and presently arrived at the port of Mingchu [in China].

Proclamation against Christians [5]
By Iyeyasu (1614)

The Positive Principle is the father, the Negative Principle the mother by whom man is begotten, and with his birth the Three Powers are complete.

Japan from the commencement was the country of the gods. The unfathomableness of the Positive and Negative Principles is called god, and who shall refuse reverence and honour to the essence of all that is Holy and Spiritual? Man owes his existence entirely to the workings of the Positive and Negative, in his five members and in the six sources of perception, in his uprising and sitting down, in moving and in being still, he is not independent of god for a single moment. The divinity is sought for elsewhere; everywhere man is provided with a divinity, and contains a complete divinity within himself. This is the form which divinity takes.

Japan is called the land of Buddha, and not without reason. It is written: "This is the country where the divine brightness reappears, this is the native-land of the Sun." The Lotus of the Law says: "The power by which Buddhas save the world, resides in their perfect omniscience, whereby they make happy all living beings, wherefore they make manifest immeasurable divine power." This is a golden saying, a miraculous passage. God and Buddha differ in name, but their meaning is one, just as if the two halves of a tally be placed together. The priests and laymen of antiquity, by the divine aid, sailed over the ocean and visited the far-off land of China in search of the law of Buddha, and the doctrines of the principles of benevolence; unweariedly they bore hither the esoteric and exoteric books. Since that time the doctrine has been handed down from teacher to teacher in unbroken succession, and the glory of the Buddhist Law has been far greater than in other lands. This exemplifies the truth that "the Law of Buddha gradually travels eastwards."

But the Kirishitan [Christian] band have come to Japan, not only sending their merchant vessels to exchange commodities, but also longing to disseminate an evil law, to overthrow right doctrine, so that they may change the government of the country, and obtain possession of the land. This is the germ of great disaster, and must be crushed.

Japan is the country of gods and of Buddha; it honours the gods and reveres Buddha. The principles of benevolence and right-doing are held to be of prime importance, and the law of good and evil is so ascertained that if there be any offenders, they are liable according to the gravity of their crime to the five punishments of branding, nose-slitting, cutting off the feet, castration and death. In the Book of Etiquette it is said: "The degrees of mourning are many, and the appropriate dresses are five. Crimes are many, and the appropriate punishments are five." If there be one suspected of crime, let the gods bear witness. By oath shall be determined the offence and its punishment, and the distinction between guilty and innocent shall not err by a hair's breadth. Criminals of every degree are detested by Buddha, god, the trinity of precious ones, mankind, Heaven and all living things. The overflowings of accumulated wickedness shall not escape; whether by crucifixion or burning in the furnace, punishment shall be meted out, for this is the way of encouraging the good and chastising the evil. Though one may desire to keep down evil, it accumulates with ease; though one desire to advance in good, it is difficult to hold by; and thus a watch must be kept. In the present life it is so, and in the next not even all the Buddhas past, present and to come, can save from the reproaches of the King of Hell, nor can the successive generations of our ancestors succour us. Fear and tremble!

The faction of the Bateren [Padres] rebel against this dispensation; they disbelieve in the way of the gods, and blaspheme the true Law, violate right-doing and injure the good. If they see a condemned fellow, they run to him with joy, bow to him and do him reverence. This they say is the essence of their belief. If this is not an evil Law, what is it? They truly are the enemies of the gods and of Buddha. If this be not speedily prohibited, the safety of the state will assuredly be hereafter imperilled; and if those who are charged with ordering its affairs do not put a stop to the evil, they will expose themselves to Heaven's rebuke.

These must be instantly swept out, so that not an inch of soil remains to them in Japan on which to plant their feet, and if they refuse to obey this command they shall suffer the penalty. We have been blessed by the commission of Heaven to be lord in Japan, and we have wielded power over this realm for years past. Abroad we have manifested the perfection of the Five Cardinal Virtues, while at home we have returned to the doctrine of the scriptures. For these reasons the country prospers, the people enjoy peace. The Scripture says: "If the present life be peaceful and tranquil, there will be a good place in that to come." Kung-fu-tze also has said: "Body, hair and skin we have received from our father and mother; not to injure them is the beginning of filial piety." To preserve one's body is to revere god. Quickly cast out the evil Law, and spread our true Law more and more; for the way of the gods and the Law of Buddha to prosper in spite of the degeneracy of these latter days is a mark of a good ruler. Let Heaven and the Four Seas hear this and obey.

From Wa Rongo, or "Japanese Analects" [6] (Ryobu Shinto)
(1669)

The Divine Ordinance, or Oracle of the Sun-Goddess Amaterasu Omikami (Tenshoko-Daijingu)

All My people! Never be crafty, but hold fast the truth, or else to your sorrow, the unseen punishment from Heaven will unfailingly come upon you, and you the wicked ones will be hurled down into Hades.

Be honest and just, then God will grant you heavenly blessedness even here on earth in compensation for your hard life of suffering and trial.

All My people! If you act against the Will of Heaven and Earth, I am sure that you will not only lose the Divine Grace, but remain eternally unsaved in Hades.

Therefore, again I say unto you! Submit yourselves disinterestedly to the never-failing Law of Nature; live, move and have your being in Her; this, indeed, is the unshaken principle of the "Way"; this is the true essence of faith in God. Not to practise hundreds of tedious ceremonies, but to reverence the One True Law of Mind, is what the Heavenly Being enjoins upon believers, and this alone pleases Him.

List ye, My people!

Enjoy your life long and happily in and through Nature. Live by the Law of Righteousness implanted in your own heart. Serve your Ancestral Deity with piety and reverence, so that our unique nationality may be well consolidated and in consequence thereof be enabled to hold sway over all other nations, making manifest how noble is the Mission which My descendants of the Imperial lineage hold in trust for the whole world!

The Oracle of the God Hachiman (Honda-No-Shohachiman) of Iwashimizu

No matter how poorly I may exist on a food of stone, or metal, and although nothing is bestowed for Me to eat, yet I will not accept any offering from those impure in heart.

Although I remain forlorn and homeless and am obliged to dwell in a stream of blazing fire, yet I am unwilling to go to the dishonest and impure and ask shelter.

All ye, My people! Know that of our innumerable deities [kami], some are great, some small, some good, whilst others are bad, so that what they like or dislike is dissimilar: the good deity never grants an unjust desire, but turns a deaf ear to the entreaties of the wicked, whilst, in striking contrast, the bad deity is content to listen to the prayer of the unjust and ready at any time to respond to it with all its mind and heart, for it takes delight in a false doctrine.

I need not add more than to say that one should walk along the Path of Righteousness in company with Honest Mind.

The Oracle of the God of Kasuga (Kasuga-Daimyojin)

Even though a man provides Me with a nice clean room, offering Me the rare and precious treasures of the land, and hanging up the sevenfold sacred ropes [shime], praying to Me earnestly with his whole heart and mind for hundreds of days, I am unwilling to favour a house with My presence, whose owner is either dishonest, harsh or greedy.

But even though one, by reason of deep mourning for a deceased parent, is polluted, and therefore cannot invite Me, nevertheless if he be always kind-hearted towards others, he may expect Me to appear in his dwelling, because I, the Kami, am truly the very Incarnation of Mercy.

Listen all ye, My people!

If you desire to obtain Divine aid, emancipate yourselves from all foolish pride and egotism, for even a hair's breadth of that kind of vanity separates you from God [Kami] as effectually as though by a mass of thick clouds.

The Oracle of the Tenjin of Kitano

Hearken all ye, My people!

If you will have your prayers granted, cleanse yourselves without, or pray with hearts pure and stainless as a mirror. If anyone who is falsely accused enquire of Me for seven days to be delivered and I fail to do so, I will confess Myself unworthy of the very title of Kami [God], because I lack the Divine Potency to give aid to the just and stand by the oppressed.

The Oracle of Fuji Daigongen

When people indulge themselves in sexual pleasures, the fountain-head of their inner virtue and wisdom is completely dried up, and consequently the moon of Divine Grace sends no spiritual light upon the surface of the water.

The Oracle of the War-God of Kashima (Kashima Daimyojin)

Ever bestowing My Divine Grace upon the people of this Central Land of Reed-Plains [i.e., Japan], and reverentially obeying the commands of the Heavenly Gods, I protect Japan against invasion by hostile foreign nations and keep her safe from the dangers of both Earthly and Heavenly demoniac powers, so that not one single native of this land is left outside My divine aid. When many people minister willingly to the national Gods, I grow in strength and the hostile Powers are subdued, but when only very few reverence the Gods, I am uneasy, for My might is weakened. It is a sad fact that the demoniacal forces frequently outweigh our Divine hosts. This is solely because some minds are blindly captivated by Confucian teachings, and others absorbed in the Buddhist creed recklessly disregard the true Original Way of the Gods [Kami], which is indigenous to the soil of the Rising Sun.

I dislike all such mental attitude towards foreign things. It is quite true that even foreign teachings—e.g., Confucianism and Buddhism— are, to some extent, useful to us, as ornaments, yet they are to the

Original Way of the Kami only what the branches of a tree are to its trunk. Indeed, Shinto is of intrinsic value to us, whilst the other alien teachings are only an auxiliary, and nothing more. Nevertheless, to my distress, people frequently think quite otherwise.

The Oracle of the God of Atsuta (Atsuta Daimyojin) Together with the Oracle of the God of Suminoe

All ye, My people under the sun! By obeying the righteous commands of the gods enjoy the happiness of the Kingdom of the gods which knows neither hatred nor sorrow, for it surpasses all the regions in the Three Worlds, and you are all the offspring of Father-Heaven and Mother-Earth, so that all beings in the world are *de facto* brothers.

Be respectful and loyal to the Mikado as the All-Illuminating August Sun-Goddess once commanded us. Should any foes arise against the Mikado, come to Me, and name them, for I will lose no time in going to destroy them for His Majesty's sake.

The Oracle of the God Tatsuta (Tatsuta Daimyojin) Together with the Saying of Ano-Hokkyo-Zenjo

All ye, My people, high and low, rich and poor! Before you pray to Heaven and Earth as well as to the myriad other deities, it is essential that you should first show filial piety by being obedient to your parents, for in them you can find all the gods of both "Within and Without." It is useless to pray to the gods that are "without," if you do not serve your parents "within" [at home] with filial piety.

The Oracle of the God Katori (Katori Daimyojin)

That the God dislikes what is unclean, is equivalent to saying that a person who is impure in heart displeases God.

He that is honest and upright in heart is not unclean, even though he be not ceremoniously so in body.

To God, inward purity is all important; mere external cleanliness avails not. This is because God is the Essential Uprightness and Honesty, and therefore, it is His Heavenly Ordinance that we should lead an honest and happy life in harmony with the Divine Will.

If a man is pure in heart, rest assured that he will ever feel the Divine Presence with him, and possess the immediate sense of the Divine within him.

The Divine Oracle from the Grand Shrine at Kitsuki

If, through the fascinating influences of the foreign civilization, men fail to observe even the least of the Laws of this Divine Kingdom, they act contrary to the commands of the national gods, and therefore I will send some of My divine messengers to annihilate such infidels.

Neither will I grant the prayers of any who do not come and worship Me before all other gods.

The Oracle of the Sea-God, Watatsumi Daimyojin, Together with the Sayings of Urabe Kanetomo Fujiwara Kanetaka, and the Buddhist Priest Jiki

Not only in Japan doth one and the same Japanese God of Heaven manifest Himself in different forms but also in many other lands.

In India He was born as the Buddha Gautama, the Supremely Enlightened One, who was the Great Teacher, the Revealer of the True Religion, and the Superior Leader of all beings, whether gods or men, in the Three Worlds.

In China, the three Sages, Kung Futsze, Laotze, and Ten-Hui, were neither more or less than our own Kami [Shinto God] himself.

You may ask: Why does one and the same God assume such varied forms? It is simply because, being one and the same God, He desires to preach the selfsame truth, and therefore He takes forms differing only in appearance from each other, so that He may best adapt His teaching to the understanding of every man.

Ponder this providential educative tactfulness and live in quiet accordance with the Law of Righteousness prescribed by our national Gods.

The Saying of Fujiwara Kinkage

The Relation between the sovereign and his subjects in this "Divine Kingdom" is like that of father and son, i.e., parental love on the one side, filial piety on the other.

The Heavenly Sovereign is high above the people here on earth beneath. As Heaven and Earth are co-eternal yet have a separate and distinct existence widely apart, so are the ruler and the ruled in Japan: they remain eternally with the same distinction.

The Saying of the Buddhist Priest Soseki, or Muso-Kokushi

It is unworthy of the Buddhist or Shinto gods to pray to them for worldly trifles. Why do you not beseech them to grant you the supreme Enlightened Knowledge which is the highest blessing? It is like asking a king or a baron for a sheet of paper worth a farthing instead of asking for the gift of a vast domain.

From "Instructions of a Mito Prince to His Retainers"

The Way of a Samurai [7]
By Mitsukuni, Prince of Mito (1628–1700)

All my retainers, high or low, should pay due attention to learning, which is nothing else than knowing the Way in which men should walk. It is needless to say that we must consider learning absolutely necessary above all things; but, to my regret, some regard it as of secondary importance; and are apt to neglect it. It is a still greater regret to hear that some of the so-called learned are far inferior to the unlearned. Such a miserable state of affairs simply results from pride in the little knowledge attained through so-called learning. The motive held by such low-minded persons in getting learning is simply to escape the contempt naturally bestowed upon the unlettered. . . .

There is another class of retainers who spend the best part of their time in reading books or writing verses for amusement only. It is quite useless to spend time in this way. What I mean by "learning" is something far different from that. It is, as I have just said, the Way in which we should walk, or the principle by which we should guide our daily conduct. This Way we must thoroughly understand and carry into practice. Without this, mankind is little better than the birds of the air and the beasts of the field. This is the reason why I advise you to regard it as of greater moment than to secure food, raiment and the other necessities of life. . . .

My retainers, be always ready to discharge your filial duties to your beloved parents, to love your brothers and sisters, and to be kind to your relatives, however remote. To friends be a true companion, not keeping in your heart the least deception, and to servants ever be a benevolent master. Don't forget these things, as they are very important. You know that these duties are minutely taught in the books of the sages; therefore, I hardly think it necessary to say much about them.

All my retainers should highly prize fidelity. No word should be uttered or deed performed in a way unsuitable to the way of an honorable samurai. To prize fidelity is nothing else than not to utter falsehoods, not to be selfish, not to run counter to proper etiquette, not to flatter a superior or to look upon an inferior with contempt, not to break a promise, not to look indifferently upon the distress of others, not to use vulgar language or to slander others. In short, one who truly prizes fidelity, ought to know the real meaning of shame, and should, even at the risk of his neck, refrain from doing those things which he ought not to do. While, at the hour of death, he must not retreat one step, but must prize *giri,* and his heart must be firm as iron and stone; yet he must also be a man of gentleness and mercy. Such we call a samurai of fidelity. . . .

If a samurai, as I have just said, prizes fidelity and his heart is sincere, he has already everything that is absolutely necessary as the qualification of a gentleman; for his lack of tact, of wit in conversation or of refinement in manner can work no harm or injury. I can not help, however, noting here, that so-called samurai of the present day are generally very clever and skilful in social intercourse, having a very refined manner in all their conduct; while, to my great sorrow, they are not a bit true to themselves or to others. . . .

There is another class of good-for-nothing fellows, whom the people ironically call *kekko-jin* [fine fellows]. They are generally effeminate in constitution and character; they are strangers both to wisdom and etiquette; by word and deed they show their dislike for virtue; and they spend their time in drinking and debauchery. Still they are not, in one sense, so detestable as the others, those hypocrites, are, for the reason that they openly behave as worthless men do without any attempt to conceal. But the abominable results of the conduct of both these two classes are evidently the same. Be careful, my retainers, to resemble neither of them.

I am informed to my great disappointment, that in social meetings retainers, both hosts and guests, are generally very rough from the point of view of etiquette, by laughing loud at nonsense, chattering too much with one another, or reproaching others without any satisfactory reason. Some, I am told, even become violently intoxicated, indulge in lewd talk, or are tempted to send for a samisen, that they may sing love songs. This is exactly like a meeting of servants or coolies. The social intercourse of samurai must be conducted in strict accordance with etiquette. We may, of course, cheerfully talk with one another in such a social gathering; but the subjects should be instructive, such as have reference to the ancients. You must surely make yourselves at home at the meeting of intimate friends, but must thoroughly understand the difference between politeness and rudeness.

You should not neglect military preparations. To provide men, horses and proper equipment according to your respective ranks, and also to practice archery, horsemanship, fencing and the use of spears, are quite necessary. By this remark, however, I do not mean to have you devote yourselves to these arts to the neglect of all other things. On the contrary, in my opinion, ordinary attention and practical skill to a moderate degree are serviceable enough, and no more is necessary. As to military tactics, however, I should like to have you pay special attention thereto. . . .

Not to forget military preparation is a prudence we should appreciate in the time of peace. It is hardly necessary to say that caution is necessary even in such a time. Therefore, while I learn with pleasure of your being duly attentive in this line, it seems to me strange enough to hear that some are so impetuous as to take up their weapons without thought or any special cause. A superficial courage of this kind only serves to give a self-evident proof of inward disturbance and of cowardice. The caution necessary to the samurai lies, not in action, but in heart. . . . To meet death with mere physical courage is an easy thing often performed by men of the lowest class. To die, therefore, in this way is not suitable for a samurai. When it becomes necessary to die, the true samurai should meet death in a spirit even more calm and composed than ordinary. That is the distinction between a samurai and a coolie. . . .

A very plain supper, as you have previously been informed, will do at your social gatherings. This is not too vulgar. Meetings of this kind are held to make friendship warmer and to exchange opinions. Entertainment does not necessarily mean nice liquor or delicious food, but it means rather a warm reception and kind treatment. . . .

As for military equipments, including harnesses, spears, swords and other things, be careful enough to keep them for practical use, not for ornament: therefore, elaborate decoration is by no means necessary. As to uniforms, the same view should be taken: no expensive stuffs should be recommended. But the styles of cut, according to your respective ranks, should be observed, as is mentioned in another document.

Some are inclined to pay too much attention to your house. It is quite enough if it be comfortable, even though not grand. If it is built so as to give protection from rain and wind, that is good enough to live in. . . . With reference, indeed, to clothes, food and dwelling, I should say that you ought to provide only the necessities of everyday use, but should include also military equipments in that category. As to other things, unless they are absolutely necessary, I see no reason why you should keep them in your houses. . . .

From ancient times the people have been divided into four classes: *Shi, No, Ko* and *Sho*. Each class has its own business. Those belonging to the *No* class are devoting themselves to agriculture; those of the *Ko* class are promoting industry; while those of the *Sho* class are engaged in trade. All of these three classes have something to contribute towards benefiting human society.

What, then, is the use of the *Shi,* or samurai, class? Its only business is to preserve, or maintain, *giri*. The people of the other classes deal with visible things, while the samurai deal with invisible, colorless and unsubstantial things. As these two divisions are so far different from each other, some may think that the members of the *Shi* class entirely unnecessary. But if there were no samurai, right would disappear from human society, the sense of shame would be lost, and wrong and injustice would prevail. In that case, a faithful subject, a dutiful son, or a trustworthy friend, would seldom be found, and such shameful acts as cheating or stealing would be a daily occurrence. In short, the whole country would be thrown into great confusion, unless it be checked beforehand by the samurai. This is the chief reason why they are placed above other people, and also why the latter are pleased to pay them great respect, in spite of their having apparently no substantial work as daily business.

Let us, then, consider for a while how the samurai of the present day are behaving. Some, they say, are given up to avarice, and sometimes are prone to take things unreasonably from innocent merchants by using august airs and threats. Some, it is said, like rank. Some, pretending to be fond of furniture, try to trade in it with the view of making a profit, just like commission merchants. Such as these are all too ignoble to be discussed here at length. But, generally speaking, they think first of their own will and pay no attention to that of others. Such selfish men are generally very clever in understanding their own interests, but very stupid in pursuing a right course. To go straight on regardless of one's own interest, whatever may be the final result, is the path in which the samurai should walk. Those who are wise in *giri* are foolish in avarice, and those who are foolish in avarice are wise in *giri*. . . .

When Kogikyu was the highest official in the time of the Ro dynasty, he happened to find vegetables of his own garden quite nice in taste and thereupon rooted them all up at once. Again, when he found the linen woven by his own maid-servant as good as that sold by merchants, he dismissed her and destroyed the loom. His reason was this: if the materials for food and clothing were raised on the premises of a gentleman of the professional class, how could those of the business class live? By this remark he meant, that the salaried samurai should not compete with the common people in pursuit of gain. Now, my retainers, you are paid to your satisfaction in accordance with your position, and, moreover, both farmers and business men are strictly enjoined to respect and obey you. The only thing left, therefore, to you is to be honest and sincere and to be well-deserving of the name of an example to the other classes. Don't forget the real motive with which Kogikyu was accustomed to act in every matter.

From the Works of Muro Kiuso

To Learn the Way [8]
By Muro Kiuso (1658-1734)

Man, endowed with feeling, and described as the soul of the universe, becomes entangled by his own craftiness, and so long as he does not learn the Way, falls short of this perfection. This is why it is necessary for him to learn the Way. To learn the Way must not be taken to be anything of a special kind, such as the spiritual vision of the Buddhists or the like. The Way is the original right principle of things. It is something which vulgar men and women know and practise as well as others. But as they do not truly know it, they do not thoroughly practise it. They learn it, but do not fully comprehend it; they practise it, but not with conspicuous success. They may go on striving to the end of their days, but they will never enter into its full meaning. Now to learn the Way is nothing more than to acquire a true knowledge of this principle, and to practise it effectively until you have the restful feeling of a fish in water, and take the same pleasure in it that a bird does in the groves. It should be made one's very life at all times, never being departed from for a moment. If, so long as we live, we follow the Way, when we die these bodies of ours and the Way come to an end together, and a long peace ensues. Living for a day, let us fulfil the Way for that day and die; living for a month, let us fulfil the Way for that month and die; living for a year, let us fulfil the Way for that year and die. If we do so, there will be left not an atom of regret, even if we die in the evening after having learnt the Way in the morning. . . .

The *Saden* [an ancient Chinese book] says, "God is uniformly just." It is his very nature to be so. Now while all men know that he is just, they do not know that he is intelligent. Yet there is nothing of so keen an intelligence as God. How is this? Man hears with his ears, and beyond their reach he hears nothing though he were as quick of hearing as Shiko; he sees with his eyes, and beyond their range he can see nothing, were he as sharp-sighted as Riro; with his heart he reflects, and, however swift his intuitions may be, still this must involve delay. God borrows not the help of ears or eyes; nor does he waste time in reflection. With him sensation is immediate, and is followed by immediate responsive action. This, be it observed, is his nature, and flows not from two or three, but from a single reality.

But although there is in heaven and earth a something infinitely quick of hearing and infinitely sharp of sight, independent of conditions of time or space, present as if actually on the spot, passing to and fro without any interval, embodying itself in all things which are, and filling the universe, it has neither form nor voice, and is therefore not cognisable by our senses. It is, however, sensible to the Real and the True. As it feels, so it responds. If there is no truth or reality, there can be no response. If it did not feel, it would not respond. The response is therefore a proof of its existence. That which responds not, of course does not exist. What a wonderful property for heaven and earth to possess! . . .

Think not that God is something distant, but seek for him in your own hearts; for the heart is the abode of God.

To forsake all evil and follow good is the beginning of the practice of our philosophy.

The Way of the Sages is not sundered from matters of everyday life.

That which in Heaven begets all things is in man that which makes him love his neighbour. So doubt not that Heaven loves goodness of heart and hates its opposite.

Has not bravery itself its root in goodness of heart, and does it not proceed from sympathy? It is only when it arises from goodness that bravery is genuine.

Once when I was in Kaga I heard a man say, "All faults whether great or small may be excused in the eyes of the world upon repentance and amendment, and leave behind no stain of deep-seated baseness." But there are two faults which are inexcusable, even when repented of—theft, and the abandonment by a samurai of a post which he is bound to defend with his life.

Avarice and cowardice are the same. If a man is stingy of his money, he will also grudge his life.

To the samurai first of all comes righteousness, next life, then silver and gold.

3. Third Period
(1700–1867)

Pure Shinto Revival

What Mabuchi Said [1] (1697–1769)

Wherein lies the value of a rule of conduct? In its conducing to the good order of the state. While the Chinese for ages past have had a succession of different dynasties to rule over them, Japan has been faithful to one uninterrupted line of sovereigns. Every Chinese dynasty was founded upon rebellion and parricide. Sometimes a powerful ruler was able to transmit his authority to his son and grandson, but they in their turn were inevitably deposed and murdered, and the country was in a perpetual state of civil war. A philosophy which produced such effects must be founded on a false system.

When Confucianism was first introduced into Japan, the simple-minded natives, deceived by its plausible appearance, accepted it with eagerness, and allowed it to spread its influence everywhere. The consequence was the civil war which broke out immediately after the death of Tenchi Tenno in 671 between that emperor's brother and son, which only came to an end in 672 by the suicide of the latter. In the eighth century the Chinese costume and etiquette were adopted by the Court. This foreign pomp and splendour covered the rapid depravation of men's hearts, and created a wide gulf between the Mikado and his people. So long as the sovereign maintains a simple style of living, the people are contented with their own hard lot. Their wants are few and they are easily ruled. But if the sovereign has a magnificent palace, gorgeous clothing, and crowds of finely dressed women to wait on him, the sight of these things must cause in others a desire to possess themselves of the same luxuries; or if they are not strong enough to take them by force, it excites their envy. If the Mikado lived in a house roofed with shingles, and whose walls were of mud, wore hempen clothes, carried his sword in a scabbard wound round with the tendrils of some creeping plant, and went to the chase carrying his bow and arrows, as was the ancient custom, the present state of things would never have come about. But since the introduction of Chinese manners, the sovereign, while occupying a highly dignified place, has been degraded to the intellectual level of a woman. The power fell into the hands of servants, and although they never actually assumed the title, they were sovereigns in fact, while the Mikado became an utter nullity. . . .

In ancient times when men's dispositions were straightforward, a complicated system of morals was unnecessary. It would naturally happen that bad acts might occasionally be committed, but the straightforwardness of men's dispositions would prevent the evil from being concealed and growing in extent. So that in those days it was unnecessary to have a doctrine of right and wrong. But the Chinese, being bad at heart, in spite of the teaching which they got, were only good on the outside, and their bad acts became of such magnitude that society was thrown into disorder. The Japanese being straightforward could do without teaching.

What Motoöri Norinaga Said [2] (1730–1801)

Japan is the country which gave birth to the goddess of the Sun, Amaterasu-oho-mi-kami, which fact proves its superiority over all other countries which also enjoy her favours. The goddess, having endowed her grandson Ninigi no mikoto with the three sacred treasures, proclaimed him sovereign of Japan for ever and ever. His descendants shall continue to rule it as long as the heavens and earth endure. Being invested with this complete authority, all the gods under heaven and all mankind submitted to him, with the exception of a few wretches who were quickly subdued.

To the end of time each Mikado is the goddess' son. His mind is in perfect harmony of thought and feeling with hers. He does not seek out new inventions, but rules in accordance with precedents which date from the age of the gods, and if he is ever in doubt, he has resort to divination, which reveals to him the mind of the great goddess. In this way the age of the gods and the present age are not two ages, but one, for not only the Mikado but his Ministers and people also act up to the tradition of the divine age. Hence, in ancient times the idea of *michi* or way [ethics] was never broached. The word was applied only to ordinary thoroughfares, and its application to systems of philosophy, government, morals, religion and so forth, is a foreign notion.

As foreign countries (China and India, particularly the former) are not the special domain of the sun-goddess, they have no permanent rulers, and evil spirits, having found a field of action, have corrupted mankind. In those countries any bad man who could manage to seize on the power became a sovereign. Those who had the upper hand were constantly scheming to maintain their positions, while their inferiors were as constantly on the watch for opportunities to oust them. The most powerful and cunning of these rulers succeeded in taming their subjects, and having secured their position, became an example for others to imitate. In China the name of *Seijin* [translated "Holy Men" by Meadows] has been given to these men. But it is an error to look upon these so-called Holy Men as in themselves supernatural and good beings, as superior to the rest of the world as are the gods. The principles which they established are called *michi* [ethics], and may be reduced to two simple rules, namely to take other people's territory, and to keep fast hold of it.

The Chinese "Holy Men" also invented the "Book of Changes" (*yeki*, or *I-king*), by which they pretended to discover the workings of the universe, a vain attempt, since it is impossible for man with his limited intelligence to find out the principles which govern the acts of the gods. In imitation of them the Chinese nation has since given itself up to philosophizing, to which are to be attributed its constant internal dissensions. When things go right of themselves it is best to leave them alone. In ancient times, although there was no prosy system of doctrine in Japan, there were no popular disturbances, and the empire was peacefully ruled. It is because the Japanese were truly moral in their practice that they required no theory of morals, and the fuss made by the Chinese about theoretical morals is owing to their laxity in practice. It is not wonderful that students of Chinese literature should despise their own country for being without a system of morals, but that Japanese who were acquainted with their own ancient literature should have pretended that Japan also had such a system, simply out of a feeling of envy, is ridiculous.

When Chinese literature was imported into Japan, the people adopted many Chinese ideas, laws, customs and practices, which they so mixed up with their own that it became necessary to adopt a special name for the ancient native customs, which were in consequence called *Kami no michi* or *Shinto,* the word *michi* being applied in the same sense as the Chinese *to* (tao), and *kami* because of their divine origin. These native customs only survived in the ceremonies with which the native gods are worshipped.

Every event in the universe is the act of the gods. They direct the changes of the seasons, the wind and the rain, the good and bad fortune of states and individual men. Some of the gods are good, others bad, and their acts partake of their own natures. Buddhists attribute events to "retribution" (*ingua*) while the Chinese ascribe them to the "decree of heaven" (*temmei,* or *tien-ming*). This latter is a phrase invented by the so-called "Holy Men" to justify murdering sovereigns and seizing their dominions. As neither heaven nor earth have minds, they cannot issue decrees. If heaven really could issue decrees it would certainly protect the good rulers and take care to prevent bad men from seizing the power, and in general, while the good would prosper, the bad would suffer misfortune. But in reality we find many instances of the reverse.

Whenever anything goes wrong in the world it is to be attributed to the action of the evil gods called *Magatsubi no kami* [gods of crookedness] whose power is so great that the sun-goddess and the creator-god are sometimes unable to restrain them; much less are human beings able to resist their influence. The prosperity of the wicked and the misfortunes of the good, which seem opposed to ordinary justice, are their doing. The Chinese, not possessing the traditions of the divine age, were ignorant of this truth, and were driven to invent the theory of "Heaven's decrees."

The eternal endurance of the dynasty of the Mikados is a complete proof that the "way" called *Kami no michi* or *Shinto* infinitely surpasses the systems of all other countries.

The "Holy Men" of China were merely successful rebels. The Mikado is the sovereign appointed by the pair of deities, Izanagi and Izanami, who created this country. The sun-goddess never said, "Disobey the Mikado if he be bad," and therefore, whether he be good or bad, no one attempts to deprive him of his authority. He is the immovable ruler who must endure to the end of time, as long as the sun and moon continue to shine. In ancient language the Mikado was called a god, and that is his real character. Duty therefore consists in obeying him implicitly, without questioning his acts. During the middle ages such men as Hojo Yoshitoki, Hojo Yasutoki, Ashikaga Takauji and others violated this duty [*michi*], and took up arms against him. Their disobedience to the Mikado is attributable to the influence of Chinese learning.

This "way" was established by Izanagi and Izanami, and delivered by them to the sun-goddess, who handed it down, and this is why it is called the "way of the gods." The nature of this "way" is to be learnt by studying the *Kojiki* and ancient writings, but mankind have been turned aside from it by the Spirits of Crookedness to Buddhism and Chinese philosophy.

The various doctrines taught under the name of *Shinto* are without authority.

Human beings having been produced by the spirit of the two Creative Deities, are naturally endowed with the knowledge of what they ought to do and what they ought to refrain from. It is unnecessary for them to trouble their heads with systems of morals. If a system of morals were necessary, men would be inferior to animals, all of whom are endowed with the knowledge of what they ought to do, only in an inferior degree to men. If what the Chinese call Benevolence (*Jin*), Righteousness (*Gi*), Propriety (*Rei*), Retiringness (*Jo*), Filial Piety (*Ko*), Brotherly Love (*Tei*), Fidelity (*Chiu*) and Truth (*Shin*) really constituted the duty of man, they would be so recognized and practised without any teaching, but as they were invented by the so-called "Holy Men" as instruments for ruling a viciously inclined population, it became necessary to insist on the more than actual duty of man. Consequently, although plenty of men profess these doctrines, the number of those who practise them is very small. Violations of this teaching were attributed to human lusts. As human lusts are a part of man's nature, they must be a part of the harmony of the universe, and cannot be wrong according to the Chinese theory. It was the vicious nature of the Chinese that necessitated such strict rules, as for instance that persons descended from a common ancestor, no matter how distantly related, should not intermarry. These rules, not being founded on the harmony of the universe, were not in accordance with human feelings, and were therefore seldom obeyed. . . .

It has been asked whether the *kami no michi* is not the same as the Taoism of Laotzu. Laotzu hated the vain conceits of the Chinese scholars, and honoured naturalness, from which a resemblance may be argued; but as he was born in a dirty country not under the special protection of the sun-goddess, he had only heard the theories of the succession of so-called Holy Men, and what he believed to be natural-ness was simply what they called natural. He did not know that the gods are the authors of every human action, and this ignorance con-stituted a cause of radical difference. . . .

The facts that the sacred mirror bestowed by Amaterasu upon Ninigi no Mikoto is still preserved at the Naiku temple in Ise; that the sword "Grass-cutter" is to this day at the temple of Atsuta in Owari; that remains which date from the divine age are even now to be found in various provinces; that the sepulchres of the Mikados from Jimmu downwards exist in parts of the Kinai; that numerous relics of the divine age remain in the possession of the Court, and that the Nakatomi, Imbe and Ohotomo families have transmitted the functions which they exercised in the age of the gods in unbroken succession to their descendants of later times, vindicate beyond the possibility of a doubt the truth of the old traditions. . . .

The goddess and the sun are one and the same. For although she will continue to shine as long as heaven and earth endure, she was born in Japan, and her descendants to this day rule over the empire. The difficulty of reconciling the statements that the world was plunged into darkness when she retired into the cavern, and that darkness did not exist before she was born is one that would strike even a child's intelligence. The critic need not make so much fuss about this point, as if it were entirely a new discovery of his own. The very inconsistency is the proof of the authenticity of the record, for who would have gone out of his way to invent a story apparently so ridiculous and incredible. The acts of the gods are not to be explained by ordinary principles. Man's intelligence is limited, and there are many things which transcend it. . . .

Even if the prince be bad, to venerate respect and obey him in all things, although it may seem like a woman's duty, is the right way of action, which does not allow of the obligations of a subject towards his prince ever being violated.

All the moral ideas which man requires are implanted in his bosom by the gods, and are the same nature as the instincts which impel him to eat when he is hungry and to drink when he is thirsty. But the morals inculcated by the Chinese philosophers are inventions, and contain something more in addition to natural morality. . . .

From the central truth that the Mikado is the direct descendant of the gods, the tenet that Japan ranks far above all other countries is a natural consequence. No other nation is entitled to equality with her, and all are bound to do homage to the Japanese Sovereign and pay tribute to him.

The True Way [3]

By Motoöri Norinaga (1730–1801)

In China all good and bad fortune of men, all order and disorder in the State—everything, in short, which happens in this world—is ascribed to the action of *Ten* [Heaven]. Using such terms as the Way of *Ten*, the Command of *Ten*, and the Principle of *Ten*, they regard it as a thing to be honoured and feared above all. China, however, is a country where the true way generally has not been handed down. There they do not know that all things are the doing of the gods, and therefore resort rashly to such inventions. Now Heaven is nothing more than the region where the gods of Heaven dwell. It is a thing destitute of sense, and it is unreasonable to talk of its "command" and the like. To fear and honour *Ten*, and not fear and honour the gods, is like yielding an idle honour and awe to the Imperial Palace, and showing no reverence or honour to its sovereign. Foreign countries, however, not having attained to the knowledge that everything is the doing of the gods, may be pardoned for believing this Doctrine of the

Way of *Ten* or the Principle of *Ten*. But what is to be thought of those who, in this imperial country, where a knowledge of the true way has been handed down, do not take the trouble to examine it, but, simply accepting the erroneous doctrines of foreign lands, imagine that that which they call *Ten* is a thing of peerless excellence, and in all matters can talk of nothing but its principle? Take again their pedantic and wearisome *Taikhi* [the Great Limit], *Mu Ki* [the Limitless], *Yin* and *Yang* [Positive and Negative Principles of Nature], *Ch'ien* and *K'un* [Celestial and Terrestrial Principles], *Pakwa* [Eight Diagrams of the Book of Changes], and *Wu-hing* [Five Elements], which are pure inventions of the Chinese, and for which there is in reality no sound reason. What consummate folly it is for those who would interpret our sacred books to rely implicitly on principles of this kind. In recent times even those who try to divest themselves of Chinese prejudices in their interpretations fail to understand the falseness of their doctrines of the Principle of Ten, and of the Positive and Negative Powers of Nature, and do not succeed in bursting the barrier because they do not put thoroughly away from them their Chinese notions, nor resolutely rouse themselves from their deluding dreams. Moreover, the refusal of some to identify Ama-terasu no Ohomi Kami [the Sun Goddess] as the Sun of Heaven is owing to their being steeped in Chinese narrow-minded reasonings, and so become blind to the wondrous and profound principle of the true way.

What Hirata Atsutane Said [4] (1776–1843)

The foundations upon which the Ancient Learning is based are the writings in which the Imperial Court has recorded the facts of antiquity. Most people are wont to suppose that the only way to attain to a knowledge of right conduct is to read books full of precepts, but they labour under a mistake. Precept is far inferior to example, for it only arises in the absence of example; while it is unnecessary when example exists. As Laotsu says, "When the Great Way decayed, Humanity and Righteousness arose." In order to spur on a warrior to valiant deeds, rather than show him a book which says, "When you go to battle, strive to be first, do not lag behind others," show him a book in which are written the facts about ancient heroes who led the way, fought bravely and achieved renown. The facts will sink deeply into his heart, and he will say to himself, "When the occasion arises, I will distinguish myself like such an one of antiquity," but the mere exhortation will scarcely stir his emotions. . . .

It is most lamentable that so much ignorance should prevail as to the evidences of the two fundamental doctrines, that Japan is the country of the Gods and her inhabitants the descendants of the Gods. Between the Japanese people and the Chinese, Hindoos, Russians, Dutch, Siamese, Cambodians and other nations of the world there is a difference of kind, rather than of degree. It was not out of vain-glory that the inhabitants of this country called it the land of the gods (*Shinkoku, kami no kuni*). The gods who created all countries belonged without exception to the Divine Age, and were all born in Japan, so that Japan is their native country, and all the world acknowledges the appropriateness of the title. The Coreans were the first to become acquainted with this truth, and from them it was gradually diffused through the globe, and accepted by every one. . . .

Amaterasu oho-mi-kami, having been appointed Queen of the sun by Izanagi, shares the government of the world with the two creators. She in turn desired to make a son of her own ruler over the terrestrial world. This was Oshi-ho-mimi no mikoto, a god who was produced from the goddess' necklace; he was married to Tamayori-hime no mikoto, a grand-daughter of the two creators. The offspring of this pair was Ninigi no mikoto, who was therefore the grandson of Amaterasu, and the title Sumemi-ma no mikoto [Sublime Grandchild] applied to him expresses this relationship. Ninigi no mikoto replaced his father as sovereign-designate of the world. . . .

As it was Japan which lay directly opposite to the sun when it had sprouted upwards and separated from the earth, it is quite clear that Japan lies on the summit of the globe. It is equally evident that all other countries were formed at a much later period by the spontaneous consolidation of the foam of the sea and the collection of mud in various localities, when Izanagi and Izanami brought forth the eight islands of Japan, and separated the land from the water. Foreign countries were of course produced by the power of the creator gods, but they were not begotten by Izanagi and Izanami, nor did they give birth to the goddess of the sun, which is the cause of their inferiority.

The traditions about the origin of the world which are preserved in foreign countries are naturally incorrect, just as the accounts of an event which has happened at the capital become distorted when they travel to a province, and it finally comes to be believed that the province was the actual scene of the event. The fact is patent that the Mikado is the true Son of Heaven, who is entitled to reign over the four seas and the ten thousand countries.

People who have been misled by their foreign studies are wont to say that Japan is a little country, as if extent of territory were any criterion of the importance or rank of a state; and they also point to her tardy civilisation. But every one knows that great minds develop late; for example Ota Nobunaga, who was commonly called *Baka dono* [Lord Idiot], until he was past the age of twenty, and the same was the case with the famous Oishi Kuranoske, whose fame will endure to the end of time. Animals and birds know how to pick up and eat grain and insects as soon as they are born, and some have offspring when they are only two or three months old. If man were to be judged by such a standard, what a helpless, good-for-nothing creature he would be. But his slow development is a proof of his superiority, and the same holds good with regard to the development of nations. . . .

The descendants of the gods who accompanied Ninigi no mikoto, as well as the offspring of the successive Mikados, who entered the ranks of the subjects of the Mikados with the surnames of Taira, Minamoto and so forth, have gradually increased and multiplied. Although numbers of Japanese cannot state with any certainty from what gods they are descended, all of them have tribal names [*kabane*] which were originally bestowed by the Mikados, and those who make it their province to study genealogies can tell from a man's ordinary surname who his remotest ancestor must have been.

From the fact of the divine descent of the Japanese people proceeds their immeasurable superiority to the natives of other countries in courage and intelligence. . . .

When the two gods lowered the spear and stirred round the chaotic mass out of which the earth was to be formed, the muck which was unfit to enter into the composition of the earth was removed by the action of the spear point, and scattered lump-wise in all directions throughout space, taking up positions more or less remote. The five planets, the twenty-eight constellations and the host of common stars being thus formed, revolve round the sun together with the earth. . . .

It is customary to suppose that the stars have no practical purpose, but it is evident that they are intended to guide the course of those barbarian mariners, who, if they knew their duty, would bring ships laden with tribute to the Emperor of Japan. . . .

The islands of Japan were begotten in exactly the same manner as human beings and everything else that has life, whether animal or vegetable, and being quite small at their birth, gradually increased in size by the accretion of matter. The result of the birth of Japan was that the sea and land were gradually parted, and the way thus prepared for the formation of foreign countries by the spontaneous condensation of the foam of the sea. . . .

The celebration of rites in honour of the gods was considered in ancient times to be the chief function of the Mikados. When Ninigi no mikoto descended from heaven his divine progenitors taught him how he was to rule the country, and their teaching consisted in this: Everything in the world depends on the spirit of the gods of heaven and earth, and therefore the worship of the gods is a matter of primary importance. The gods who do harm are to be appeased, so that they may not punish those who have offended them, and all the gods are to be worshipped, so that they may be induced to increase their favours. To compel obedience from human beings, and to love them was all the sovereign had to do, and there was no necessity for teaching them vain doctrines such as are preached in other countries. Hence the art of Government is called *Matsurigoto,* which literally means "worshipping." Accordingly the early sovereigns worshipped the gods in person, and prayed that their people might enjoy a sufficiency of food, clothing and shelter from the elements, and twice a year, in the 6th and 12th months, they celebrated the festival of the "General Purification," by which the whole nation was purged of calamities, offences and pollutions.

Although in later ages many foreign customs were adopted we find that the religious rites of Shinto always occupied the first place in the books wherein are recorded the rules and ceremonies of the court. . . .

As it is the duty of subjects to imitate the practice of the incarnate god [*arahito-gami*] who is their sovereign, the necessity of worship-

ping his ancestors and the gods from whom they spring, is to be enjoined upon every man.

As the number of the gods who possess different functions is so
great, it will be convenient to worship by name only the most important and to include the rest in a general petition. Those whose
daily affairs are so multitudinous that they have not time to go
through the whole of the following morning prayers, may content
themselves with adoring the residence of the Emperor, the domestic
kami-dana, the spirits of their ancestors, their local patron god and
the deity of their particular calling in life.

In praying to the gods the blessings which each has it in his power
to bestow are to be mentioned in a few words, and they are not to be
annoyed with greedy petitions, for the Mikado in his palace offers
up petitions daily on behalf of his people, which are far more effectual
than those of his subjects.

The Superiority of the Ancients [5]
By Hirata Atsutane

In ancient times great care was taken in worshipping, and this resulted in peace on earth. There were no famines or pestilences and all
people lived peacefully. This is the reason that later it was said that
worship and government were one. It appears that in ancient times
China worshipped the gods. In etiquette the principal place was given
to worship of the gods and the gratitude of the people of the earth
for the beneficence of the first ancestors. But as the connection with
heaven was not the same in China as in Japan it can be seen that
naturally the fear of the gods was weak and there was no faith in
the gods.

The emperors, though they were themselves gods for generations,
specially reverenced in ancient times, without the slightest failure,
the spirits of their ancestors. But after Confucianism and Buddhism
crossed over into Japan, it is a sad fact that the worship of the gods
was neglected. Notwithstanding how much foreign religion may be
said to have spread, there is no reason why the worship of the souls
of ancestral parents should be carelessly carried out and filial piety
to living parents discontinued.

In the regulation made for the household first pay attention to the ancestors and let other matters be attended to afterwards. Let the heart without fail at sunset and sunrise reverence the ancestors. Never for an instant turn your backs to the god shelves and burying grounds.

The love of the gods of heaven and earth is great beyond words, but this love spreads over heaven and earth and is wide reaching, but the gods who are closely attached to my house and person are truly, as Motoöri says, the souls of my ancestors and we ought to be specially careful not to treat them with neglect.

The man who understands and treats the gods and his parents with care is one who is strong in the right, and he will of course behave loyally in his heart toward his lord and will be true to his friends and loving and charitable toward his wife and children. The foundation of the "Way" therefore is where man is mindful of his ancestors.

To receive kindness from a person without the intention of returning it and to forget this kindness is to be lower than the birds and beasts, and such a one is below all consideration. Formerly when a person showed ungratefulness to me I showed my anger, now when I am charitable to a person, I think no more about it; when I am in receipt of kindness I think of how I am going to return it. And when I lend anyone money I do not lend it expecting to get it returned. It is better from the first to lend it as a gift.

Men are born by nature to know that their parents are above them through the soul of the great god Mimusubi, hence they naturally grow up and copy the deeds of their parents. And looking upon mankind you can easily discern a child born of a family where the parents worshipped Buddhist idols and are silly about the Buddhist scriptures. This child will be steeped in Buddhism and will as a natural thing remember the stinking Buddhist verses. The parent is the instructor when his actions are imitated by the child. If the parent's actions are wrong and he scolds the child for doing wrong, this is unjust.

It is not a good custom of the present age that no matter whether a person be high or humble he is taught from childhood to read Chinese books. Chinese learning is one form set up to teach people to do good. But it reasons things too minutely and shows right and wrong too closely, and makes a man think too highly of his knowledge and think himself cleverer than others, and instead of improving a man's heart it makes it bad. One who has not the determined heart of a Japanese gentleman, or in the case of children those who study Chinese learning, never become ripe scholars.

That which naturally ought to be understood is understood by birth. I do not know about foreign countries, but it is surely so in Great Japan. Therefore the nature which comes by birth is the one that ought to be followed and is the path of man. I am therefore against people reading too many books. Even if people are caused to read books there are seldom any who read enough. They read just enough to do them harm, and become ridiculous persons.

Looking at the people of this age relative to the worshipping of their ancestors, we find that we do not fully realize what is the foundation of the way. Confucianists and such like say there is no such thing as the soul, and that after death everything is dispersed and lost like wind and fire and cannot be known. Such sayings are spread and people's minds become steeped in such false sayings. As they are not sure whether the soul exists they make offerings before the souls in a careless way. In preparing food for themselves they will add dried bonito and so forth and make a most tasty relish, and even then if the taste is not right they will scold the household and the cook. But when they make offerings to the soul shrines of their ancestors the taste does not matter. This is a great mistake arising from not being sure that the soul of man exists, because they have been misled by the false doctrines spread by the Confucianists and the Buddhists. After death a person becomes a soul and a god and this condition is beyond the boundary between the seen and the unseen world, and this is the reason that things are not eaten up as by the living. The reason the quantity of food remains unchanged is that just a little of the flavor has been sucked up. If there is anyone who doubts this let him compare the flavor of the offerings after they have been taken down from the shelf with some food which has simply been put in one side, and he will be able to taste a slight difference.

In the Omine and Mitsumine mountains there are many wolves which are called the messengers of the gods of these mountains, and people from other parts of the country come and, applying through the guards of these mountains, choose and borrow one of these wolves as a defense against fire. That is to say they only arrange to borrow it and really do not take a wolf to their place. And from the day of borrowing they offer daily food to the spirit of the wolf. But if through neglect several days pass without food being offered then the wolf chosen becomes thin, emaciated, and weak. There is a case where a man I know borrowed a wolf and neglected to offer food for four or five days, and misfortune came to him from that source and he was fearfully surprised.

Therefore in offering food to the spirits and looking to see whether it decreases or not, we find it just as it was and we ask ourselves the reason of this. Is not the reply that we cannot explain the things of the unseen world? I cannot make light of these awful things, and though it may not be necessary to quote stories like that of the wolves, there is not any doubt that souls exist. And as they are without doubt in the shrine shelves of every house it is best to treat them carefully and not carelessly. The origin of thus treating lightly the worship of ancestors by the people of this day is the artificial knowledge of those rotten Confucianists and the allurements of the sellers of quack medicines of Buddha, Bosatsu, Amida, and so forth.

What Hatori Nakatsune Said [6] (1791)

The accounts given in other countries, whether by Buddhism or Chinese philosophy, of the form of the heavens and earth and the manner by which they came into existence, are all of them inventions of men, who exercised all their ingenuity over the problem, and inferred that such and such things must actually be the case. . . .

The principles which animate the universe are beyond the power of analysis, nor can they be fathomed by the human intelligence, and all statements founded upon pretended explanations of them are to be rejected. All that man can think out and know is limited by the powers of sight, feeling and calculation, and what goes beyond these powers cannot be known by any amount of thinking.

How is it then possible for men who were born hundreds and thousands of myriads of years after the origin of the universe, to know how it originated and the successive steps by which it assumed its present form? Our country, owing to the facts that it was begotten by the two gods Izanagi and Izanami, was the birth place of Amaterasu oho-mi-kami, and is ruled by her Sublime Descendants for ever and ever, as long as the universe shall endure, is infinitely superior to other countries, whose chief and head it is; its people are honest and upright of heart and are not given to useless theorizing and falsehoods like other countries, and thus it possesses correct and true information with regard to the origin of the universe. This information has descended to us unaltered from the age of the gods, and unmixed, even in the slightest degree with unsupported notions of individuals. This indeed is the genuine and true tradition. The Chinese accounts sound as if based on profound principles, and one fancies that they must be right, while the Japanese accounts sound shallow and utterly unfounded in reason. But the former are lies, while the latter are the truth, so that as time goes on, and thought attains greater accuracy, the erroneous nature of these falsehoods becomes ever more apparent, while the true tradition remains intact.

West Meets East [7]

Perry and the Lord Rector

(Excerpts from a Conversation Between Commodore Perry and an Official of the Shogunate During Perry's Visit to Japan in 1854.)

Perry: You must pardon me for bringing up this matter so abruptly, but a member of the crew of one of my ships, a man of low rank, has just died. If his death had occurred in any other country, he would have been buried without delay, but I understand that the laws of your country are particularly severe, and I wish, therefore, first to ask where he may be buried. After examining the shore, I observe that the island of Natsushima, which lies off Kanagawa, has upon it no houses or dwellings, and I assume, therefore, that there will be no objection to his burial there. If it should not cause you any inconvenience, I wish to consider his burial there to be a settled matter. (At this moment, one of the barges, bearing a white flag, returned to Kanagawa from Uraga. It was beached on Natsushima, and four or five persons landed and walked about as though searching for a burial plot.)

The Lord Rector: It is indeed sad that one coming from so far a place should die. Even the life of one of humble rank is not a light matter. In Japan, we bury persons in temples and not in places where there are no human habitations. True, he was not one of our countrymen, but how disconsolate would be burial in an uninhabited place! We will select a place where he may be buried. Natsushima is an uninhabited island belonging to certain lords and nothing can be done on it without the permission of the authorities. He should be buried at the foot of the Uraga Lighthouse.

Perry: Whether the remains can be sent to Uraga will depend upon the state of the weather, and will entail much trouble. I intend to remain here until the present negotiations are concluded, even if that should require one or two years. During this period, others will die; and it would be extremely inconvenient to remove the remains each time to Uraga. Dead men can do no wrong.

The Lord Rector: As foreign vessels are not permitted to enter the bay beyond Uraga, your countrymen will be unable in later years to worship at his grave; but if this is not a matter of importance to you, he may be buried in a temple near by; and the grave may be removed later, if circumstances require this. (This matter was raised unexpectedly, and we, as well as the foreigners, wished to settle it without delay. For this reason, a reply was made at once.)

Perry: I thank you very much. If you will agree to this arrangement, it would be most convenient, on the understanding that the graves may be removed later, if necessary. The fact that our countrymen will be unable later to worship before these graves is not of importance, and I hope that you will accede to my request. (Perry appeared to be extraordinarily grateful, to the extent even of shedding tears.)

We have in our country always regarded human life as of the first importance in the conduct of our government, and, therefore, whenever any of our countrymen—of course—or persons belonging to another country or even to a country with which we do not ordinarily have intercourse, reach our shores after having been shipwrecked, we exert every effort to rescue them, and we treat them with kindness. I perceive no sign, however, that human life is counted in your country to be of great importance; for whenever a vessel of any foreign country approaches your shores, you repel it with guns; and when shipwrecked persons reach the shore, you treat them like slaves and keep them in harsh imprisonment. Whenever Japanese are shipwrecked off our shores, my countrymen rescue them and send them back to their own country; but when such persons return to their own country, you will not receive them. You thus seem to have no regard even for your own countrymen and to be exceedingly inhumane. Our country has become one of the great powers, despite various circumstances; our California faces Japan, the two being divided, not by another country, but by the Pacific Ocean. In a short time, the ships frequenting Japanese waters will greatly multiply in number, and if the government of your country continues to adhere to its harsh practices and a large number of lives are sacrificed, we would not overlook it. If your country should persist in its present practices and fail to mend them, and if ships are not helped, it will surely be looked upon with hostility. If your country becomes an enemy, we will exhaust our resources if necessary to wage war. We are fully prepared to engage in a struggle for victory. Our country has just had a war with a neighboring country, Mexico, and we even attacked and captured its capital. Circumstances may lead your country also into a similar plight. It would be well for you to reconsider.

The Lord Rector: If forced by circumstances, we also will go to war; but many of your statements are not true, due, I assume to the fact that many of your ideas have been created by mistaken reports. It is only natural, perhaps, that as we have no intercourse with other countries you should have mistaken ideas about our government. Our government is not the inhumane thing you describe. First, we excel any other country in the importance we attach to human life. For this reason, we have enjoyed peace for more than 300 years. If we were so inhumane as to consider human life cheaply, the state I have described could not have been possible. Our laws forbid the construction of large vessels and their navigation to foreign countries, so we cannot rescue vessels on the high seas; but when foreign vessels are in distress along our shores and ask for fuel, water or provisions, we have been accustomed to mete out kindly treatment. It is not true, as you said, that we do not help ships in distress wrecked along our coasts. We will continue to supply fuel, water and provisions. Then, your statement that shipwrecked persons have been thrown like slaves into prison must be due to false reports. According to our laws, shipwrecked persons wherever they may be found, are to be treated with kindness and sent to Nagasaki and there delivered to the Dutch captain, by whom they are returned to their respective countries. Some time ago, certain of your countrymen arrived in distress at Matsumae, which is a place in the north; they were all taken to Nagasaki and from there sent to your country. There are persons who, even though in distress, are not of good character: they violate our laws and do as they please. Such we are obliged to detain temporarily before sending them to Nagasaki; but it is the unlawful behavior of persons of this character which alone brings about such treatment. It is quite possible that upon their return, they assert that they were treated like slaves, and otherwise circulate false reports. There is nothing inhumane about our government; and I am certain that if you will examine the state of our country and study the facts, your doubts will be dissolved. If you in your country truly value human life, you will not allow the resentment of successive years to crystallize. These are not matters so grave as to make war necessary. It would be well for you indeed to reconsider.

Perry: I have heard that your country has issued an order to supply foreign ships with fuel, water and provisions, and to rescue vessels in distress, as you have said; but our ships have frequently approached this country and have met with nothing but refusals; and they have not readily been able to obtain fuel and water. If your government is in fact as you describe it to be, and if you continue hereafter to supply fuel, water and provisions, and give help to those in distress, nothing more can be said. I desire, however, that a decree may be issued concerning the method by which you will hereafter supply fuel, water, provisions and coal. I shall be satisfied also if you reply to me that you will hereafter treat shipwrecked persons in as kindly a manner as you have just described.

Why do you not allow commerce? Commerce has to do with the things which a nation has and with what it lacks; it is a source of great profit and now flourishes between the countries of the world day and night. It brings great wealth to each country. If you open your country to commerce it will bring to you great profit and will surely be to your great advantage.

The Lord Rector: However much commerce has to do with what a nation has or lacks and would therefore be to its advantage, our

country since the beginning has found the things which it produces
to be sufficient for its own needs. We are not discontented at being
without the products of other countries. Having decided that we
shall not permit commerce, we cannot easily decide to permit it. You
say that your principal purpose in coming was to have greater value
placed on human life and to have help given to ships. You have attained your purpose. Now, commerce has to do with profits, but has
it anything to do with human life? Is it not enough that you have
gained what you sought?

Perry cogitated for some time and then said: You are right. As
you say, I came because I valued human life, and the important thing
is that you will give our vessels help. Commerce brings profit to a
country, but it does not concern human life. I shall not insist upon it.

4. Intermediate
(1867–1890)

Documents of the Restoration Period [1]
(1867–1889)

Imperial Rescript to the Daimyo
(March 21, 1868)

We have just succeeded to the Imperial Throne and the Empire is
now undergoing a thorough reformation. We ourselves exercise
supreme and sole decision in both civil and military matters. The
national dignity and happiness depend upon Our fulfilling the duties
of Our high office, and We are constantly and unrestingly applying
Our thoughts to this subject.

Unworthy as We are for the task, We desire to continue the work
begun by Our wise ancestors, and to carry out the policy bequeathed
Us by the late Emperor by giving peace to the clans and the people

at home, and abroad by making the national glory to shine beyond the seas. Because Tokugawa Keiki harbored lawless schemes, the empire has fallen to pieces, and the result has been civil war, inflicting the greatest injuries upon the people. We have therefore been compelled to resolve on taking the field in person against him.

As has already been notified, the existence of relations with foreign countries involves very important questions. We are willing therefore for the sake of the people of the Empire to brave the perils of the deep and to undergo the greatest hardships; to swear to spread the national glory abroad, and to satisfy the departed spirits of Our ancestors and of the late Emperor. . . .

The Imperial Oath (1868)

I. An Assembly widely convoked shall be established, and thus great stress shall be laid upon public opinion.

II. The welfare of the whole nation shall be promoted by the everlasting efforts of both the governing and the governed classes.

III. All subjects, civil and military officers, as well as other people shall do their best, and never grow weary in accomplishing their legitimate purposes.

IV. All absurd usages shall be abandoned; justice and righteousness shall regulate all actions.

V. Knowledge shall be sought for all over the world, and thus shall be strengthened the foundations of the Imperial Polity.

Return of the Fiefs
(March 5, 1869)
(A Memorial to the Emperor from the Lords of the Satsuma, Choshu, Hizen, and Tosa clans.)

Since the time when Your Majesty's ancestors founded this country and established a basis of government, all things in the wide expanse of heaven and all things on earth to its furthest limits, have belonged to the Emperor from generation to generation. This is what is known as "one central government." And the sole power of giving and of taking away, which renders it impossible for the nobles to hold the people in subjection in virtue of their land, or to deal with the smallest piece of ground at their pleasure, or to seize and treat despotically any individual of the humbler classes, this is what is understood by the term "one universal authority."

The administration of the Emperors was conducted entirely on this principle. They conducted the government in their own persons, the name and reality of power were combined, and consequently the nation was tranquil and contented. But from the time of the middle ages the administration became lax, and the authority of the Emperors came to be a plaything. All men fighting for power, changes of government followed each other in rapid succession, until half of the country fell into the hands of men who dealt with the people and the land at their pleasure; and in the end a state of things was reached where there was nothing but open contention and acts of violence. The government having no body of administration to protect, and no effective power, was unable to control matters. Everywhere men of influence, but of unprincipled character, took advantage of the existing disorder to promote their own interests, and the weak became food for the strong.

The most powerful barons took possession of fourteen or fifteen provinces while those of less influence collected bodies of armed retainers to the number of five or six thousand. Successive Shoguns seized land and people arbitrarily whenever they thought fit, and by this means extended their influence. Finally the Mikado's government lost all real authority, and was entirely dependent upon the will of the Shogunate. The boundless despotism of the Shogunate lasted for over six hundred years, and during this interval violent dealings with land and with the people were carried out by stealth under pretence of the Imperial authority. These acts were rendered possible owing to the existence of people who could not dissociate themselves from the time-honored observances of the past, and were still guided by the reverence due from a subject to his sovereign, and by a proper sense of the relation which should exist between high and low.

The ancient family of the Tokugawa dynasty of Shoguns and their relatives held half the country; as a natural consequence fresh families were constantly springing up; and it became a precedent founded on long custom which has lasted up till the present time for these numerous branches of the Tokugawa family to take no heed of the question as to whether their lands and subjects had been received in grant from the proper government or not. It was commonly said by members of these families: "These possessions of ours were gained by the military power of our ancestors." But there is little doubt that those ancestors had originally raised forces, plundered the Imperial storehouses, and laid forcible hands on the treasures contained, and had braved the penalty of death in the execution of their designs. Those who break into storehouses are commonly termed robbers, but no suspicion was attached by the nation to those who seized upon the land and people. It is terrible indeed this confusion between right and wrong.

It is now sought to establish an entirely new form of government. Care must, therefore, be taken to preserve intact both one central body of government, and one universal authority. The land in which your servants live is the land of the Emperor, and the people whom they govern are his subjects. Neither the one, therefore, nor the other can belong to your servants.

Your servants accordingly beg respectfully to surrender to Your Majesty the registers of the population, and beg Your Majesty to deal with everything as you may think fit, giving what should be given and taking away what should be taken away. They entreat Your Majesty to issue such Imperial Decrees as may be deemed necessary to deal with the lands and people of the four clans represented in this memorial, and to make such changes as Your Majesty may think proper. They also beg that all laws, decrees, and military regulations, extending even to military dress and accoutrements, may be issued by the Central government, so that all matters of state may be decided by one and the same authority. In this way both name and reality will be secured, and this country will be placed upon a footing of equality with foreign powers.

Your servants share the responsibility which the present critical condition of affairs entails upon the Mikado's government. It is this which has led them to represent their foolish views for the consideration of Your Majesty.

The Promise of a Parliament
(October 12, 1881)

We, sitting on the Throne which has been occupied by Our dynasty for over 2500 years, and now exercising in Our name and right all authority and power transmitted to us by Our ancestors, have long had in view gradually to establish a constitutional form of government, to the end that Our successors on the Throne may be provided with a rule for their guidance.

It was with this object in view that in the 8th year of Meiji We established the Senate, and in the 11th year of Meiji authorised the formation of Local Assemblies, thus laying the foundation for the gradual reforms which We contemplated. These Our acts must convince you, Our subjects, of Our determination in this respect from the beginning.

Systems of government differ in different countries, but sudden and unusual changes cannot be made without great inconvenience.

Our ancestors in Heaven watch Our acts, and We recognize Our responsibility to them for the faithful discharge of Our high duties, in accordance with the principles, and the perpetual increase of the glory, they have bequeathed to Us.

We therefore hereby declare that We shall, in the 23rd year of Meiji, establish a Parliament, in order to carry into full effect the determination We have announced, and We charge Our faithful subjects bearing Our commissions to make, in the meantime, all necessary preparations to that end.

With regard to the limitations upon the Imperial prerogative, and the constitution of the Parliament, We shall decide hereafter and make proclamation in due time.

We perceive that the tendency of Our people is to advance too rapidly, and without that thought and consideration which alone can make progress enduring, and We warn Our subjects, high and low, to be mindful of Our will, and that those who may advocate sudden and violent changes, thus disturbing the peace of Our realm, will fall under Our displeasure.

Extracts from the Constitution of 1889
(February 11, 1889)

Having, by virtue of the glories of Our Ancestors, ascended the Throne of a lineal succession unbroken for ages eternal; desiring to promote the welfare of, and to give development to the moral and intellectual faculties of Our beloved subjects, the very same that have been favoured with the benevolent care and affectionate vigilance of Our Ancestors; and hoping to maintain the prosperity of the State, in concert with Our people and with their support, We hereby promulgate in pursuance of Our Imperial Rescript of the 12th day of the 10th month of the 14th year of Meiji [October 12, 1881], a fundamental law of State, to exhibit the principles, by which We are to be guided in Our conduct, and to point out to what Our descendants and Our subjects and their descendants are forever to conform.

The rights of sovereignty of the State, We have inherited from Our Ancestors, and We shall bequeath them to Our descendants. Neither We nor they shall in future fail to wield them, in accordance with the provisions of the Constitution hereby granted.

We now declare to respect and protect the security of the rights and [of the] property of Our people, and to secure to them the complete enjoyment of the same, within the extent of the provisions of the present Constitution and of the law.

When in the future it may become necessary to amend any of the provisions of the present Constitution, We or Our successors *shall assume the initiative right,* and submit a project for the same to the Imperial Diet. The Imperial Diet shall pass its vote upon it, according to the conditions imposed by the present Constitution, and in no other wise shall Our descendants or Our subjects be permitted to attempt any alteration thereof.

I. The Empire of Japan shall be reigned over and governed by a line of Emperors unbroken for ages eternal.

III. The Emperor is sacred and inviolable.

VIII. The Emperor, in consequence of an urgent necessity to maintain public safety or to avert public calamities, issues, when the Imperial Diet is not sitting, Imperial Ordinances in the place of law.

Such Imperial Ordinances are to be laid before the Imperial Diet at its next session, and when the Diet does not approve the said Ordinances, the Government shall declare them to be invalid for the future.

XI. The Emperor has the supreme command of the Army and Navy.

XII. The Emperor determines the organization and peace standing of the Army and Navy.

XIII. The Emperor declares war, makes peace, and concludes treaties.

XXVIII. Japanese subjects shall, within limits not prejudicial to peace and order, and not antagonistic to their duties as subjects, enjoy freedom of religious belief.

Instructions to Governors
(September 28, 1887)

Now that His Majesty's judgment has become ripened after years of thought, has become strengthened more than ever, and now that the work of the Restoration is so near its completion that "only a cart-load of earth," so to speak, is needed to give the last finish to the hills we have been building up, should any of the people in the country, not clearly understanding His Imperial Majesty's views, be led astray into erroneous ideas by doubts or misgivings, no small injury will be inflicted upon the great work in hand. We hereby inform you, in respectful obedience to the gracious will of His Imperial Majesty, of a general view of the policy of the country, both as to internal and external affairs, and point out to you the course of administration to be pursued.

Firstly, the fundamental principles of our constitutional system of government shall be based upon the historical traditions of the country and the principles that have been handed down by the Imperial Ancestors, modified by careful consideration of the actual circumstances of the times; respect shall be paid to the rights of the subject and extension be given to the power of public representation. These things, it must be observed, are gracious gifts which His Imperial Majesty is pleased to grant to his subjects upon His own judgment and condescension. These points may without difficulty or elucidation be understood, if one but glances at the dignified and majestic character of our national polity since the days of the first Imperial Ancestor, and of the Imperial Rescripts of April, 1875 [8th year of Meiji] and of October, 1881 [14th year of Meiji].

In foreign countries the course each nation pursues is different from that pursued by others, owing to the historical peculiarities of each nation. Opinions are consequently divided according to the different schools of thinkers, and these opinions are as yet far from being unified. Different scholars maintain different theories, and each advocating his own ideas by copious arguments they do not seem to come to any agreement. They have each of them more or fewer reasons for the support of their positions, which are plausible enough to effect an agitating influence upon the general public. It cannot but follow from such a state of things that men holding opinions more or less coinciding with each other's should gradually form themselves into a combination, and should be in perpetual conflict with those differing from them. Such is indeed what is very frequently observed in other countries. Yet in this country the upholding of the divine emblems of the Imperial Ancestors in a position permanent and inviolable, the maintenance of the dignity of the Imperial Family, while on the other hand the granting to subjects the right of representation, are matters of the most significant importance in their bearing upon the national policy and upon the great aims of the Imperial Ancestor. With regard to this matter, therefore, neither the one nor the other of His Majesty's subjects has the slightest shadow of right to attempt an intrusion. Should any of them either before or after the proclamation of the Constitution offer any objection to the determination of it according to His Majesty's own personal judgment, he should be looked upon as having overstepped the limits of freedom of speech and that of holding public meetings and of petition; and should any individual, under pretext of such objection, instigate or persuade others to plan insurrection, such necessary measures as expediency may require should be adopted for the maintenance of the public peace.

As to the opinion that diplomatic affairs should be submitted to the public deliberation of the people, it must be observed that no such course is followed in any constitutional monarchy. The supreme powers connected with military and foreign affairs are exclusively in the hands of sovereigns, and excepting in certain cases no such affairs are submitted to the public deliberation of the people. Were the power of declaring war and of concluding peace and treaties to be delegated to the public, where it must be asked would be the supreme power of the Sovereign? For these reasons, the proposition above alluded to must be rejected according to our future constitution. This is also a point which you shall bear in mind in guiding the course to be followed by the people.

A Memorial from the Samurai of Kochi Ken
(October 1874)

Education should consist, first of all, in the study of our native writings by which we learn the superiority of our national constitutions over those of all foreign nations, and next in acquiring a knowledge of the doctrines of the [Chinese] sages, by which we learn the virtues of loyalty, filial piety, benevolence, and justice. After that the pupil should be taught to read European books, by which his understanding may be more and more enlarged. Any other course will end in exalting them and in thinking meanly of others and must speedily result in causing us to fall into the snares of an evil religion. Even now the religion of Jesus is flourishing in the metropolis, and there is danger of it spreading over the empire. Now the religion of Jesus is one which shows its respect for heaven by misrepresenting heaven, and whose mode of teaching men is to lead them astray. It is a religion which has the evil result of causing men to make naught of their lords and parents. If it is not now strictly prohibited, it threatens to raise its hopes even to the Imperial throne. Is not this a truly alarming state of things? We have humbly observed that the fact of the Imperial line having remained unbroken from the first foundation of the Empire until now is due to the Imperial glory being shed abroad throughout the land, and the people enjoying the blessing of Imperial favor, to the hearty observance of the respective duties of lord and vassal, and to a just distinction being maintained between high and low. But the students of western learning call those bigots who respect the religion of our empire, and ridicule as students of a far-fetched philosophy those who read Chinese books. But what do we mean by "bigot"? Is it not a person who holds fast to one thing and is incapable of progress, and would not we call it a far-fetched philosophy when a man is ignorant of the good and bad qualities of things that are before his eyes, and starts off in pursuit of that which is high and distant? Is not the bigotry of the students of western learning of the worst kind, for they do nothing but assert the fitness of the customs of foreign countries distant 10,000 ri, and are ignorant of the reverence due to the gods, and of the utility of the doctrines of the sages.

We pray that Your Majesty will encourage the true learning, and prohibit evil doctrines, thereby maintaining sternly the right system of education.

There are at present many matters with which the State has to deal, but among them none is more pressing than to stir up the spirit of the samurai, and to calm the minds of the people. The reason why our empire has never been exposed to insult since its foundation is that the original high spirit of the samurai has been preserved. If it had not been preserved, how should we ever have been able to confront all the great continents on equal terms? In spite of this, however, the samurai have been relieved of their proper office and a system introduced which brings them to the same level as all classes of subjects. This is a name and not a reality. The samurai devotes his powers to the acquirement of learning and the art of war, and turns his attention to matters of State, and although it is desired to deprive him of the one thing in which his forte lies, and to convert him all at once into a peasant, it is impossible to do so, nor is it possible for him to become an artisan or merchant, however much this may be wished for. He only gives himself up to indolent habits, and consumes to no purpose the allowance issued to him. If a danger arises to our country, of what service will he be in defending it? Under the feudal system a standard of learning and accomplishments was set up, which the samurai were required to attain, but in spite of this some of them gave way to indolence. Now that there is no such control, all, without distinction of rank, prize luxury and rival each other in adopting new things; they love what is strange, and great and small alike look to foreign countries as their model in all things. No matter what merits a Japanese thing may have they despise and disregard it. What an unnatural state of things is this!

We hope that the samurai may be at once restored to their ordinary functions, that their high spirit may be encouraged, that frugality may be earnestly practised, and that morals may be rendered pure. If these things are not attended to, all our efforts after progress towards enlightenment and civilization will be in vain.

In all our reforms of our government there is none in which foreign institutions have not been imitated. We ought certainly to have adopted those inventions in which foreigners excel, viz., fire-arms, ships of war and fortifications, and to have guarded our coast vigilantly by means of them. But since the revolution we have not heard of one great gun having been cast or a single fort having been erected. It is perhaps the plan of our statesmen to conduct our relations with foreign countries in accordance with foreign international law. They think that in our commerce with foreigners sincerity and justice should be the rule. They say that we have already entered into friendly relations with foreigners and if we treat them with sincerity and justice they can certainly have no pretence for invading us. These are not our views. We believe that it is our servile attitude towards foreigners that has hitherto prevented them from attacking us. If in our relations with them we took our stand on our warlike prestige they would certainly become enraged and attack us, even though we committed no breach of faith. We may see that this is so if we observe from what causes they go to war with each other. Their wars are not always owing to unavoidable causes; they often proceed from a conflict of interests, or from a rivalry in power and prestige. Ever since 1853 foreigners have despised and mocked us for our servility and have not scrupled to use their military prestige to bring pressure upon us. They have tricked us by their international law and deluded us by their false religion. The spirit they have shown toward us is greatly to be detested. Their international law and good faith and justice are certainly not to be relied on. Why therefore does our government not adopt those things in which they excel and use them for the vigilant defence of our coasts? Large sums of money are now being spent on railways and stone houses. In our opinion if these sums were to be expended on the erection of works for the defence of our own coast this object might easily be attained.

In ancient times Toyotomi Hideyoshi wielded the military power of the empire with unexampled ability. He sent Kato Kiomasa and other valiant generals with an army of 160,000 brave samurai on an expedition against Korea. There they had several engagements with an auxiliary force from China, but although they were victorious none of our troops could ever get west of the O-rioku-ko [Arinare]. At last after seven years, during which time the army was never disbanded, Hideyoshi died and the troops returned to Japan. In the end we were unable to retain possession of a foot of Korean soil. And this was not owing to the want of skill on the part of our generals, or to cowardice in our troops. They labored under the disadvantage of fighting in a foreign country and were overpowered by numbers. Your Majesty is gifted with great discernment and will not require to ask scholars to tell you whether our present generals are more or less effective than those of Hideyoshi's time. To attack China suddenly with a small army would be a very dangerous step. But your servants are still unacquainted with the circumstances of the case. If our differences with China have arisen from unavoidable causes and it is necessary to send an expedition to deal out to her a just punishment, full of loyal impulse and righteous indignation, we shall of course do our best to make the Imperial glory shine out brightly beyond the seas. And if they take the initiative and invade Japan, it will be the time for us to spare no effort and even to lay down our lives in gratitude for our country. If we are unsuccessful what better can we demand than to die for Japan?

The Nature of the Japanese
(1889)
By Fukuzawa Yukichi

In the West parliamentary institutions have been called into being by the advancing requirements of the times. As the people grew in knowledge, and consequently in power, despotic government showed features alike distasteful to men's sense of freedom and opposed to their rights, and thenceforth the admission of the important factor, public opinion, to a share in government became a foregone conclusion. In the Japan of to-day, however, a widely different state of affairs exists. The general mass of the nation is indifferent to political power, and ignorant of its value; people mostly occupy themselves with their own personal affairs and are well content, no matter whose hands hold the reins of rule, if only their burdens are lessened and their condition ameliorated. The rivalry which in the West leads people to compete for power, is due simply to the high value they place upon their personal rights; in this country, owing to the peculiar customs which have for so long existed, we are not at all sensitive about our privileges and our rights. From this indifference arises the fact that, as compared with Western nations, the Japanese are not so strongly moved by sentiments of self-respect and self-assertion. It is enough that an order should issue from the government; it is at once submissively obeyed, even though it may be inconsistent with reason. We need not say that personal rights are before political rights in importance; that is a fact which is beyond discussion, for the former must be recognized and established on a sound and solid basis before the latter can come into existence. Nevertheless the Japanese people have not yet recognized or appreciated the value of their personal rights; how, then, can they understand their political rights? We, therefore, assert without fear of contradiction that the nation generally has not yet manifested any desire to take part in politics, or at any rate if such a wish has been expressed, it has not been so formulated as a result of mature deliberation on the subject.

A people who so readily adapted themselves to the greatest changes their country had undergone since its foundation are not the least likely to be bewildered by the inauguration of a Parliament. Difficulties may arise at the outset; there may be misunderstanding on the part both of the government and the people; undesirable or rash persons may inadvertently be admitted to Parliament. But rashness is not a quality which recommends itself to the Japanese people, and such errors will soon be remedied. These difficulties need not be dreaded. If we remember that society is in this country under the final control of the sacred Throne, which sheds a benign influence all around, we shall have no cause to fear that political excitement will lead our people to stray from the path of order and duty. We may be told that the quality of obedience, though hereditary in the Japanese nation, can be affected by the influence of the ever changing times. We do not think that is probable. We cannot believe that an hereditary quality will so easily yield to external circumstances, or that even education will quickly impair it. Though the institution of Parliament is a novel and unprecedented one in this country, we firmly believe that both government and people will by virtue of their hereditary spirit of obedience faithfully observe and conform to the duties required of them.

A Gift from the Throne
(From Prince Ito's remarks on the Constitution, 1889)

If we carefully regard the method in which public education has advanced, from the cultivation of knowledge in connection with political economy, law, and kindred branches, to commerce, trade, and industries, and compare the present state of affairs with that which existed some twenty years ago, we shall not exaggerate if we say that the country has undergone a complete metamorphosis. If we reflect upon the history of civilization in this country it will be perceived, I think, that while several influences have been at work, still the introduction of such alien religious systems as Confucianism and Buddhism, which were largely instrumental in elevating our people, and the development of such works as have conduced to their welfare, have been due to the benevolent guidance and encouragement of the Sovereign. We may therefore say with truth that the civilization which we now possess is a gift from the Throne. These facts, which are plainly apparent in the pages of our history, will clearly demonstrate to others the nature of our national life.

Under an absolute system of government the Sovereign's will is his command, and the Sovereign's command at once becomes law. In a constitutional country, however, the consent of that assembly which represents the people must be obtained. It will be evident, however, that as the supreme right is one and indivisible, the legislative power remains in the hands of the Sovereign and is not bestowed on the people. While the supreme right extends to everything, and its exercise is wide and comprehensive, its legislative and executive functions are undoubtedly the most important. These are in the hands of the Sovereign; the rights pertaining thereto cannot be held in common by the Sovereign and his subjects; but the latter are permitted to take part in legislation according to the provisions of the

Constitution. In a country which is under absolute rule the view of the Sovereign is at once law; in a constitutional country, on the other hand, nothing being law without a concurrence of views between the Sovereign and the people the latter elect representatives to meet at an appointed place and carry out the view of the Sovereign.

Emperor Meiji's Imperial Rescript to Soldiers and Sailors [2]

The forces of Our Empire are in all ages under the command of the Emperor. It is more than twenty-five centuries since the Emperor Jimmu, leading in person the soldiers of the Otomo and Mononobe clans, subjugated the unruly tribes of the land and ascended the Imperial Throne to rule over the whole country. During this period the military system has undergone frequent changes in accordance with those in the state of society. In ancient times the rule was that the Emperor should take personal command of the forces; and although the military authority was sometimes delegated to the Empress or to the Prince Imperial, it was scarcely ever entrusted to a subject. In the Middle Ages, when the civil and military institutions were framed after the Chinese model, the Six Guards were founded, the Right and Left Horse Bureaus established, and other organizations, such as that of the Coast Guards, created. The military system was thus completed, but habituated to a prolonged state of peace, the Imperial Court gradually lost its administrative vigour; in course of time soldiers and farmers became distinct classes, and the early conscriptive system was replaced by an organization of volunteers, which finally produced the military class. The military power passed over entirely to the leaders of this class; through disturbances in the Empire the political power also fell into their hands; and for about seven centuries the military families held sway. Although these results followed from changes in the state of society and were deeply to be deplored, since they were contrary to the fundamental character of Our Empire and to the law of Our Imperial Ancestors. Later on, in the eras of Kokwa and Kaei, the decline of the Tokugawa Shogunate and the new aspect of foreign relations even threatened to impair our national dignity, causing no small anxiety to Our August Grandfather, the Emperor Ninko, and Our August Father, the Emperor

Komei, a fact which We recall with awe and gratitude. When in youth We succeeded to the Imperial Throne, the Shogun returned into Our hands the administrative power, and all the feudal lords their fiefs; thus, in a few years, Our entire realm was unified and the ancient regime restored. Due as this was to the meritorious services of Our loyal officers and wise councillors, civil and military, and to the abiding influence of Our Ancestors' benevolence towards the people, yet it must also be attributed to Our subjects' true sense of loyalty and their conviction of the importance of "Great Righteousness." In consideration of these things, being desirous of reconstructing Our military system and of enhancing the glory of Our Empire, We have in the course of the last fifteen years established the present system of the Army and Navy. The supreme command of Our forces is in Our hands, and although We may entrust subordinate commands to Our subjects, yet the ultimate authority We Ourself shall hold and never delegate to any subject. It is Our will that this principle be carefully handed down to posterity and that the Emperor always remain the supreme civil and military power, so that the disgrace of the middle and succeeding ages may never be repeated. Soldiers and Sailors, We are your supreme Commander-in-Chief. Our relations with you will be most intimate when We rely upon you as Our limbs and you look up to Us as your head. Whether We are able to guard the Empire, and so prove Ourself worthy of Heaven's blessing and repay the benevolence of Our Ancestors depends upon the faithful discharge of your duties as soldiers and sailors. If the majesty and power of Our Empire be impaired, do you share with Us the sorrow; if the glory of Our arms shine resplendent, We will share with you the honour. If you all do your duty, and being one with Us in spirit do your utmost for the protection of the State, Our people will long enjoy the blessings of peace, and the might and dignity of Our Empire will shine in the world. As We thus expect much of you, Soldiers and Sailors, We give you the following precepts:

(1) The soldier and the sailor should consider loyalty their essential duty. Who that is born in this land can be wanting in the spirit of grateful service to it? No soldier or sailor, especially, can be considered efficient unless this spirit be strong within him. A soldier or a sailor in whom this spirit is not strong, however skilled in art or

proficient in science, is a mere puppet; and a body of soldiers or sailors wanting in loyalty, however well ordered and disciplined it may be, is in an emergency no better than a rabble. Remember that, as the protection of the State and the maintenance of its power depend upon the strength of its arms, the growth or decline of this strength must affect the nation's destiny for good or for evil; therefore neither be led astray by current opinions nor meddle in politics, but with single heart fulfil your essential duty of loyalty, and bear in mind that duty is weightier than a mountain, while death is lighter than a feather. Never by failing in moral principle fall into disgrace and bring dishonor upon your name.

(2) The soldier and the sailor should be strict in observing propriety. Soldiers and sailors are organized in grades, from the Marshal and the Admiral of the Fleet down to the private soldier or ordinary seaman; and even within the same rank and grade there are differences in seniority of service according to which juniors should submit to their seniors. Inferiors should regard the orders of their superiors as issuing directly from Us. Always pay due respect not only to your superiors but also to your seniors, even though not serving under them. On the other hand, superiors should never treat their inferiors with contempt or arrogance. Except when official duty requires them to be strict and severe, superiors should treat their inferiors with consideration, making kindness their chief aim, so that all grades may unite in their service to the Emperor. If you, Soldiers and Sailors, neglect to observe propriety, treating your superiors with disrespect and your inferiors with harshness, and thus cause harmonious co-operation to be lost, you will not only be a blight upon the forces but also be unpardonable offenders against the State.

(3) The soldier and the sailor should esteem valour. Ever since the ancient times valour has in our country been held in high esteem, and without it Our subjects would be unworthy of their name. How, then, may the soldier and the sailor, whose profession it is to confront the enemy in battle, forget even for one instant to be valiant? But there is true valour and false. To be incited by mere impetuosity to violent action cannot be called true valour. The soldier and the sailor should have sound discrimination of right and wrong, cultivate self-possession, and form their plans with deliberation. Never to despise an inferior enemy or fear a superior, but to do one's duty as soldier

or sailor—this is true valour. Those who thus appreciate true valour should in their daily intercourse set gentleness first and aim to win the love and esteem of others. If you affect valour and act with violence, the world will in the end detest you and look upon you as wild beasts. Of this you should take heed.

(4) The soldier and the sailor should highly value faithfulness and righteousness. Faithfulness and righteousness are the ordinary duties of man, but the soldier and the sailor, in particular, cannot be without them and remain in the ranks even for a day. Faithfulness implies the keeping of one's word, and righteousness the fulfilment of one's duty. If then you wish to be faithful and righteous in anything, you must carefully consider at the outset whether you can accomplish it or not. If you thoughtlessly agree to do something that is vague in its nature and bind yourself to unwise obligations, and then try to prove yourself faithful and righteous, you may find yourself in great straits from which there is no escape. In such cases your regrets will be of no avail. Hence you must first make sure whether the thing is righteous and reasonable or not. If you are convinced that you cannot possibly keep your word and maintain righteousness, you had better abandon your engagement at once. Ever since the ancient times there have been repeated instances of great men and heroes who, overwhelmed by misfortune, have perished and left a tarnished name to posterity, simply because in their effort to be faithful in small matters they failed to discern right and wrong with reference to fundamental principles, or because, losing sight of the true path of public duty, they kept faith in private relations. You should, then, take serious warning by these examples.

(5) The soldier and the sailor should make simplicity their aim. If you do not make simplicity your aim, you will become effeminate and frivolous and acquire fondness for luxurious and extravagant ways; you will finally grow selfish and sordid and sink to the last degree of baseness, so that neither loyalty nor valour will avail to save you from the contempt of the world. It is not too much to say that you will thus fall into a lifelong misfortune. If such an evil once makes its appearance among soldiers and sailors, it will certainly spread like an epidemic, and martial spirit and morale will instantly decline. Although, being greatly concerned on this point, We lately issued the Disciplinary Regulations and warned you against this

evil, nevertheless, being harassed with anxiety lest it should break out, We hereby reiterate Our warning. Never do you, Soldiers and Sailors, make light of this injunction.

These five articles should not be disregarded even for a moment by soldiers and sailors. Now for putting them into practice, the all important is sincerity. These five articles are the soul of Our soldiers and sailors, and sincerity is the soul of these articles. If the heart be not sincere, words and deeds, however good, are all mere outward show and can avail nothing. If only the heart be sincere, anything can be accomplished. Moreover, these five articles are the Grand Way of Heaven and Earth and the universal law of humanity, easy to observe and to practice. If you, Soldiers and Sailors, in obedience to Our instruction, will observe and practice these principles and fulfil your duty of grateful service to the country, it will be a source of joy, not to Ourself alone, but to all people of Japan.

The 4th day of the 1st month of the 15th Year of Meiji.

[Imperial Sign Manual]

5. Fourth Period

Modern State Shinto Period
(Since 1914)

The Religion That Includes All Others

Shinto is a great religion that includes all others. For example, Shinto may be compared to a tree while all other religions are fertilizers. Thus Shinto, by absorbing and assimilating various fertilizers, as a result of a process of inclusion and selection, must increase and expand itself. A religion like Christianity, however, which neglects both the family system and nationalism, is not a fertilizer. On the other hand it is a great evil. If the usages of the existing family system should become extinct in Japan and we should come to pure in-dividualism, or if, again, we should abandon nationalism and be-come altogether humanitarian, the results would be disastrous.

—Editorial in *Kami Kaze,* a Shinto magazine (Tokyo, July 1, 1921). Translated and cited by D. C. Holtom in *The Political Philosophy of Modern Shinto,* *T.A.S.J.,* Vol. XLIX, Part II (1922), pp. 125, 126.

The Spiritual Mission of the Emperor

The people and gods . . . are only working to accomplish this greatest and loftiest task of unifying the world under the sway of the Emperor of Japan. . . . We are only aiming at making the Emperor of Japan rule and govern the whole world, as he is the only ruler in the world who retains the spiritual mission inherited from the re-motest ancestors in the Divine World.

—*Taisho Nichi-Nichi Shimbun* (Osaka, December 21, 1920). Cited by D. C. Holtom, *The Political Philosophy of Modern Shinto,* p. 126.

The Salvation of Mankind

It is now most clear that the salvation of the entire human race is the mission of our empire. Nations are now in a condition of disorder. There are classes within the nations, each class struggling for its own interests and each thinking the other an irreconcilable enemy. Radi-calism is spreading abroad. The poison of the disease penetrates flesh and bones and threatens to overthrow the state. The idea of reliance upon the state is conspicuously weakened. The heart of man has lost its power to co-operate. Individuals do as they please, acting dis-solutely without restriction. The capitalistic class of England and America, flushed with the victory of the Great War, have become arrogant and domineering throughout the world and are giving rein to unbounded greed. Behold the world is full of the struggle between capital and labor. They are fallen into the pit. The hell of fighting and bloodshed has appeared on earth.

When we observe such conditions there is not one of our people who does not believe that, if only they had our emperors, they would not come to such extremity. . . . Our people, through the benevolent virtue of the emperors, have attained a national constitution that is without parallel in the world. . . . Now if all the world should come to look up to the virtue of our emperor and should come to live under that influence, then there could be light for the future of humanity. Thus the world can be saved from destruction. Thus life can be lived within the realms of goodness and beauty. Of a truth great is the mission of our nation.

—Uesugi Shinkichi, *Kokutai Sikwa Hatsuyo,* "The Exaltation of the Essence of the National Constitution" (Tokyo, 1919). Translated and cited by D. C. Holtom, *The Political Philosophy of Modern Shinto.*

The White Heat of Faith

In our country acts of loyalty to the Emperor as the head of our collective family system partake of a moral nature, so that it is hardly necessary to say that one aspect of loyalty permits of an ethical explanation. But as much as the Emperor, who constitutes the object which imparts life to this loyalty considered as morality, is equipped conjointly with divine and human natures, it follows that that which from an external point of view is regarded as an ethical element, when considered in its deeper aspects, becomes transfused with the white heat of a religious faith. Indeed the loyalty of Japanese has been so conspicuously transformed into faith and religion as to lead foreign scholars to go so far as to say that loyalty constitutes the religion of the Japanese people. The Emperor is Incarnate Deity and occupies in Japanese faith the position which Jehovah occupied in Judaism. It has also been made clear that the spirit of loyalty which impels our goodly subjects is nothing other than the heat of faith which controlled the chosen Hebrew people.

Therefore, for the Japanese standpoint, that attitude of consciousness which stimulates loyalty to the Emperor, regarded as man, when he is regarded as Deity, immediately becomes filled with the content of an enthusiastic religious faith which offers body and spirit as a holy sacrifice. Wherefore, if one regards this merely from the standpoint of morality, it may be designated the unique patriotism of the Japanese. This is the secular aspect of Shinto. It must not be forgotten, however, that Shinto possesses fundamental aspects as well as external, that it is a national religion which worships the Emperor as divine.

—Genchi Kato, *Waga Kokutai to Shinto,* "Our National Organization and Shinto" (Tokyo, 1919). Translated and cited by D. C. Holtom, *The Political Philosophy of Modern Shinto.*

The Meaning of Life

Even though there were no temples or churches, the Empire would still exist. On the other hand, if the Shinto shrines should cease to exist, the Empire would come to an end. This is because the shrines are an epitome of the Empire, that is, they are the Empire itself.

The deities of the shrines are fundamentally related to the establishment of the nation, and to honour and worship them is to unite oneself with the Empire. This is because the shrines are a part of the Empire and an expression thereof. While faith in Buddha and Jesus may separate one from his duty as a subject of the state, such faith can never be a manifestation of the nation. The worship of the deities of the Shinto shrines gives support to the Emperor's supreme authority over ceremonies. On the other hand, the worship of Buddha and God at the temples and churches has no connection whatsoever with the matter of His supreme authority over ceremonies.

The essential nature of the shrine exists in the worship of their deities. The center of the shrine activities is the worship of the gods and the surrender of everything in the attainment of union with them. By union with a divine life that transcends the individual self, the individual becomes god. God is worshipped in the individual self and god is made to exist therein. Hereby the little individual self becomes the expression and manifestation of the gods who are rulers with boundless and supreme power.

By virtue of the worship of the gods, the individual, who in his physical life cannot escape change and destruction, comes to possess an existence that is deathless and eternal, one that flourishes more and more for ever. Hereby stability is imparted to the activities of the individual; the individual existence gains inner serenity and life is given meaning.

What is here meant by imparting meaning to life is not to be judged by the standard of personal gain, but rather it means participation as subjects in the support of Imperial rule. It means to become of one body with our ancestors, to make the traditional spirit of our ancestors our spirit. It means the spirit with which our ancestors worshipped and served the gods, in brief, the Great Imperial Parent, with a dedication that took them through the waters of the sea, though their bodies were left there in heaps, and across mountains, though they died there to become grasses by the way. For us, it means that in the same way, knowing that we shall be burned we enter fire and determined to be drowned we go into water. It means a fervent pushing on to spread the Imperial rule and to extend the Imperial glory.

—Takemoto Toyonosuke (a priest of the Atago shrine in Kyoto), in *Yomiuri Shimbun* (1937). Cited by D. C. Holtom, *The National Faith of Japan* (London: Kegan Paul, Trench, Trubner and Co.; New York: E. P. Dutton and Co., 1938).

War, the Father of Creation

War is the father of Creation [*Sozo no chichi*] and the Mother of Culture [*Bunkwa no haha*]. Rivalry for supremacy does for the state what struggling against adversity does for the individual. It is such impetus, in the one case, as in the other, that prompts the birth and development of Life and Cultural Creation [*Bunkwa-teki sozo*].

War, in this sense, does not conform to the generally accepted conception in which it is held to consist of a series of terrific destructive acts perpetrated by massed people for unrelenting slaughter and devastation. War, thus characterized, is simply an inevitable outcome of the application of the idea that "might makes right," an insatiable thirst after sheer conquests. Such definition of war must be rejected forthwith by our people, who have an unshakable faith in the Life of the Universe [*Banyu-no-seimei*], and who are animated by the belief that it is their heaven-sent mission to participate in the great work of helping the Life of the Universe to unfold and infinitely to develop. Accordingly the greatest responsibility imposed upon our Empire is that, on the one hand, of checking all forms of the idea that "might makes right," which naturally stand in the way of our efforts to discharge our great mission in our pursuit of righteousness, and of our creative activities, and, on the other hand, of taming, correcting, and directing all evil forces that tend, with baneful will, toward the grasping of power for power's sake. And we must do this in such manner as to cause our endeavors to be transformed into, or to be assimilated with, the benign and magnanimous soul of Japan [*Wakon*] and to flow into the majestic and all-embracing course of universal justice [*Kodo*], or the Imperial Way. To exalt war to such a high level is, in short, the mission of national defense.

—*Kokubo no Hongi to Sono Kyokwa no Teisho*, "Principles of National Defense and Proposals for its Augmentation" (Tokyo, 1934). Quoted in Kenneth W. Colegrove, *Militarism in Japan* (Boston and New York: World Peace Foundation, 1936).

The Meaning of Kami

The Japanese *kami* . . . as used in National Shinto, does not have a religious meaning, although it possesses a spiritual content. . . . *Kami* is not a religious word. Inasmuch as this word, as used in Shinto shrine terminology, is an important agency for the fostering of the national spirit, no change in content is permissible. The declaration of the Christian world that "God is the one and only creator of the universe, that he is uniquely omnipotent with no other gods beside him," is not realized in any term in the Japanese language. The Japanese *kami* is not a word that indicates such a Christian meaning, and since the significance of this word cannot be changed, Christianity on its part must select another word in place of *kami* for the expression of its religious terminology.

—*Zaidan Hojin Meiji Seitoku Kinen Gakkai Kiyo*, "Transactions of the Meiji Japan Society," No. 52 (Autumn 1939). Translated and cited by D. C. Holtom in "The Meaning of Kami," *Monumenta Nipponica*, Vol. III, Nos. 1 and 2, and Vol. IV, No. 2 (Tokyo: Sophia University, 1940–1941).

The God in the Emperor

What is the essence or nature of Amaterasu Omikami? It signifies the sublime and mightiest power of the nation, namely the throne, and the great-august-heart or the soul of the ruler, which is embodied in the Throne. In other words it represents the divine soul of the ruler of the empire, the Emperor. The Emperor is the divine manifestation of Amaterasu Omikami and rules the empire in accordance with her will. Thus the Emperor and the imperial Throne, transmitted in an unbroken line, are sacred and inviolable. . . .

About seven centuries ago the word *jinno* was first used. This word originated from the faith that the Emperor and Amaterasu Omikami were identical and were of one august body. . . . This spirit or faith, . . . the guiding light in every respect of the Meiji Restoration, . . . was what united Japan, making her realize both her divine lineage and her divine nationality, and awakening a racial determination.

Lastly it must be mentioned that the faith of *Kannagara* expresses within it a feeling of assimilation and harmony, a tendency towards avoiding argumentation and wilful adherence to one's personal opinions, the result of submitting to one's superiors and respecting them. These characteristics come from the fact that the faith of *Kannagara* expresses one's small self or ego through society or the nation, and acts and works in accordance with a great family and the will of the ancestors of that family, and not through the small will of an individual. . . .

The spirit of *Kannagara* . . . developed through a racial faith based upon the spirit of the establishment of the empire which later in the Nara period produced a culture indigenous to the nation. During this same period the nationalistic idea that Japan is "a nation which, as it is with the gods, makes no unnecessary argumentations," was born. This idea is that Japan, being a divine nation, finds it unnecessary to argue or discuss over superfluous matters. In other words, it is a nation of deeds, not words.

—Shozo Kono, *Kannagara no Michi*, "The Meaning of Kannagara," in *Monumenta Nipponica*, Vol. III, No. 2 (Tokyo: Sophia University, 1940).

The Essence of Shinto

Shinto . . . has culminated in Mikadoism or the worship of the Mikado or Japanese Emperor as a divinity during his lifetime as well as after his death. . . . Herein lies even at the present day, in my opinion, the essence or life of Shinto inseparably connected with the national ideals of the Japanese people. Japanese patriotism or loyalty as you might call it really is not simple patriotism or mere loyalty as understood in the ordinary sense of the word, that is, in the mere ethical sense of the term. It is more—it is the lofty self-denying, enthusiastic sentiment of the Japanese people toward their august ruler, believed to be something divine, rendering them capable of offering up anything and everything all dearest to them willingly, that is, of their own free will, of sacrificing not only their wealth and property, but their own life itself, for the sake of their divinely gracious sovereign. . . . All this is nothing but the actual manifestation of the religious consciousness of the Japanese people.

—Kato Genchi, *A Study of Shinto* (Tokyo, 1937).

The Trunk and the Branches

The Japanese Empire is founded upon the spirit of profound reverence for Amaterasu Omikami from whom our emperors are directly descended. This spirit or principle may be analyzed into two constituents, namely, ancestor worship and god-worship. Ancestor worship has given rise to the consanguineous unity of the nation, and god-worship to our spiritual unity; and the two elements in combination have formed the foundations of the typical and unique national constitution of our Empire.

The Japanese people as subjects of the Emperor have inhabited this archipelago for so many centuries without interruption, and without interference from outside, that their families have closely mixed and mingled with one another and formed a race of admirable tendencies. And the fact is worthy of note that the Imperial Family has stood at the very center of this national process of common assimilation, so that the imperial blood may be said to run in the veins of all Japanese, who have thus become kinsmen with one another, descended from a common ancestor. That common ancestor, or ancestress, is Amaterasu Omikami. The relations between the Imperial House and the people today may therefore be likened to those between the trunk and branches of a gigantic tree, for if we were to trace the genealogy of each Japanese subject, we would find that he belongs to a family which centuries ago was either a direct or an indirect offshoot of the Imperial Family. . . . In other words, the Imperial Family and the people having a common ancestor in Ama-

terasu Omikami, our sovereign and his subjects are completely united
like one man to form the Japanese nation and state.

—Koya Nakamura, *History of Japan,* translated by M. G. Mori (Board of Tourist Industries, Japanese Government Railways, 1939).

We Bathe in His Glory

We say the Emperor is like a father and mother to us, but that is
an inadequate comparison. The Emperor is a personage far above
and superior to our fathers and mothers. We who exist today were
born through the august power of the Emperor. Whoever we are,
old or young, we bathe in his glory. Assuming that there were no
Emperor, not one of us could by any possibility have been born.

—Karsuhiko Kakehi, *Kokka no Kenkyo,* "A Study of the State" (Tokyo, 1938).
Cited by Otto D. Tolischus, *Through Japanese Eyes* (New York: Reynal and
Hitchcock, 1945).

Beyond Men's Power

Japan's national polity is unique in the world. Heaven sent down
Ninigi-no-Mikoto to Kashihara, Yamato Province, with a message
that their posterity should reign over and govern Japan for ages
eternal. It was on this happy day, 2601 years ago, that our first Emperor, Jimmu, ascended the throne. Dynasties in foreign countries
were created by man. Foreign kings, emperors and presidents are all
created by men, while Japan has a sacred throne, inherited from the
Imperial ancestors. Japanese Imperial rule, therefore, is an extension
of Heaven. The dynasties created by men may collapse but the Heavenly created throne is beyond men's power.

—Baron Kiichiro Hiranuma, Home Minister, in speech to schoolteachers at
celebration of the "2601st" anniversary of the foundation of the Japanese
Empire, February 11, 1941. Cited by Otto D. Tolischus, *op. cit.*

The Emperor of All Mankind

The Emperor is not to be worshipped exclusively by the Japanese,
nor to be represented as Emperor of Japan alone. The Emperor gov-
erns Japan and is the Emperor of mankind the world over. He rules
the universe with Amaterasu-o-Mikami and Taka-mi-Musubi-no-

Mikami. Therefore Japan exists not only for Japan but for the whole world, and as a representation of the High Plain of Heaven must be expanded through the universe. Our national law is the representation of the Great Way of the High Plain of Heaven, which is the way of the Gods, and is creating the law of the Universe.

—Sadao Kiyohara, *Shintoshi,* "History of Shinto" (Tokyo, 1935). Cited by Otto D. Tolischus, *op. cit.*

A Mother Chastises a Child

It is the foremost axiom of the Way of the Gods that without the Japanese Emperor no nations of the world would have ever come into existence, because he proves the sole successor to the Progenitress of the whole cosmos—the Sun Goddess. He cares for all individuals and nations as if they were born as his own beloved children; he beseeches them to assist him wholeheartedly in the accomplishment of His divine mission bequeathed by his deified forebears.

However, should any perverse nation dare obstruct the Emperor in the carrying out of his celestial undertaking, he will resort, though reluctantly, to arms for the purpose of constraining that nation to come back to the right path and to collaborate with the Emperor once more with fidelity. It is just as a mother chastises a naughty child into obedience so that his conduct may be rectified. This noble sentiment is fully manifest in the Imperial Rescript issued December 8, 1941, which reads in part:

"It has been truly unavoidable and far from Our wishes that Our Empire has now been brought to cross swords with America and Britain."

—Professor Chikao Fujisawa, *The Great Shinto Purification Ritual and the Divine Mission of Nippon* (Tokyo, February 1942). Cited by Otto D. Tolischus, *op. cit.*

Second Coming

It may be intimated that the present Greater East Asia War is virtually a second descent of the Grandchild, who perpetuates himself in the everlasting life of the Emperor.

—*Ibid.*

The World of Light

It is my conviction that the mission of the Yamato race is to prevent the human race from becoming devilish, to rescue it from destruction and lead it to the world of light.

As we see the failure of modern civilization based mainly on European and American culture, which overestimates material things, falls into individualism and sinks into selfishness, we feel more and more the urgency of reviving the essential character of Japanese civilization, based on the natural development of the natural man and the principle of unity within the nation and thence unity of human society.

—Yosuke Matsuaka, *Showa Ishin*, "The Showa Restoration" (Tokyo, 1938). Cited by Otto D. Tolischus, *op. cit.*

The Hopes of Confucius

Now Chinese civilization, the so-called Hun civilization, in its basic elements and nature was entirely dependent on foreign influences. Especially its fundamental principles were developed and formed under the great spiritual leadership of Japan. In the spring and autumn period, during the decline of the Chou dynasty, when the national unity was disturbed by invasions of the Hun people from the South and West, Confucius, in the ancient Japanese cultural sphere of Shantung preached "the way of the ancient Kings" to revive the Chou dynasty. Truly, he was hoping for the continental revival of Imperial Japan.

Now, awaken the Chinese to the realization that they are Japanese, and in amalgamation of Japan and China, create a stable life and a Japanized New Continent!

—From *Shinajin wa Nipponjin nari*, "The Chinese are Japanese" (Tokyo: Asiatic Problems Society, 1939). Cited by Otto D. Tolischus, *op. cit.*

The Great Ideal

Needless to say, the aim of Japan's foreign policy is that of enabling all nations of the world each to take its own proper place in accordance with the spirit of Hakko Ichiu, the ideal which inspired the foundation of our Empire. The object of the three power pact, concluded between Japan, Germany and Italy, on September 27 last, is none other than the realization of the same great ideal.

—Foreign Minister Yosuke Matsuoka to Diet, January 20, 1941. Cited by Otto D. Tolischus, *op. cit.*

Japan's "Good Neighbor" Policy

Japan's foreign policy is in conformity with the spirit of Hakko Ichiu which inspires it, and the aim of which is universal peace and good neighborliness. But we must be quick in action in order to cope with the momentous needs of the times.

—Yosuke Matsuoka, Foreign Minister, on return from Moscow, April 22, 1941. Cited by Otto D. Tolischus, *op. cit.*

Life in Death

To give up one's life for the sake of the Emperor cannot be called self-sacrifice. It is rather discarding one's lesser self to live in the great Imperial Virtue, and exalting one's true life as a national subject.

—*The Basic Meaning of the National Policy* (Tokyo: Department of Education, 1939). Cited by Otto D. Tolischus, *op. cit.*

Great Japan

Great Japan! Great Japan!
Our seventy million citizens
Look up to the Emperor even as to God,
And love and serve him even as a parent.

—*National Reader for Ordinary Elementary Schools* (Tokyo: Department of Education, 1926). Quoted by D. C. Holtom, *The National Faith of Japan.*

The Land of the Gods

The just order of the world is concentrated in Japan as the land of the gods.
If this order were to take the shape of a mountain
It would excel all others like the eternal Fuji-san.

If it were to take the shape of water
It would be a measureless ocean surrounding the island of Japan.
If it were to take the shape of a flower
It would be a wild cherry blossom, the beauty of which is incompara-
    ble.
If it would take the shape of a sword
It would be a steel so sharp and fine as to cut through the hardest
    helmet.

—Famous Japanese poem quoted by Karl Lowith in "The Japanese Mind," an
    article in *Fortune* (December 1943).

6. The Week of Surrender
(AUGUST 12–19, 1945)

"For the Happiness of All Nations"

To our good and loyal subjects:

After pondering deeply the general trends of the world and the
actual conditions obtaining in our empire today, we have decided
to effect a settlement of the present situation by resorting to an extraordinary measure.

We have ordered our Government to communicate to the Govern-
ments of the United States, Great Britain, China and the Soviet
Union that our empire accepts the provisions of their joint declaration.

To strive for the common prosperity and happiness of all nations
as well as the security and well-being of our subjects is the solemn
obligation which has been handed down by our imperial ancestors
and which we lay close to the heart.

Indeed, we declared war on America and Britain out of our sincere desire to insure Japan's self-preservation and the stabilization

of East Asia, it being far from our thought either to infringe upon the sovereignty of other nations or to embark upon territorial aggrandizement.

But now the war has lasted for nearly four years. Despite the best that has been done by every one—the gallant fighting of the military and naval forces, the diligence and assiduity of our servants of the State and the devoted service of our 100,000,000 people—the war situation has developed not necessarily to Japan's advantage, while the general trends of the world have all turned against her interest.

Moreover, the enemy has begun to employ a new and most cruel bomb, the power of which to do damage is, indeed, incalculable, taking the toll of many innocent lives. Should we continue to fight, it would not only result in an ultimate collapse and obliteration of the Japanese nation, but also it would lead to the total extinction of human civilization.

Such being the case, how are we to save the millions of our subjects, or to atone ourselves before the hallowed spirits of our imperial ancestors? This is the reason why we have ordered the acceptance of the provisions of the joint declaration of the powers.

We cannot but express the deepest sense of regret to our allied nations of East Asia, who have consistently co-operated with the Empire towards the emancipation of East Asia.

The thought of those officers and men as well as others who have fallen in the fields of battle, those who died at their posts of duty, or those who met with death [otherwise] and all their bereaved families, pains our heart night and day.

The welfare of the wounded and the war sufferers and of those who have lost their home and livelihood is the object of our profound solicitude. The hardships and sufferings to which our nation is to be subjected hereafter will be certainly great.

We are keenly aware of the inmost feelings of all of you, our subjects. However, it is according to the dictates of time and fate that we have resolved to pave the way for a grand peace for all the generations to come by enduring the [unavoidable] and suffering what is insufferable. Having been able to safeguard and maintain the structure of the imperial state, we are always with you, our good and loyal subjects, relying upon your sincerity and integrity.

Beware most strictly of any outbursts of emotion that may engender needless complications, of any fraternal contention and strife that may create confusion, lead you astray and cause you to lose the confidence of the world.

Let the entire nation continue as one family from generation to generation, ever firm in its faith of the imperishableness of its divine land, and mindful of its heavy burden of responsibilities, and the long road before it. Unite your total strength to be devoted to the construction for the future. Cultivate the ways of rectitude, nobility of spirit, and work with resolution so that you may enhance the innate glory of the imperial state and keep pace with the progress of the world.

—Radio Rescript read by Emperor Hirohito, August 15, 1945.

Bushido and the Atomic Bomb

Rather than accuse those who used the fateful atomic bomb, it will be more Bushido-like to give due credit to the scientific superiority of those who were capable of producing such a weapon. It would be much to our good if we could accuse ourselves of being so capable. The Japanese must now learn to look into the face of reality. There is a reason for victory just as much as there are causes for defeat. We had neglected to gauge our limitations and we did not know enough of our adversary.

—*Yomiuri Hochi*, Tokyo newspaper, August 16, 1945.

The Voice of Reason

There is no use thinking of what is past. Once the imperial decision is given us, we must entrust everything to the mercy of His Imperial Majesty.

At this time the national feeling is no doubt a desire to rise anew and in the years to come to advance science to the point where some weapon superior to the new type bomb may be devised in revenge. However, we must cast aside this narrow viewpoint, and, no matter how difficult life may be, we must adopt an entirely new and broad outlook and liquidate the military for the sake of the Japanese people today.

The fact that the blood of our warriors was unable to set the world on a new path can be seen in the imperial message at this time as a revelation of God.

I believe that we should now divert all our efforts to the enhancement of culture through science. This is the path for the Japanese people who must start out anew.

In this "culture" we must show superiority in the science of living and also in the science of food production. Furthermore, by the grace of His Majesty, we must look up to the imperial way and entrust ourselves to His Majesty's vast and infinite will, unswervingly following the path of righteousness.

Furthermore, a new great religion and a great religious leader must be born to give succor to the bewildered populace.

—Statement by Lieutenant General Reickichi Tada, President of the Japanese Board of Technology, August 15, 1945, following Emperor Hirohito's surrender rescript. (An hour after this statement was issued, Domei, the official Japanese news agency, broadcast instructions to newspaper editors not to print it or further disseminate it.)

"This Is Temporary"

We have bowed to the enemy's material and scientific power. However, in spiritual power we have not lost yet. We do not think the way we have thought has been wrong. We are still fighting for the independence of East Asia. We have lost, but this is temporary.

—Kusuo Oya, Japan Broadcasting Corporation, August 16, 1945.

The Quintessence of the Nation

To the officers and men of the imperial forces:

Three years and eight months have elapsed since we declared war on the United States and Britain. During this time our beloved men of the Army and Navy have been sacrificing their lives valiantly on disease-stricken and barren lands and on tempestuous waters in the blazing sun, and for this we are deeply grateful.

Now that the Soviet Union has entered the war against us, to continue the war under the present internal and external conditions would be only to increase needlessly the ravages of war finally to the point of endangering the very foundation of the empire's existence.

With that in mind, and although the fighting spirit of the imperial army and navy is as high as ever, and with a view to maintaining and protecting our noble national polity, we are about to make peace with the United States, Britain, the Soviet Union and Chungking.

To a large number of loyal and brave officers and men of the imperial forces who have died in battle and from sicknesses goes our deepest grief. At the same time we believe the loyalty and achievements of you officers and men of the imperial forces will for all time be the quintessence of our nation.

We trust that you officers and men of the imperial forces will comply with our intention and will maintain a solid unit and strict discipline in your movements and that you will bear the hardest of all difficulties, bear the unbearable and leave an everlasting foundation of the nation.

—Rescript of Emperor Hirohito to the imperial forces, August 17, 1945.

"The Light of the Ideal"

The light of the ideal for the racial emancipation enkindled by the War of Greater East Asia will keep burning despite the tragic finale of the conflict.

—Broadcast from Tokyo, directed to East Asiatic peoples, August 17, 1945, two days after Emperor Hirohito's surrender rescript.

"The National Might"

Local governors, school principals, teachers, and students, should be determined to recover the national might from the scorched earth.

—Broadcast from the Japanese Ministry of Education, Tokyo, August 17, 1945.

"For the Revival of the Japanese Race"

To the spirits of members of the Special Attack [suicide] Corps: I express my deep gratitude to you who have fought so well. Ever convinced of final victory, you fell gallantly as human bullets. But that conviction finally has not been fulfilled. With my death I desire to make atonement to the souls of my former subordinates and to members of their bereaved families.

I also have a message to young men at large. If my death should prove to be any admonition to you to be cautious and endure all hardships, always aware that any ill-advised conduct will invite disastrous consequences, thereby following His Imperial Majesty's will, I shall be very happy.

In your patience and endurance never lose your qualities as Japanese. You are the treasure of the nation. Attend properly to your peacetime circumstances and maintain steadfastly the spirit of the Special Attack Corps by your utmost for the revival of the Japanese race and for world peace.

—Note written by Vice Admiral Takijiro Onishi, formerly Commander-in-Chief of Japanese forces in the Philippines, before committing hara-kiri, August 17, 1945.

"Racial Spirit Has Been Established"

The situation confronting us at present is indeed regrettable to us who devoted our efforts to prosecuting the Greater East Asia war. Through the granting of His Majesty's gracious decision, however, our national policy, which is the foundation of our nation, is safe. Thinking of this, I am moved to tears of gratitude.

Today, when the imperial decision has been granted, the way has become clear. There is need for renewed efforts, without any misconception of loyalty and treason, for the future construction of a new Japan. It goes without saying that it is necessary to change speedily our way of thinking. The price that must be paid for this defeat in battle is very high, but as the consequence of such an all-out war, that cannot be helped.

We cannot, however, build a future Japan if we are overoptimistic now. We must have the courage to face the present severe situation. Have we Japanese not been overoptimistic in the past in our foreign policy? Can we say there have never been any errors in the prosecution of the war caused by overoptimistic thinking? If we are lax at this time when we are face to face with defeat, it will be impossible to pave our way to a better future.

There is need to investigate thoroughly the conditions of the Potsdam Declaration and to understand the terms.

With regard to the high price of the war, I would like to discuss whether or not it was worth the price. I shall not go into details but will consider it only from the diplomatic standpoint. This war has proved that Japan, on the basis of maintaining friendly relations with the nations of the world, can rebuild herself by peaceful, though strenuous, efforts. Racial spirit, respecting each other's position based on friendship among the Greater East Asia nations, has been established. These have been the great results of the war.

From the establishment of such a spirit and faith in the spirit are born the great efforts to plunge into the future.

From what then, does the reconstruction for the future begin? The first thing is to face the present crisis and launch forth with courage on the path of moral principles. To carry out the terms of the Potsdam Declaration manfully and with good grace, is, I believe, the first step toward building the future.

We cannot say that there have been no examples in our history wherein the way for the nation's future was opened by surmounting troubles both at home and abroad. This is not an identical example, but at the time of the Meiji Restoration, when reverence of the Emperor and expulsion of the barbarians was debated, an imperial decision was granted, whereby through the policy of a foreign nation, Japan's future was laid open in a day.

Reflecting how in the Meiji Restoration, the people united together under His Imperial Majesty to face the troubles both within and without and made way for Japan's future by co-operating with foreigners, there is no need to harbor gloomy thoughts over the present situation. If we carry on with perseverance and with clear understanding, Japan's future is sure to brighten.

—Statement to the Japanese People by Foreign Minister Mamoru Shigemitsu, August 18, 1945.

"The Grave Mistake"

[The Japanese nation must] reflect seriously upon the grave mistake it made in the past of following Government leadership blindly and without proper criticism. Only by active participation of the people in politics can a change in national thought be effected and a new outlook for Japan established.

—Editorial in Tokyo *Asahi*, August 19, 1945.

"The People Know"

The first matter that comes to mind is the stern self-reflection of those leaders of today who brought their nation into the present state of affairs.

The people have studied the past political history and know just what it was that led the present leaders to become the unsuitable leaders that they are for the present state of affairs. The people know how to select their own leaders and how to make up their own minds in such matters.

—Editorial in Tokyo *Mainichi*, August 19, 1945.

7. Doctrines of Sectarian Shinto

The Way of Nature
(Shinto Honkyoku)

Shinto, or Kamu-Nagara, is a Way of Nature. This does not mean that it is a primitive and inferior nature worship. It means that Shinto is a spontaneous and real manifestation of the true nature of things, taking form in human affairs in proportion as this nature is given opportunity for sincere and unperverted expression. Thus, Shinto can be explained from the standpoint of the true, the good, and the beautiful.

The truth of Shinto is to be seen in the inevitability of its underlying doctrine. This is apparent on consideration of the real significance of the great deities introduced in the oldest Yamato literature. Ame-no-Minaka-Nushi-no-Kami [The Deity Who is Lord of the

Center of Heaven], the first god named in the *Kojiki,* is correctly understood as the central existence of the universe, the primary source of all things, both animate and inert. All the phenomena presented to human senses are the manifestations in time of this absolute god. The Absolute functions in time in the form of the two-fold creation *kami,* Taka-Mimusubi-no-Kami and Kami-Musubi-no-Kami. These two beings represent activities of opposite kinds, from which the phenomenal world has had its rise. The positive-negative, or male-female, potency appears in Japanese history as the great father and mother of the race, Izanagi and Izanami, from whom is born the Sun Goddess, Amaterasu-Omikami, who in turn is the progenetrix of the Imperial Family and the Japanese people. Amaterasu-Omikami, in her position among the historical personages of Japan, is like the sun in heaven about which planetary bodies revolve. The aptness of this solar metaphor accounts for the sun imagery of the early mythology. The statements just made point to undeniable facts in Japanese history. This is not a matter of mere chance or coincidence, but is so by inner necessity. This is the Truth of the Way of the Gods.

Then there is the Good. The original positive-negative creative potencies of Old Shinto are the two beings or forces named above, Taka-Mimusubi-no-Kami and Kami-Musubi-no-Kami. The word *musubi* as employed in their descriptive titles expresses the original and correct idea of their functions. *Musu* means "to have life"; *bi* is "spirit." The total word means "life-spirit" or "life-giving spirit." They are thus the creative energy of the universe which appears as life. They are the living, changing, progressing life itself. There is an utmost good and this goodness is a part of the Way of the Gods.

In the third place there is the Beautiful. The world of nature bears within itself a spontaneous beauty. In particular the land of Japan reveals in its endowment of loveliness the very essence of this natural beauty. Furthermore, in the simplicity, the dignity and the charm of the shrines, where the most impressive attitudes of the Japanese spirit are nourished, and in the stately worship of the gods, one may see an untrammelled revelation of the undefiled and unpretentious grace which lies at the heart of nature. This is the Beauty of the Way of the Gods.

Another distinguishing characteristic of Shinto lies in what may be called corporateness. In many other religions men as individuals are set over against the gods. In Shinto we are merged with our fellow-men about us and with the unseen host of ancestors that have gone before us and, as a great spiritual body, united with the divine. We are made of one line with the *kami* through our ancestors. We are united, divine and human, past and present, into a totality of warp and woof, interpenetrated and coherent. We are recipients from the *kami* by direct descent through the ancestors of a specific endowment of tendencies and aptitudes, and if we permit this innate disposition to find normal expression, we achieve spontaneously, filial piety, loyalty, and love of fellowmen. There is no conflict of individualism here, and no placing of the gods outside the world of men. We are all one with our ancestors and, as a race, a part of divine nature. Accordingly it is involved in the natural unfolding of the Way of the Gods that we should be prudent regarding self, that we should make room for personal development, that we should keep household and business in order, that we should contribute to national progress and anticipate the future peace of the whole world. This is true ancestral-ism. The ancestor worship of the ancient Greeks presented similar features but it was smothered in an invasion of monotheism. It is common for monotheism to decry ancestralism as an expression of ignorance, but genuine ancestralism, far from being inferior, is in reality a spontaneous expression of the truth, the goodness, and the beauty in nature. There are three things which are inseparable: our race which is our ancestral inheritance, our country, which is our ancestral home, and our faith, wherewith our loyalties are sustained. This is the true Way of the Gods.

Finally, Shinto has been called the Wordless Way. This means that practice is more important than mere words, that the hand is mightier than the mouth, that deeds are weightier than rhetoric, that actualities are the greatest of arguments. This practical tendency reflects an in-born aptitude of the Japanese people. The finest expression of this passion for reality is in the patriotism with which we guard and protect the welfare of our country—a patriotism which, on the one hand, is centralized in devotion to our Imperial Family and which exalts our race and supports our homes and our magnificent national organization on the other. All this is not a formal achievement, the-oretically fostered with words, but is the natural registration of our racial characteristics, manifested in all its purity in the past, handed on unimpaired through our ancestors and maintained without flaw in the present. This is true Shinto.

—Kanzaki Kazusaku, *The Doctrine of Shinto Honkyoku,* in *Uchu* (January 1930). Quoted by D. C. Holtom, *The National Faith of Japan.*

Ten Precepts of Shinri Kyo

1. Do not transgress the will of the gods.
2. Do not forget your obligations to ancestors.
3. Do not transgress the decrees of the State.
4. Do not forget the profound goodness of the gods whereby misfortune is averted and sickness is healed.
5. Do not forget that the world is one great family.
6. Do not forget the limitations of your own person.
7. Even though others become angry, do not become angry yourself.
8. Do not be slothful in your business.
9. Do not be a person who brings blame to the teaching.
10. Do not be carried away by foreign teaching.

—Translated from an article by Sano Itohiko in *Uchu* (January 1930). Quoted in D. C. Holtom, *The National Faith of Japan.*

Tenets of Taisha Kyo

1. To make our hearts upright and to govern our bodies.
2. To have compassion on those who are less fortunate than ourselves and, by giving instruction to those who defy the divine will, to lead them to enter our upright fellowship.
3. To devise ways of realizing genuine happiness and of attaining that spiritual power which pierces through all things both revealed and unrevealed and which exists both now and hereafter. Therefore those who have entered into this church, while reverently thanking and worshipping the divine goodness, should first and foremost accept and embody the divine purpose of loving their fellowmen, should keep in mind the duty of improvement and achievement, and should give expression to moral sincerity. If one is merely greedy of divine blessings and is regardless of human duties, if one is selfishly lacking in concern for others, such a person desecrates the divine goodness and defies the divine purpose of love

for others. He does not understand human duty and betrays the principles of the church. One should abandon the distinction of "other" and "self" and should consummate a heart of compassion for his fellowmen, ever mindful of the fact that acts of knowing the truth and doing it are not performed merely for the sake of one's own interests, ever knowing that suffering and blessing, advantage and disadvantage, are to be shared widely with others and not in violation of the divine purpose of compassion and equality and not in injury of the good faith of one's fellow men. We believe that these are the main principles of human morals and the gist of one's duty in giving thanks for divine blessings.

Therefore the believers of our church, by adding to and extending the benevolence of spirit which we have received as a natural endowment and by showing gratitude for divine goodness, should perform in the world the common duties of humanity. In the world to come such people will shine with the glory of those who have become Kami.

—Kono Shozo, *Shinto Taiko,* "The Gist of Shinto" (Tokyo, 1927). Quoted in D. C. Holtom, *The National Faith of Japan.*

Essential Doctrines of Shusei Ha

1. The myriad forms and manifold network of the universe, including man and the moral world and all things whatsoever, have come into being through the spiritual activity of the triune deity of creation, and the soul of man is of one substance with this heavenly deity. The principles of this sect consist in the protecting and the careful fostering of this superlatively good soul.

2. The two deities, Izanagi and Izanami, at the command of the deities of heaven, improved and consolidated this country, including peoples, creatures, grasses, trees, and all things whatsoever. Accordingly in *shuri kosei* [*shuri*—"strengthening," *kosei*—"making secure"] lies the fundamental law of the evolution of the universe and, in truth, the progress of mankind and the advancement of society are due to the operation of this one principle.

3. *Shuri kosei* is also the process whereby man faithfully observes the moral law and the means by which the affairs of family and society

are administered. This purpose is brought to realization through the glorious and radiant virtue of Amaterasu-Omikami.

—*Ibid.*, p. 207.

Precepts of Taisei Kyo

1. To observe the worship of the kami of heaven and earth and the distant worship of the spirits of successive generations of emperors and of the deities of the Imperial sanctuaries.
2. To observe the divine commandments which are as imperishable as heaven and earth and to strengthen the national organization.
3. To make clear the way of human conduct as revealed by Heaven.
4. To train ourselves in devotion to the true law and to strengthen the foundations of inner tranquillity.
5. To unite the temporal and spiritual worlds with a clear understanding of the meaning of life and death.
6. To study science and technique and to encourage business enterprise.
7. To carry on religious rites and ceremonies after the manner of successive generations of royal courts.

—*Ibid.*, p. 212.

Tenets of Mitake Kyo

1. To follow the instructions of the teachers of the church, to exemplify divine reason and human benevolence in conduct and not to violate the sacred will of the great Gods of Mitake.
2. Especially to preserve in their hearts reverence for the gods and love of country, to honor and obey the Emperor, to conform to the decrees of the state and, by constant diligence in business to lay the foundations of a prosperous land and a strong soldiery.
3. To follow the teachings of the great deities, to keep the peace in patience, never to slander others, and to reveal modesty and reverence in conduct.
4. Always in uprightness and integrity to value the truth and never to speak words of deception.
5. To practice fraternity and be as brothers together, and as evidence

of the possession of such spirit, to labor to succor travelers, of whatever country they may be, in their troubles and sickness.

—*Uchu* (January 1930). Quoted in D. C. Holtom, *The National Faith of Japan*, p. 231.

Ten Precepts of Shinshu Kyo

1. Worship the great deities of this sect.
2. Pacify thy spirit, for it is part of the spirit of deity.
3. Practice the Way of the Gods.
4. Revere the divine origin of the state.
5. Be loyal to the ruler.
6. Be zealous in filial piety toward thy parents.
7. Be kind to others.
8. Be diligent in business.
9. Preserve steadfastness within thy breast.
10. Cleanse away the rust of thy body.

—Sugano Masateru, *Kyogi no shori*, "A Guide to Teaching" (Tokyo, 1928). Quoted in D. C. Holtom, *The National Faith of Japan*, p. 236.

Proverbs of Kurosumi Kyo

When the Heart of Amaterasu-Omikami and the heart of man are one, this is eternal life.

When the Heart of Amaterasu-Omikami and our hearts are undivided, then there is no such thing as death.

When we realize that all things are the activity of Heaven, then we know neither pain nor care.

Forsake flesh and self and will, and cling to the One Truth of Heaven and Earth.

Happy is the man who cultivates the things that are hidden and lets the things that are apparent take care of themselves.

Of a truth there is no such thing as sickness.

If you foster a spirit that regards both good and evil as blessings, then the body spontaneously becomes healthy.

In truth the Way is easy. He who abandons self-knowledge and spends his days in thankfulness grows neither old nor weary. He knows only joy and happiness.

Both heaven and hell come from one's own heart. Oh the sadness of wandering in the devil's prayers.

If in one's heart one is a kami, then one becomes a kami; if in one's heart one is a Buddha, then one becomes a Buddha; if in one's heart one is a serpent, then one becomes a serpent.

Nothing in all the world calls forth such gratitude as sincerity. Through oneness in sincerity the men of the four seas are brothers.

All men are brothers. All receive the blessings of the same heaven. The suffering of others is my suffering; the good of others is my good.

—*Kurosumi Kyosho,* "The Texts of Kurozumi Kyo." D. C. Holtom, *The National Faith of Japan,* p. 252.

Proverbs of Konko Kyo

God is the Great Parent of your real self. Faith is just like filial obedience to your parents.

Free yourself from doubt. Open and behold the great broad way of truth. You will find your life quickened in the midst of the goodness of God.

With God there is neither day nor night, neither far nor near. Pray to him straight forwardly and with a heart of faith.

With sincerity there is no such thing as failure. When failure to accomplish your purpose in prayer arises then know that something is lacking in sincerity.

Bring not suffering upon yourself by indulgence in selfishness.

One who would walk in the Way of Truth must close the eyes of the flesh and open the eyes of the spirit.

In all the world there is no such thing as a stranger.

Your body is not for your own freedom.

Do not bring bitterness to your own heart by anger at the things that are past.

Do not profess love with your lips while you harbor hatred in your heart.

One should not be mindful of suffering in his own life and unmindful of suffering in the lives of others.

—*Konko Kyo Kyoten,* "The Sacred Texts of Konko Kyo" (Okayama City, 1929). D. C. Holtom, *The National Faith of Japan,* pp. 261, 262.

Part III

NOTES

BIBLIOGRAPHY

INDEX

Notes

(Throughout these notes the abbreviation *T.A.S.J.* stands for Transactions of the Asiatic Society of Japan, published in Tokyo by the Society, and in London by Kegan Paul, Trench, Trubner and Co.)

Holders of the publication rights who granted permission to use texts quoted in this book are listed in the notes below.

PART I

CHAPTER 1

1. D. C. Holtom, *Modern Japan and Shinto Nationalism* (Chicago: University of Chicago Press, 1943).

CHAPTER 2

1. Inazo Nitobe, *The Japanese Nation* (New York: G. P. Putnam's Sons, 1912), p. 52.
2. H. G. Quaritch Wales, "Shinto's Place in World Culture," *Asia and the Americas* (April 1945).
3. D. C. Holtom, "The Meaning of Kami," *Monumenta Nipponica,* Vol. III, Nos. 1 and 2, and Vol. IV, No. 2 (Tokyo: Sophia University, 1940–41).
4. Saeki Ariyoshi, in *Shinto Encyclopedia* (Tokyo, 1937). Translated and cited by D. C. Holtom, *op. cit.*
5. D. C. Holtom, *op. cit.*
6. Geoffrey Gorer, "Themes in Japanese Culture," *Transactions of the New York Academy of Sciences* (March 1943).
7. *Nihongi,* Vol. II, translated by W. G. Aston (London: Kegan Paul, Trench, Trubner and Co., 1896).
8. D. C. Holtom, *Modern Japan and Shinto Nationalism.*

CHAPTER 3

1. W. G. Aston, *Shinto, the Way of the Gods* (New York: Longmans, Green and Co., 1905).
2. Percival Lowell, "Esoteric Shinto," *T.A.S.J.,* Vol. XXI (1893).

CHAPTER 4

1. Inazo Nitobe, *Lectures on Japan* (Tokyo: Kenkyusha, 1936).

CHAPTER 5

1. W. E. Griffis, *The Religions of Japan* (New York: Charles Scribner's Sons, 1896).

CHAPTER 6

1. G. B. Sansom, *Japan: A Short Cultural History* (New York: D. Appleton-Century Co., 1943).
2. Harper, Havelock Coates, and Ryugaku Ishizuka, *Honen, the Buddhist Saint* (Kyoto: Chionin, 1925).
3. Kaiten Nukariya, *The Religion of the Samurai: A Study of Zen Philosophy and Discipline in China and Japan* (London: Luzac and Co., 1913).
4. W. G. Aston, *A History of Japanese Literature* (New York: D. Appleton-Century Co., 1937).
5. Inazo Nitobe, *Bushido, the Soul of Japan* (Philadelphia: The Leeds and Biddle Co., 1900).
6. Tasuku Harada, *The Faith of Japan* (New York: The Macmillan Co., 1914).
7. United Press dispatch in the New York *World-Telegram*, June 6, 1945.
8. Quotations in this paragraph are from Tasuku Harada, *The Faith of Japan*.
9. Yoshi S. Kuno, *Japanese Expansion on the Asiatic Continent* (Berkeley: University of California Press, 1937).
10. Koya Nakamura, *History of Japan*, translated by M. G. Mori (Tokyo: Board of Tourist Industry, Japanese Government Railways, 1939).

CHAPTER 7

1. Kamo-no-Mabuchi, *The Revival of Pure Shintau*, translated by Sir Ernest Satow, *T.A.S.J., Reprints*, Vol. II (1927).
2. *Ibid.*
3. *Ibid.*
4. This digest of Ichikawa's doctrine is paraphrased from Ernest Satow, *op. cit.*
5. Hirata Atsutane, *Zoku Shindo Taii*, "The Great Principles of Shinto." Text in *Shinto Daijiten*, "The Shinto Encyclopedia," Vol. I (Tokyo, 1939). Translated and cited by D. C. Holtom, *Modern Japan and Shinto Nationalism*.

CHAPTER 8

1. Arthur May Knapp, *Feudal and Modern Japan* (Yokohama: The Advertiser Publishing Co., 1906).
2. *Ibid.*
3. G. B. Sansom, *Japan: A Short Cultural History* (New York: D. Appleton-Century Co., 1943).
4. Otto D. Tolischus, *Through Japanese Eyes* (New York: Reynal and Hitchcock, 1945).

CHAPTER 9

1. Shozo Kono, *Jingishi Gaiyo*, "An Outline of Shinto History" (Tokyo, 1927). Translated and cited by D. C. Holtom, *Modern Japan and Shinto Nationalism*.
2. *Ibid.*

3. Hirobumi Ito, *Commentaries on the Constitution* (Tokyo, 1889). Translated and cited by D. C. Holtom, *Modern Japan and Shinto Nationalism*, p. 9.

4. Nagao Ariga, *Shinto Kokkyo Ron*, "Shinto as a State Religion" in *Tetsugaku Zasshi*, "Philosophical Magazine" (June 1910). Translated and cited by D. C. Holtom, *The National Faith of Japan* (London: Kegan Paul, Trench, Trubner and Co., 1938; New York: E. P. Dutton and Co., 1938).

5. Arthur May Knapp, *Feudal and Modern Japan*.

6. Hillis Lory, *Japan's Military Masters* (New York: The Viking Press, 1943).

7. G. Etsujiro Uyehara, *The Political Development of Japan, 1867–1909* (New York, 1910). Quoted by D. C. Holtom, *Modern Japan and Shinto Nationalism*.

8. Shinkichi Uesugi, *Kokutai Seika no Hatsuyo*, "Exalting the Essence of the National Structure" (Tokyo, 1919). Quoted by D. C. Holtom, *Modern Japan and Shinto Nationalism*.

9. Sadao Araki (then Minister of Education), "State and Education," *Contemporary Japan* (December 1938). Quoted by D. C. Holtom, *Modern Japan and Shinto Nationalism*.

10. Genchi Kato, *Waga Kokutai to Shinto*, "Our National Structure and Shinto" (Tokyo, 1919). Quoted by D. C. Holtom, *Modern Japan and Shinto Nationalism*.

11. Genchi Kato, *A Study of Shinto, the Religion of the Japanese Nation* (Tokyo: The Meiji Japan Society, 1926).

12. *Time*, May 21, 1945.

13. John Morris, *Traveler from Tokyo* (New York: Sheridan House, 1944).

14. H. J. Timperley, *Japan, A World Problem* (New York: John Day, 1942).

15. Tetsujiro Inouye, *Shukyo to Kyoku no Shototsu*, "The Conflict of Religion and Education" (Tokyo, 1932). Translated and cited by D. C. Holtom, *Modern Japan and Shinto Nationalism*, p. 81.

16. Hiroyuki Kato, *Waga Kokutai Kyo*, "Our National Structure and Christianity." Translated and cited by D. C. Holtom, *Modern Japan and Shinto Nationalism*.

17. Cited by Basil Hall Chamberlain, *The Invention of a New Religion* (London: Watts and Co., 1912).

18. Ebira Ebisawa, in *Bulletin of the National Christian Council of Japan*, translated by Bishop J. C. Mann (June 1939). Quoted by D. C. Holtom, *Modern Japan and Shinto Nationalism*.

19. Karl Lowith, "The Japanese Mind," *Fortune* (December 1943).

CHAPTER 10

1. The following list is from D. C. Holtom, *The National Faith of Japan*.

2. *Japanese Government Documents, 1867–1889. T.A.S.J.*, Vol. XLII. Part I (Tokyo, 1914).

3. Inazo Nitobe, *Lectures on Japan* (Tokyo: Kenkyusha, 1936).

PART II

CHAPTER 1

1. All selections from the *Kojiki*, with the exception of Section IV, are taken from the translation by Basil Hall Chamberlain, in *T.A.S.J.*, Supplement to Vol. X (1882).
2. Translated by William George Aston, *Shinto, the Way of the Gods* (New York: Longmans, Green and Co., 1905).
3. Selections from the *Nihongi* are reprinted from *The Nihongi*, translated from the original Chinese and Japanese by W. G. Aston. *Transactions and Proceedings of the Japan Society*, Supplement I (London: Kegan Paul, Trench, Trubner and Co., 1896).
4. Selections from the *Manyoshu* reprinted from *The Manyoshu: One Thousand Poems* (Tokyo: The Iwanami Shoten, 1940; Chicago: University of Chicago Press, 1941).
5. Condensation of a synthesis of three *norito*, Nos. 16, 17, and 19, of the *Engi Shiki*, used at the monthly service in the sixth month. Translated by Ernest Satow in "Ancient Japanese Rituals," *T.A.S.J.*, Vol. VII, IX.
6. The *norito* is read by a church dignitary who is supposedly speaking for the emperor. The "He" thus refers to the emperor.

CHAPTER 2

1. All selections from the *Shoku Nihongi* marked [1] are from *Shoku Nihongi*, "Chronicles of Japan," translated by J. B. Snellen, *T.A.S.J.*, Vol. XI, 2nd series (1934). Note the mixture of Buddhism and Shinto.
2. Selections from the *Shoku Nihongi* marked [2] are from *The Imperial Edicts in the Shoku Nihongi*. Translated with introduction and notes by G. B. Sansom, *T.A.S.J.*, Vol. I, 2nd series (1924).
3. Extract from the *Jinkoshotoku*, cited by W. G. Aston in *A History of Japanese Literature* (New York: D. Appleton–Century Co., 1937).
4. Extract from *Taiheiki Somoku*, "Record of Great Peace," cited by W. G. Aston, *A History of Japanese Literature*. The great wind which destroyed the Mongol fleet was called a *Kami Kaze* (god-sent wind) by the Japanese. In World War II the term was applied to suicide pilots.
5. From remarks by Ernest Satow at a Meeting of the Asiatic Society of Japan, October 27, 1877, *T.A.S.J.*, Vol. VI, Part I (1888). Note the thorough admixture of Shinto, Confucianism, and Buddhism in the remarks of this seventeenth-century shogun.
6. All selections from *Wa Rongo* are reprinted from "The Wa Rongo or Japanese Analects," translated by Genchi Kato, *T.A.S.J.*, Vol. XLV, Part II (1917).
7. Extracts from Ernest W. Clement, "Instructions of a Mito Prince to His Retainers" (a translation of Mitsukuni's *Giko Meirei*), *T.A.S.J.*, Vol. XXVI (1898).
8. Extracts from the *Shundai Zatsuwa*. Cited by W. G. Aston, *A History of Japanese Literature*.

CHAPTER 3

1. Digest of Mabuchi's teachings from E. M. Satow, *The Revival of Pure Shintau, T.A.S.J.*, Vol. III, Part I, Appendix.
2. Digest of Motoöri's teachings by E. M. Satow, *The Revival of Pure Shintau.*
3. Extract from the *Tamagatsuma.* Cited by W. G. Aston, *A History of Japanese Literature*, p. 330.
4. Ernest Satow, *The Revival of Pure Shintau.*
5. From the *Lectures of Hirata Atsutane,* translated by R. J. Kirby in "Ancestral Worship in Japan," *T.A.S.J.*, Vol. XXXVIII, Part IV (1911).
6. Ernest Satow, *The Revival of Pure Shintau.*
7. Extracts from "Diary of an Official of the Bakufu," *T.A.S.J.*, Vol. VII, 2nd series (1930).

CHAPTER 4

1. Reprinted (with the exception of the last selection) from *Japanese Government Documents, T.A.S.J.*, Vol. XLII, Part I (1914).
2. Cited by Hillis Lory in *Japan's Military Masters* (New York: Viking Press, 1943).

Annotated Bibliography

The following books, articles, and pamphlets recommended for further reading cover many phases of the Japanese problem discussed in this book and are all works which have been consulted in its preparation. Some of them duplicate some of the information in others, but since many of them are now rare, an extensive list is given in the hope that enough of them may easily be located by anyone to make further study of Shinto and its implications possible to the average reader. The abbreviation *T.A.S.J.* in this bibliography stands for *Transactions of the Asiatic Society of Japan,* published in Tokyo by the Society, and in London by Kegan Paul, Trench, Trubner and Co., Ltd.

Aston, W. G. *A History of Japanese Literature.* New York: D. Appleton–Century Co., 1937.

Since the earliest books of the Japanese are the classics of Shinto, and since most of Japan's later literature reflects her religious beliefs, this, the outstanding book in its field, is essential to the study of Shinto. It includes many selections from Japanese texts.

———— (tr.). *Nihongi. Chronicles of Japan, from the Earliest Times to* A.D. 697. *Transactions and Proceedings of the Japan Society.* Supplement I. 2 vols. London: Kegan Paul, Trench, Trubner and Co., 1896.

The second of Japan's two earliest books of history and legend, and basic book of Shinto. It is on the cosmological myth related in this book and the *Kojiki* that Japan's doctrine of divinity, racial superiority, and world-conquering destiny is based.

———— "Shinto." Article in *Encyclopedia of Religion and Ethics.* Edited by James Hastings. New York: Charles Scribner's Sons, 1922.

An excellent historical outline and interpretation.

———— *Shinto, the Way of the Gods.* New York: Longmans, Green and Co., 1905.

The outstanding work of its time for the study of Old Shinto and still a standard work. Written as it was before the strength of State Shinto had begun to be felt, it underestimates the importance of state indoctrination. Indeed the closing paragraphs say that "the official cult . . . has little vitality. . . . As a national religion Shinto is almost extinct." Also the findings of more recent scholarship may set aside some of Aston's conclusions. Yet it remains as a clear and fascinating study of the basic aspects of Shinto, and is noteworthy for being one of the earliest detailed studies in English in its field.

Barton, George A. *The Religions of the World*. Chicago: University of Chicago Press, 1920.

The Chapter on "The Religions of Japan" includes a short discussion of Shinto and the impress made upon it by Buddhism.

Borton, Hugh. *Japan Since 1931*. New York: Institute of Pacific Relations, 1940.

A review of the political developments of Japan during the decade before the attack on Pearl Harbor, with informative discussion of the control of government by the militarists and the regimentation of public opinion.

Buchanan, Rev. D. C. *Inari: Its Origin, Development, and Nature*. T.A.S.J. Vol. XII. 2nd series. December 1935.

An intensive short study of the cult of Inari, worship of the food goddess, first conceived as the spirit of rice, and later symbolized by the fox.

Chamberlain, Basil Hall. "Notes on Chinese and Japanese Art by Motoöri." *T.A.S.J.* Vol. XII. Part III.

This translation of a treatise on art by one of the three leaders of the Pure Shinto Revival reveals much of the revival's point of view toward China.

———— (tr.) *The Kojiki, or Record of Ancient Matters*. T.A.S.J. Vol. X. Supplement.

Japan's earliest book and the most important book of Old Shinto.

Clary, William W. *Japan: the Warnings and Prophecies of Lafcadio Hearn*. "Claremont Oriental Studies," No. 5. Claremont, California, April 1943.

A review of Lafcadio Hearn's interpretations of the Japanese, whom he called "a race . . . five thousand years at least emotionally behind us."

Clement, Ernest W. (tr.) "Instructions of a Mito Prince to his Retainers." *T.A.S.J.* Vol. XXVI. December 1898.

In this seventeenth-century pamphlet, written by a lord of the Tokugawa period to his Samurai, is contained much of the code of Bushido which formed so great a part of Japanese feudal ethics and has been so influential in the national tendency to worship the emperor and glorify war since that time. It is also an excellent revelation of the thorough admixture of Shinto, Buddhism, and Confucianism in Japanese thought of this period.

Coates, Harper Havelock, and Ryugaku Ishizuka. *Honen, the Buddhist Saint*. Kyoto: Chionin, 1925.

An exhaustive biography of Honen Shonin, founder of the Jodo Sect of Japanese Buddhism, which greatly influenced Japanese thought in the Middle Ages, and left a deep impress on Shinto. With discussions of Honen's teachings, and extracts from his works.

Colegrove, Kenneth W. *Militarism in Japan*. New York: World Peace Foundation, 1936.

A discussion of the military tradition in Japan, military control of government, and emperor worship.

Crucifixion of the Twenty-Six in 1597. T.A.S.J. Vol. XLIV. Part I. 1916.

Account of the crucifixion of twenty-six Catholic missionaries on the order of Hideyoshi, sixteenth-century regent of Japan, with valuable comments on the attitudes of feudal Japan.

Daisetz Teitaro Suzuki. *Japanese Buddhism*. Board of Tourist Industry, Japanese Government Railways, 1938.

A brief discussion of the rise of Buddhism in Japan by a modern Japanese scholar.

Diary of an Official of the Bakufu. (Name of translator not given.) *T.A.S.J*. Vol. VII. 2nd series. December 1930.

Translation of a diary kept by an unidentified official of the shogun's government during the visit of Perry to Japan, recounting details of Perry's conversations with the "Lord Rector."

Embree, John F. *The Japanese*. Washington: The Smithsonian Institution, 1943.

An excellent forty-two page discussion of the general characteristics, habits, and background, of the Japanese people, with a short exposition of the part Shinto plays in their national consciousness. With sixteen pages of photographs.

——————— *The Japanese Nation*. New York: Farrar and Rinehart, Inc., 1945.

A careful study of the major social, economic, and cultural forces which sway modern Japan, with due attention to the powerful function of State Shinto in Japanese education. There is also a good chapter on the influence upon modern Japan of the Tokugawa period.

Fleisher, Wilfrid. *What to Do With Japan*. New York: Doubleday, Doran and Co., 1945.

A realistic appraisal of the ideological strength of Japan at war, with factual comment on the contribution of Shinto to that strength and speculation on the importance of emperor worship in postwar regulation of the Japanese.

Fortune, Editors of. *Japan and the Japanese*. Washington: The Infantry Journal, 1945.

A somewhat superficial review of Shinto is related to Japan's conduct in World War II. A good background work for conditions which surround the government and the people of modern, militaristic Japan.

Friess, Horace L., and Schneider, Herbert W. *Religion in Various Cultures*. New York: Henry Holt and Co., 1932.

Historical and critical discussions of Shinto and Japanese Buddhism form a part of this important survey of the cultural influence of religions throughout the world.

Gorer, Geoffrey. "Themes in Japanese Culture." Article in *Transactions of the New York Academy of Sciences*. Series II. Vol. V, No. 5. March 1943.

A fascinating study in the effect which Shinto has had on the rigid training of Japanese children.

Griffis, William Elliot. *The Religions of Japan*. New York: Charles Scribner's Sons, 1896.

A standard early study of Old Shinto, Confucianism, Buddhism, Ryobu, and Christianity in Japan up to the time of the Meiji Restoration.

Gubbins, J. H. "Laws of the Tokugawa Period." Article in *T.A.S.J.* Vol. XXVI. December 1898.

An excellent résumé of Japanese feudal laws which demonstrate the close supervision of the individual Japanese exercised by the Tokugawa shoguns and their *daimyos.*

Hepner, Charles William. *The Kurozumi Sect of Shinto.* Tokyo: Meiji Japan Society, 1935.

A clear statement of the historical development of Shinto, with especial attention to the history and doctrines of the Kurozumi sect.

Holtom, D. C. *Modern Japan and Shinto Nationalism: A Study of Present Day Trends in Japanese Religions.* Chicago: University of Chicago Press, 1943.

The most important of recent scholarly contributions to an interpretation of the political significance of State Shinto. Uses some of the material in Mr. Holtom's earlier paper in *T.A.S.J.,* "The Political Philosophy of Modern Shinto."

——————— "Some Notes on Japanese Tree Worship." *T.A.S.J.* Vol. VII. 2nd series. December 1931.

A discussion of the important place which trees occupy in Shinto devotions.

——————— *The Japanese Enthronement Ceremonies.* Tokyo: The Kyo Bun Kwan, 1928.

A detailed description of the ceremony of enthronement of the Japanese emperor, with interpretations of the meaning of the imperial treasures (the mirror, the jewels, and the sword) and of the ceremonial ritual which accompanies the ascent to the throne of one who is looked upon as a god incarnate.

——————— "The Meaning of Kami." Article in three parts in *Monumenta Nipponica.* Vol. III, Nos. 1 and 2, Vol. IV, No. 2. Tokyo: Sophia University, 1940–1941.

Clarification of the attitude of the Japanese toward the Shinto gods, sacred persons, and all else designated by the term *Kami,* in the light of recent scholarly research.

——————— *The National Faith of Japan: A Study in Modern Shinto.* London: Kegan Paul, Trench, Trubner and Co., 1938; New York: E. P. Dutton and Co., 1938.

The most important of recent works on Shinto. The history of Shinto, the origin and development of the state doctrine, the infiltration of Buddhism, the development and content of the Shinto sects. Probably the most valuable of the books here listed for anyone who wishes to make a serious study of the meaning and history of Japan's national religion.

——————— "The Political Philosophy of Modern Shinto." *T.A.S.J.* Vol. XLIX. Part II.

One of the earliest and most important statements showing the direction being taken by the Japanese government in total indoctrination of its people.

Hume, Robert Ernest. *The World's Living Religions.* New York: Charles Scribner's Sons, 1931.

The chapter on Shinto in this standard work furnishes a good, brief outline.

Ichuro Kurata. *"Yama-nokami."* (Mountain Deities.) *Contemporary Japan,* October 1940.

A study of the worship of the gods who dwell in (and sometimes are) the mountains of Japan.

Inazo Nitobe. *Bushido, the Soul of Japan.* Philadelphia: The Leeds and Biddle Co., 1900.

A discussion of the code of the Samurai of feudal Japan, written from the point of view of honest Japanese bias which marks all of the work of this highly respected Japanese scholar.

———— *Lectures on Japan.* Tokyo: Kenkyusha, 1936.

A collection of lectures given by this modern Japanese scholar in the United States in an attempt to interpret the Japanese character, Shinto, and Japanese thought in general, to the people of the United States.

———— *The Japanese Nation: Its Land, Its People, and Its Life.* New York: G. P. Putnam's Sons, 1912.

A historical, social, and political evaluation of the Japanese by one of the most respected of Japanese scholars, who spent much of his adult life in working for understanding between his people and the Western nations. Though many of his conclusions are discredited by contemporary history, the obvious sincerity and social purpose of Inazo Nitobe stand as an example of the social forces potential in Japanese thought.

Johnstone, William C. *The Future of Japan.* New York: Oxford University Press, 1945.

Sound and well-considered suggestions for our postwar treatment of Japan and the Japanese in light of their thorough indoctrination in the tenets of State Shinto and their well-organized industry. Mr. Johnstone writes hopefully of the possibility of a Japanese liberal movement which may be Japan's salvation if properly encouraged by the victorious United Nations.

Kaiten Nukariya. *The Religion of the Samurai: A Study of Zen Philosophy and Discipline in China and Japan.* London: Luzac and Co., 1913.

A study of Zen Buddhism in Japan with especial attention to its influence upon *bushido* and the military and social ideology of the Middle Ages, so clearly reflected in modern Japan. Mr. Kaiten was, at the time he wrote this book, a professor at Keo-O-Gi-Jiku University and So-to-shu Buddhist College, Tokyo.

Kato, Genchi. *A Study of Shinto, the Religion of the Japanese Nation.* Tokyo: The Meiji Japan Society, 1926.

A valuable historical study by a highly respected modern Japanese scholar. Mr. Kato, in a laudable effort to further understanding, has made an attempt to reconcile Shinto beliefs with those of Western religions which is not convincing, but his work is of great value not only as representative of scholarship, but as a Japanese point of view.

Kato, Genchi. "A Study of the Development of Religious Ideas Among the Japanese People as Illustrated by Japanese Phallicism." *T.A.S.J.* Vol. I. 2nd series. Supplement. December 1924.

A historical interpretation of the part phallicism has played in Shinto from the earliest times to the present day.

————— "The Naoe Matsuri." *T.A.S.J.* Vol. VII. 2nd series. December 1931.

A description of one of the important Shinto ceremonies of exorcism which includes symbolic human sacrifice—a residual evidence of early actual sacrifice of human beings.

————— (tr.) "The Wa Rongo, or Japanese Analects." *T.A.S.J.* Vol. XLV, Part II. December 1917.

One of the most famous of the writings of late Ryobu Shinto.

————— *What is Shinto?* Tokyo: The Maruzen Co., Ltd., 1935.

One of a series of short studies issued for propaganda purposes by the Board of Tourist Industries, Japanese Government Railways. An interesting example of scholarship harnessed for the uses of the Japanese state.

Kirby, R. J. "Ancestral Worship in Japan." *T.A.S.J.* Vol. XXXVIII. Part IV. 1911.

A digest of the teachings of Hirata Atsutane, one of the three great leaders of the Pure Shinto Revival, in regard to reverence of ancestral spirits.

Kishio Sutomi. *Japanese Civilization.* New York: E. P. Dutton and Co., 1924.

A review of Nichirenism, a Japanese Buddhist cult, which excellently illustrates how the nationalistic principles of Shinto were taken into Japanese Buddhism.

Knapp, Arthur May. *Feudal and Modern Japan.* Yokohama: The Advertiser Publishing Co., 1906.

Though clouded with the author's obviously romantic love for all things Japanese which makes his conclusions frequently worthless in the light of those of more objective and exacting scholars, this book has value for its colorful picture of the life of the people in the days of the shoguns and immediately following.

Koya Nakamura. *History of Japan.* Board of Tourist Industry, Japanese Government Railways, 1939.

A brief historical outline, the chief value of which is its revelation of the point of view which the modern Japanese government would like to have accepted by the Western world.

Lamott, Willis Church. "What Not to Do With Japan," *Harper's Magazine,* June 1945.

A contemporary summing up of the attitude of the Japanese people toward their sacred emperor, the effects upon them of Bushido, and the postwar problems posed by these factors, by a man who lived in Japan, as missionary and teacher, from 1919 to 1938.

Lay, Arthur Hyde. "Japanese Funeral Rites." *T.A.S.J.* Vol. XIX. Part III. October 1891.

A discussion of the funeral rites of the early Japanese and their attitude toward death during the Old Shinto period. Important in evaluating the modern conception of the desirability of death for the emperor as an escape from the pathological horror of dissolution which burdened the early Japanese mind.

Lory, Hillis. *Japan's Military Masters.* New York: Viking Press, 1943.

The rise of modern militarism in Japan, with a very valuable chapter on "The Religion of the Army" showing the intimate connection between emperor-worshiping Shinto and the training of a Japanese soldier.

Lowell, Percival. "Esoteric Shinto." Article in four parts. *T.A.S.J.* Vol. XXI and XXII.

A discussion of the magic rites, superstitions, and pilgrimages of the esoteric Shinto sects.

Maki, John M. *Japanese Militarism: Its Cause and Cure.* New York: Alfred A. Knopf, 1945.

An important historical survey of the forces (including Shinto) which have contributed to Japan's conviction of supremacy, and a keen evaluation of our postwar problem in the Pacific by a man (born in America of Japanese parents) who has spent most of his adult life in Japanese studies.

Manyoshu: One Thousand Poems. (Translator's name not given.) Tokyo: The Iwanami Shoten, 1940; Chicago: University of Chicago Press, 1941.

Japan's classic anthology of ancient poetry originally collected some time between the middle of the eighth and the beginning of the tenth centuries. One of the basic books of Old Shinto.

Masaharu Anesaki. "Japanese Criticisms and Refutations of Christianity in the Seventeenth and Eighteenth Centuries." *T.A.S.J.* Vol. VII. 2nd series. December 1930.

A part of the story of persecution of Christianity under the Tokugawa shoguns, who were interested in furthering Zen Buddhism and Ryobu Shinto as a means of keeping their Samurai loyal to government and the people docile.

Mason, Joseph Warren Teets. *The Meaning of Shinto.* New York: E. P. Dutton and Co., 1935.

A book to avoid because of extremely biased interpretations which see Shinto through a haze of cherry blossoms surrounded by sweetness and light.

McLaren, W. W. (ed.). *Japanese Government Documents, 1867–1889. T.A.S.J.* Vol. XLII. Part I. Tokyo, 1914.

An invaluable collection of government documents during the first half of the Meiji era, revealing the governmental point of view immediately after the Restoration.

Mears, Helen. *Year of the Wild Boar.* New York: J. B. Lippincott Co., 1942.

An account of a year which Miss Mears spent in Japan just before the outbreak of war with the Western allies. Her keen analyses of customs, religious observances, and Japanese thought form a valuable addition to evidence useful in any evaluation of Shinto.

Morris, John. *Traveler from Tokyo*. New York: Sheridan House, 1944.

A British teacher in Tokyo for four years interprets the mind of the Japanese on the basis of close observation and acquaintanceship with students and Japanese liberals.

Motohiko Anzu. "Shinto as Seen by Foreign Scholars." Tokyo: Nippon Bunka Chuo Renmei, *Cultural Nippon*. Vol. VI. No. 4. 1938.

A brief history of scholarly Western research in Shinto, with short discussions of the findings of such men as Aston, Chamberlain, Florenz, and Holtom, and a general thesis that only the Japanese themselves are capable of interpreting the Japanese national religion correctly.

"National Cult in Japan," *Japan Chronicle,* July 20, 21, 1918 [Kobe].

A Roman Catholic Study of Shinto's opposition to Christianity.

Norman, E. Herbert. *Japan's Emergence as a Modern State*. New York: International Secretariat, Institute of Pacific Relations, 1940.

An excellent historical study of late feudalism, the Restoration, and the post-Restoration industrialism of Japan. An essential book for all who are interested in the practical background of Japan's modern ideology.

Otoo Huzii. *Japanese Proverbs*. Board of Tourist Industries, Japanese Government Railways, 1940.

A collection of, and comment upon, Japanese folk sayings, many of which reflect the temper of Shinto and Bushido.

Reischauer, A. K. (tr.) "Genshin's *Ojo Yoshu:* Collected Essays on Birth into Paradise." *T.A.S.J.* Vol. VII. 2nd series. December 1930.

Translation of a classic of the Jodo or "Pure Land" sect of Buddhism which had a notable effect on the code of the Samurai through advancing the idea of the worthlessness of life and the consequent desirability of death.

Ryusaku Tsunada. "Two Tales of Historic Japan." Article in *Columbia University Quarterly*. Vol. XXVII. No. 2. June 1935.

A discussion of the *Genji Monogatari* and the *Heike Monogatari,* two classic tales of feudal Japan centering in the stories of the Genji (or Minamoto) and the Heike (or Taira) families, the two powerful military clans who struggled for dominance of Japan during the Middle Ages. Mr. Ryusaku's article explains much of the background of this struggle, and shows how the religious forces at work during this period contributed greatly to the "death for the emperor" doctrine.

Sansom, G. B. (tr.) "The Imperial Edicts in the *Shoku Nihongi.*" *T.A.S.J.* Vol. I. 2nd series. December 1924.

See note on Snellen, J. B., "The Shoku Nihongi."

——— *Japan: A Short Cultural History*. New York: D. Appleton–Century Co., 1931, 1943.

An exhaustive cultural and social history of the Japanese from their beginnings to the Meiji Restoration. The outstanding one-volume work of its kind.

Satow, Ernest. "Ancient Japanese Rituals." *T.A.S.J.* Vol. VII. Parts II and IV and Vol. IX. Part II. September 1889.

An important account of the rites and ceremonies of Old Shinto, their origins and meanings to the Japanese.

——————— *The Revival of Pure Shintau. T.A.S.J.* Vol. III. Part I. Appendix.

A digest of the teachings of Mabuchi, Motoöri, Hirata, and others of the Pure Shinto Revival period which laid the basis for State Shinto.

———————, and Florenz, Karl. "Yengi-Shiki." (Institutes of the Period of Yengi.) *T.A.S.J.* Vol. VII. Vol. IX. Vol. XXVII.

Translation of the *norito,* or prayers, used in Shinto rituals.

Shozo Kono. "Kannagara no Michi: the Meaning of Kannagara." Article in *Monumenta Nipponica.* Vol. III. No. 2. Tokyo: Sophia University, 1940.

Clarification by a modern Japanese scholar of the doctrine of the identity of the Japanese emperor with Amaterasu Omikami, chief goddess of the Shinto pantheon, and the Japanese attitude of unified loyalty to this concept and its implications.

Sinto Shrines: with a Brief Explanation of Sinto Ceremonies and Priesthood. (Anonymous.) Board of Tourist Industries, Japanese Government Railways.

An official Japanese government description and interpretation of the shrines, the emblems, the music, and the rites of State Shinto.

Smith, Guy-Harold, Good, Dorothy, and McCune, Shannon. *Japan, a Geographical View.* New York: American Geographical Society, 1943.

An examination into the part which geography, climate, national resources, industry, and population have played in Japan's national character.

Snellen, J. B. (tr.). *Shoku Nihongi: Chronicles of Japan from 697–791* A.D. *T.A.S.J.* Vol. XI. 2nd series. 1934.

A continuation of the *Nihongi* chronicle, reflecting much that is pertinent concerning the imperial consciousness of divinity, and the life of the Japanese during the eighth century A.D., when the country was being consolidated and Buddhism was sweeping the land, making its ineradicable impress on Shinto.

Tasuku Harada. *The Faith of Japan.* New York: The Macmillan Co., 1914.

An outline of Shinto and Japanese Buddhism and their effect upon Japanese patriotism by a modern Japanese scholar. Its conclusions are charged with the emotional bias toward idealization of Japanese thought which marks the mind of a loyal Japanese, but which perhaps adds to the strength of his thesis.

"The God Emperor." Article in *Time,* May 21, 1945.

A somewhat superficial discussion of emperor worship in Japan, with a biographical discussion of Emperor Hirohito and speculations as to the significance of Shinto in postwar relations.

Timperley, H. J. *Japan, A World Problem*. New York: The John Day Co., 1942.

A short general book reviewing briefly the background of early expansion, feudalism, imperialism under the shoguns, economic maladjustment, and the totalitarian spirit in Japan.

Tolischus, Otto D. *Through Japanese Eyes*. New York: Reynal and Hitchcock, 1945.

Of unique value because of the large number of direct quotations from Japanese sources, many of which reveal to what an amazing degree State Shinto ideology has dictated the convictions of the Japanese people.

Wales, H. G. Quaritch. "Shinto's Place in World Culture," *Asia and the Americas*, April 1945.

Discussion by an archaeologist of the international implications of Shinto, with a speculation on the possibility that the religion may be an offshoot of the Royal God cult of the Mayans.

Ward, Robert S. *Asia for the Asiatics*. Chicago: The University of Chicago Press, 1945.

A valuable study of the technique of the Shinto-indoctrinated Japanese in regulating the "inferior" subject peoples of occupied territories, based upon Mr. Ward's own experience in occupied Hong Kong.

Yone Noguchi. *Japan and America*. New York: Orientalia, 1921.

Lectures on Japan given in America by a modern Japanese poet. Not of great value save as they reveal the mind of an educated Japanese conditioned by Shinto concepts.

Yoshida, K. *Japanese Education*. Board of Tourist Industry, Japanese Government Railways, 1937.

An official history of education in Japan and a superficial account of the present Japanese educational system written for Western consumption, carefully avoiding the matter of nationalist indoctrination in the public schools.

Zachert, Herbert. "Social Changes During the Tokugawa Period." *T.A.S.J.* Vol. XVII. 2nd series. December 1938.

Social life in Yedo during the two centuries immediately preceding the Restoration, during which the influence of the Samurai declined and that of the merchants rose, thus contributing to the overthrow of the shogunate.

Zenichi, Itani. "The Economic Causes of the Meiji Restoration." *T.A.S.J.* Vol. XVII. 2nd series. December 1938.

A short study of the combination of external and internal forces which brought about the downfall of the shogunate and the restoration of the imperial government.

Index

Kanzaki Kazusaku, 203
Karsuhiko Kakehi, 189
Kasuga shrine, 38
Kato, Genchi
  on God-emperor doctrine, 183–84, 186–187
  on jewel spear of heaven, 20
Katori, oracle of, 135
Kiichiro Hiranuma, 189
Kikuchi family, 35
Kiri-sute-gomen, 53
Kitabatake Chicafusa, quoted on divinity of Japan, 53, 126
Kiujiki, 26
Knapp, Arthur May
  quoted on "Japanese Sphere of Influence," 69
  quoted on position of medieval Japanese farmer, 53
  quoted on Tokugawa laws, 54
Kobo Daishi, 30
Kochi Ken, Samurai of, 171
Kogoshui, possible debt to Buddhism, 32
Kojiki
  as authority for restoration, 59
  as base of Motoöri's teachings, 46
  as source of Pure Shinto Revival, 45
  expounded by Hirata, 50
  history of, 19
  importance of, in Shinto, 19
  mythology of, compared with that of Old Testament, 81
  myths taught as history, 71
  poetry from, 98, 99
  possible debt of, to Buddhism, 32
  selections from, 91–99
Kojiki den of Motoöri, 50
Kojima, 127
Kokubo no Hongi to Sono Kyokwa no Teisho, 185–86
Konko Kyo, doctrine of, 207
Kono Shozo, doctrine of Taisha Kyo, 203
Korea
  early Japanese attempts to conquer, 43
  invasion of, by Japan in 16th century, 43
  migrations from, 7
Kotoku, Emperor, 17
Kuammu Tenno, ancestor of Hirata, 49
Kublai Khan, 5n
Kuge, 58
Kukai (see Kobo Daishi)
Kung-fu-tze (see Confucius)
Kuniaki Koiso, expounds hakko ichi-u, 24
Kurosumi Kyo, doctrine of, 206

Kuzuhana, 48
Kusuo Oya, 196

Lady Otomo of Sakanoe, 113
Lament for Childlessness, 99
Land of the Gods, The, 192
"Land of the Rising Sun," derivation of, 7
Lao Tze, identified with kami, 136
Laotzu (see Lao Tze)
Liberalism in Japan
  at time of Restoration, 61
  evidenced by Ichikawa Tatsumaru, 83
  evidenced by Inazo Nitobe, 84
  evidenced by Memorial of 1874, 83
  evidenced by Nihongi, 82, 83, 104–107
  evidenced by opposition to Pure Shinto Revival, 47
  evidenced by Reickichi Tada statement, 195
  evidenced by statements during week of August 12, 1945, 85
  evidences of, discussed, 82–85
Life in Death, 192
"Life of the Universe" doctrine, 38, 185
Light of the Ideal, The, 197
Liu Chiu (or Loo choo), 43
Lory, Hillis, quoted on emperor worship, 71
Lowell, Percival, quoted on meaning of Shinto, 22, 23
Lowith, Karl, quoted, 75

Mabiki, 56
Mabuchi
  as co-founder of Pure Shinto Revival, 45
  attacks on Chinese doctrines, 45
  attacks on shogunate, 45
  influence of Taoism on, 45
  selections from writings of, 144, 145
Mahayana Buddhism (see Buddhism in Japan)
Mana, relation to kami, 11
Mainichi, 200
Manifest God, A, 124
Manyoshu
  possible debt of, to Buddhism, 32
  selections from, 108–16
Marco Polo, 7
Matsudaira Sadanobu, 54
Matsurigoto
  as doctrine of Pure Shinto Revival, 46
  discussed by Hirata, 154
Meaning of Kami, The, 186
Meaning of Life, The, 184
Meiji, Emperor
  assumes authority in Restoration, 58

human sacrifice in, 11, 28, 103, 104
importance of dreams in, 12
importance of signs in, 12
impossible to reconcile with Christianity, 74
Inari cult, 65
influence of, on Japanese Buddhism, 32, 33
justification for medieval expansion, 43
Konko Kyo doctrine, 207
Kurosumi Kyo doctrine, 206
lack of moral code praised by Pure Shinto Revival, 27
list of names of sects, 76
literature of state doctrine, 181–93
Mitake Kyo doctrine, 205
morality in, 26
mountain sects listed, 76
mourning houses of, 28
musicians and dancers in, 27
naming of, 9
nature worship in, 9, 22, 27
number of adherents to sects, 76
opposition to pure Shinto Revival, 47
origin of name discussed by Motoöri, 147
phallicism in, 12–15, 20
"popular" Shinto, 65
possible connection with Mayan Cult, 8
possible sources of, 8
prayers of, 26
priests of, 27
priests regulated by state, 63
purification sects discussed, 77
purification sects listed, 76
pure Shinto Revival, 25, 27, 39, 45–51
reconciled with Christianity, 74, 75
repudiated by Reickichi Tada, 195
rites in hara-kiri, 42
ritual and ethics of, 26
"ritualists" in, 27
ritual of, discussed by Hirata, 154
ritual regulated by government, 71
Ryobu, 30–33
sectarian, after adoption of constitution, 67
sectarian, as distinct from state and popular, 66
sectarian in social welfare work, 66
sects as allies of liberalism, 79
selections from Old Shinto texts, 91–118
Shingon or "True Word" Sect, 30
selections from texts of Pure Shinto Revival, 144–59
selections from texts of second period, 118–44

selections from texts of third period, 144–63
Shinri Kyo doctrine, 203
Shinshu Kyo doctrine, 206
shrines of, 38
Shusei Ha doctrines, 204
source of Bushido, 40
sources of State Shinto in Pure Shinto Revival, 45
State, declared not religion, 6, 9, 10
State Shinto, 39
Suiga movement, 39
Sun worship in, 9
superiority expounded by Motoöri, 148
Taisei Kyo doctrine, 205
Taisha Kyo doctrine, 203
Tree worship in, 13, 14, 15
uncleanness in, 27
Watarai Movement, 39
worship of living in, 10
worship of mountain gods in, 13
Yang and Yin influence, 9
Yiu-itsu movement, 38
Yoshida movement, 38
Shinto Honkyoku, doctrines of, 200–203
Shinto, The Way of the Gods, cited on phallicism, 12
Shogun (*see* Seii-Tai-Shogun)
Shogunate
    attacked by Mabuchi, 45
    beginnings of dissolution, 56
    condemned by leading nobles, 165
    dissolution of, 58
    establishment of, 36
    opposed by Samurai, 58
    taxes under, 54
    Tokugawa, 52–58
    weakened by Perry visits, 57
Shojiroku, 26
Shoku Nihongi, selections from texts of, 118–26
Shozo Kono, 186
Shrines of Shinto
    as alternate habitations for tree gods, 14
    "foundation of the empire," 184
    Ise, 30
    Kasuga, 38
    number of state shrines, 75
    origin of grand shrine of Ise, 103
    Yasukuni, 71
Shusei Ha, doctrines of, 204
Signs, Portents, Magic, and Remedies, 120
Sin in Shinto, 27
Stars, their function defined by Hirata, 154
State Shinto,
    declared not a religion, 69